# MUSIC FOR THE PEOPLE

# GARETH MALONE

# MUSIC FOR THE PEOPLE

## The Pleasures and Pitfalls of Classical Music

Collins

First published in 2011 by Collins
an imprint of HarperCollins*Publishers*
77–85 Fulham Palace Road
London W6 8JB

www.harpercollins.co.uk

10 9 8 7 6 5 4 3 2 1

Extract from *Fanfare for the Common Man* by Aaron Copland (p. 134) © Copyright 1944 by the Aaron Copland Fund for Music, Inc. Copyright renewed. Boosey & Hawkes Inc., sole licensee. Reproduced by permission of Boosey & Hawkes Music Publishers Ltd.

Extract from 'Somewhere' from *West Side Story* by Leonard Bernstein (p. 134) © 1956, 1957, 1958, 1959 by Amberson Holdings LLC and Stephen Sondheim. Copyright renewed. Leonard Bernstein Music Publishing Company LLC, publisher. International copyright secured. Reproduced by permission of Boosey & Hawkes Music Publishers Ltd.

Add.30014 ff.124v-125 The Virgin with angels, from the 'Hymn book of the St Saviour's Monastry, Siena', 1415 (vellum) by Italian School, (15th century) British Library, London, UK (p. 246) © British Library Board. All Rights Reserved/The Bridgeman Art Library.

Autograph score of Handel's *Jeptha* (p. 247) © The British Library Board. R.M.20.e.9.

Music origination by Barnes Music Engraving Ltd.

Extract from *Second String Quartet* by Brian Ferneyhough © Copyright 1978 by Hinrichsen Edition, Peters Edition Limited, London. Reproduced by permission of Peters Edition, London.

Extract from *Treatise* by Cornelius Cardew © Copyright 1967 by Hinrichsen Edition, Peters Edition Limited, London. Reproduced by permission of Peters Edition, London.

A catalogue record for this book is
available from the British Library

ISBN: 978-0-00-738305-4

Printed and bound in Great Britain by
Clays Ltd, St Ives plc

**Mixed Sources**
Product group from well-managed
forests and other controlled sources
www.fsc.org  Cert no. SW-COC-001806
© 1996 Forest Stewardship Council

FSC is a non-profit international organisation established to promote the responsible management of the world's forests. Products carrying the FSC label are independently certified to assure consumers that they come from forests that are managed to meet the social, economic and ecological needs of present and future generations.

Find out more about HarperCollins and the environment at
www.harpercollins.co.uk/green

*For Becky and Esther*

# Contents

# Part 4: APPENDICES

*There are a million things in music I know nothing about. I just want to narrow down that figure.*

ANDRÉ PREVIN (1972)

*Why does everyone else in the office think you're from Mars if you ever go to the opera?*

MY MATE CHRIS (2010)

# Introduction

I've always listened to classical music because my parents carefully indoctrinated me from birth. As a baby I would go to sleep to *This is the Record of John* by Orlando Gibbons (think men in ruffs singing in high voices). As a young child I felt that classical music was more interesting that popular music; I remember clearly, aged eight, being very disappointed when a girl told me that she only liked pop music. The relationship would never have worked. Over the intervening 27 years I've dabbled in all sorts, including pop, rock and acidjazzfunk. I'm always excited when I hear something that I haven't heard before. Music knits together the tapestry of my life; it reflects my mood and it offers me nourishment. I love to read about it, to perform it but most especially to listen to it.

Next to my CD player I have a pile of music that I'm currently listening to: Stile Antico singing Tudor Christmas music; Muse's *The Resistance*; and *Verklärte Nacht* by Schoenberg. In my office I have the music that I listen to less regularly: Nicolai Gedda singing opera arias; 'Living Toys' by Thomas Adès; and almost the complete works of Bach. In the loft is a huge box of music I don't need to listen to again for a very long time (mostly from my teenage years): the KLF back catalogue, six versions of *Progen* by The Shamen and all my Janet Jackson records. I've always been obsessive and when I get my teeth into a piece it can be a year before I relegate it to the dustier sections of my CD rack.

If you are just coming to classical music for the first time, then it might seem as impenetrable as fine wine, learning Greek or taking up mountaineering. It's true that there is a mountain of music to listen to and if I started listening now I'm sure it would take me the rest of my life to work my way through the back catalogue of recordings stocked in my local classical CD shop (HMV on Oxford Street, as regretfully the small independent stores are now few and far between, thanks to internet downloads). But it isn't necessary to sample every piece to feel that you are getting a handle on this amazing music. When you know a couple of works well and understand how they fit into the general picture of music, you will quickly overcome your initial trepidation.

This book isn't comprehensive – it's a tour guide and a personal ramble through music based on my own interests and discoveries. The intention is to spark connections and points of departure for you. I will take you through the history of music later in the book, but this isn't a lesson, it's an impassioned plea to give this music a chance and a pocket guide (if you've got big pockets) to help you when you need assistance. Let us forage together.

# Part 1
# LISTENING

Chapter **1**

# You Love Classical Music – *Yes, You Do!*

Before we start let's get a few things straight:

1 There is so much to know about music that a lifetime's study couldn't hope to tell you everything.
2 There are so many hidden alleyways, nooks and crannies in music that it's quite possible to get stuck in just one area and neglect all the other music. There is much to challenge you, expand your horizons and generally give your musical taste a spring clean.
3 You are in control of what you listen to, where you start and where you finish. Only you know what you like and what you don't like. It's fine to admit that you simply don't 'get' a piece – sometimes music takes time to get to know, or sometimes you'll just never be friends.
4 There is no one correct way to listen to classical music or any other kind of music because it's an intensely personal business.

## Discovery

'Discovery' is the name given to the London Symphony Orchestra education and outreach department by its founder Richard McNicol, my mentor and music education guru. He chose this name because for him that's the best way for people to connect with music: when they make the discovery themselves. This is your guide to discovering music.

Richard told me a story which illustrates the importance of feeling that music *belongs to you.* He encouraged a group of children to create music based loosely on ideas taken from a piece for full orchestra by the great Russian composer Igor Stravinsky. The children worked on these pieces for weeks before performing them to their schoolmates. At the end of the project the schoolchildren attended a concert of Stravinsky's work. After the concert a young boy spoke to Richard and asked him 'Here, mister, how did that Stravinsky know *our* music?'

I was lucky enough to work closely with Richard for two years at the LSO, watching how he brought people to music and not the other way round. An overly didactic approach often fails with music because I can't *make* you like something. I can only point you in the direction of it and hope that you hear what I hear. I also hope that through using this book you will come to feel that music does indeed belong to everyone and that much of this wonderful repertoire can be *yours.* There's no instant answer to understanding or knowing about classical music; the first step is building a positive relationship with the music.

Inexplicably, certain works have a hold on me and refuse to let go. I could listen to Bach's Mass in B Minor every day without growing tired, whereas some pieces, although fascinating, don't put down roots in the way that a truly great work does. What appeals to me might not appeal to you and although I do make recommendations in this book I'm aware that my evangelism for a piece may fall on stony ground. This book is *not* a prescriptive list of works that you *should* appreciate. The purpose is to give you the tools to make your own discoveries.

Most people struggle with pieces that are too complex or simply not tuneful enough for their taste. Length and complexity are factors in limiting appreciation of music but there is much to recommend on the musical nursery slopes before you tackle the great summits.

Music appreciation is as subjective as any other artistic discipline because our brains are changed by any musical experience we have during our lives and that in turn affects how we listen to new pieces. Although I make a case for the importance of a little background research in Chapter 4 there is no right way to listen to Mozart and there never will be. You should not feel that Mozart is somehow superhuman and therefore beyond your comprehension.

I have seen time and time again how anyone can learn to appreciate music. During my years working for English National Opera's Baylis Programme (their community and education wing) I was sent to schools in deprived areas of London. From Hackney to the less salubrious parts of Ealing, if there was a school whose pupils knew nothing of opera then I'd be sent there, armed only with a score, an opera singer and a *répétiteur* (official term for an opera rehearsal pianist). What I observed was the dramatic effect these workshops had on students' attitudes towards opera.

One of the most striking examples of the success of this practical approach to learning about music was working with some young homeless people at St Martin-in-the-Fields. We brought a singer from the ENO Chorus to sing 'Vissi d'Arte' ('I lived for art') from Verdi's *Tosca*. For most people it's rare to get so intimate with a voice that has been trained to fill every corner of an opera house. It's like standing next to a jumbo jet on a runway (though it does sound a bit better). Huddled round in their slightly shabby canteen, drinking strong, sugary tea from polystyrene cups, these young people were profoundly affected by the physical presence of a large operatic voice: they couldn't believe it. The voice didn't belong in that space and it transported us all. We explored the story of *Tosca* – a bleak and violent opera – and I genuinely believe that their opinion of the art-form was transformed. They spoke with the singer, they heard from us about

production at ENO and most importantly they took part by singing sections of the opera.

I'm not saying that they all became opera fans, but it was clear
that until then they had completely the wrong impression of
opera: 'fat ladies screaming'. It's interesting how many people
can carry a vivid – and sometimes prejudiced – impression of
what opera is like, having only experienced it from those adverts
for 'Go compare' or 'Just one Cornetto'. Within a few hours we
started to recalibrate that popular misconception, using a little
knowledge of the story, a basic understanding of how some of the
music was composed and the unforgettable experience of hearing an opera singer in the flesh. Given this sort of preparation the
most unlikely children can sit through up to three hours of opera,
something many adults struggle with.

For me these workshops were a baptism of fire, because in
order to prepare I would often be sent the music just a few days
in advance and I'd have precious little time to get to know a new
opera before being sent into a school as an evangelical advocate.
The discipline of sitting with a score (the written musical notes),
reading the synopsis (the plot), digging out the programme (if I
could find one), reading the director's production notes (if
they'd written any) and living with the music for a few days
before being hurled into a school was an excellent cramming
course. The job gave me the opportunity to talk to singers from
the production, to grapple with the themes during workshops –
and finally after all that I'd go to see the opera for the first time.
If they'd known then how little I knew about opera, and how
much study I was having to do, perhaps they'd have employed
someone else. It proved an excellent training for opera
appreciation.

So sometimes, in order to appreciate music, a little homework
is required. My dad's school motto was *nil sine labore* – 'Nothing without work' (how I loathed it when he stood over my piano
practice quoting this aphorism). I'm afraid it applies here, but it
needn't be a chore. Of course I understand that by some

definitions music that requires 'work' is an anathema – surely we should love a great piece of music at first listening? But think how often you meet someone and fall in love at first sight – once in a lifetime? Many pieces of music take time to get to know.

I'm assuming if you've bought this book about classical music then you are ready to apply yourself. So let's move on.

## You know more than you think you do

Whether you notice it or not, classical music is everywhere, keeping teenagers at bay in train stations,[1] persuading you to buy wine on TV adverts and pulling no punches in film soundtracks. I believe it is the ultimate destination for all true music lovers. Once the sheen has rubbed off lesser forms, the gems of classical music shine even brighter.

If you're reading this book, then it probably means that you already feel that you know a little something about classical music. Maybe you'd like to know more. Or perhaps, like Socrates, you know enough to know that you don't know anything. Hopefully you have been enticed to dip into this strange and wonderful world. This book is intended to build on your tentative enthusiasms; I'm here to help. If, as I hope, you have enjoyed any classical music, there will be something in this book for you. Once you discover an area of music that you like, given the number of composers and over 500 years of Western musical history, there are hundreds of discoveries to be made.

## Don't panic

You'll never get to know every piece of music because there's just too much out there and you may not like everything you hear, but that doesn't mean you don't like classical music. There are pieces of music I haven't got my head round – either they are too sickly sweet or too bitter, too angular and modern or not modern enough. I think it's important not to feel that if you don't like a piece you should give up on it straight away. Having said that, I gave up on Bruckner a few years ago after a spectacularly tiresome concert experience, but who knows, perhaps I'll grow back into it. And it's important not to feel overwhelmed by how much music there is to listen to.

The chief difficulty in learning about any art-form is the 'emperor's new clothes' effect. We've all been there – a friend eulogises about a piece of music. 'You've got to hear this! It's amazing! Listen to that cymbal crash!' Their face is terrifyingly alive. Their hair is standing on end. They are in the throes of what can only be described as a personal moment. Meanwhile, you are wondering what all the fuss is about. Everybody experiences music differently. Several factors can affect this: the context, how much you know about the piece and how often you have heard it before.

Try listening to a piece of classical music that you know well in a variety of contexts: (1) while washing up; (2) while looking at cherished photographs; (3) while keeping an eye on the sports result as your favourite team loses/wins. You'll find that the atmosphere of the piece changes and affects the activity as much as the activity affects the music.

## Technical language

In this book I will tell you what I consider helpful in understanding how melody, harmony and the structure of music work but without turning this into an A-Level textbook. Terms such as *staccato* and *legato* may be alien to you but the concepts they signify will be familiar (they mean 'short/detached' and 'smooth', respectively). Getting to grips with how music works is a technical business and unwrapping a technical term reveals yet more layers of technical terms underneath, like an endless game of pass the parcel. Technical terms can be daunting but I make no apologies for taking you through the first few layers and teaching the basics that you need to enhance your understanding. You need them because they stand for concepts for which there is no other word: harmony, melody, sonata, symphony, concerto, etc. But wherever possible I will explain any terms, avoid overly technical language and use everyday alternatives where they exist.

There are many books available which attempt to explain everything there is to know about how music functions but which for the beginner are utterly bewildering in their depth and density of language: it's not necessary to be a mechanic to drive a car. Music is at once incredibly simple – a child can appreciate and perform it – and also complex – philosophers, scientists and musicians are still perplexed by many of the mysteries of music; for example, why exactly are we moved by certain pieces and not others? Why exactly do some people love Bach while others cannot abide him? Despite years of study and masses of knowledge, these are still matters for debate. Some technical aspects of music can be left unexplained without impairing your appreciation.

## Over-familiarity breeds contempt

These days I wouldn't choose to go to a concert of Ravel's *Boléro* despite it having a terrific melody and for many years being one of my favourites. I first heard it when it was about seven years old when Torvill and Dean were at the Olympics: I thought it was very stirring. It was then used on television programmes for the next ten years, almost on a loop; when I got to secondary school we studied it for GSCE; when I started to work at the LSO it was part of an education concert to show the different sections of the orchestra. It's a pretty simple piece: the melody repeats itself around the entire band before building to a grand finale for full orchestra. Ravel issued a warning about the piece before its first performance: 'a piece lasting seventeen minutes and consisting wholly of orchestral tissue without music ... There are no contrasts, and there is practically no invention except in the plan and the manner of execution.'[2] I still feel that it's a great piece of music, but I just can't listen to it any more because not only is the *Boléro* itself repetitive but I've also heard it repeated everywhere from lifts to restaurants.

If pressed, most experts will acknowledge that such familiar pieces are in many ways wondrous compositions; it's just that they wouldn't pay money to hear them again because over-familiarity has set in and hardened minds. I am guilty of this attitude because I've been listening to classical music for most of my life, and I think that regardless of the musical genre people take a similar position towards music they think of as less complicated or lower-brow. It's a matter of perspective: after listening to heavy rock music, pop-rock might seem rather tame; likewise if you've just been listening to a Mahler symphony, which may have a profoundly intense and emotional effect on you, then a waltz by Johann Strauss may feel light and frivolous and less than satisfying.

Making a discovery of a piece of music is a very personal business. The first time you hear a melody and it connects with you can be highly significant; I can recall the first hearing of all my favourite music with startling immediacy. It's extremely discouraging to discover that a piece you have fallen in love with is not considered 'great'. For example my friend Aaron when he was about twenty had one piece of 'serious' (i.e. classical) music in his collection: *Má Vlast* by Smetana. It's a glorious piece of music whose second movement describes the River Vltava from its early springs to the confluence of the river as it flows towards Prague. The structure is simple but effective, the melody (based on a folksong) is appealing and the orchestration is stirring, plus it was a piece he liked.

We sat in our university halls and listened to it, and I found it incredibly moving, not having heard the piece for many years (my primary school music teacher Mr Naylor played it to me in 1986). However, Aaron was humiliated when speaking to a music student of 'serious classical music' about Smetana, who somewhat sniffily said they 'considered *Má Vlast* to be rather lowbrow'. I can imagine the avant-garde music that this music student was being exposed to in music college and I suppose that Aaron's Smetana CD must have seemed naïve by comparison.

Don't let this put you off. If you like a piece then that's just fine. Perhaps by the time you have listened to *The 100 Greatest Classical Hits in the Universe ... Ever* a few times you'll be screaming for something different. Until that time, just enjoy.

## Film scores

If you watch films then you probably know more classical music than you think you do. Many directors edit their films to existing works. The most famous example of this was Stanley Kubrick, who was a musical magpie. *2001: A Space Odyssey*, *Eyes Wide Shut*, *The Shining*, *Barry Lyndon* and *A Clockwork Orange*, among others, contain classical music used to piercing effect. Nevertheless many composers have created original works for the cinema and great composers of the twentieth century took up the challenge of composing for film.

However, composing for film is a very different business. Film composers are not in charge of their own work; the director is the boss. In 1948 the Englishman Ralph Vaughan Williams wrote the score for *Scott of the Antarctic*. In a salutary lesson to all students of film composition, he wrote the music *before* seeing the film. The result was that much of the music never made it on to the screen because the film that the director had made did not require all of the music that Vaughan Williams had written. But no matter, because Vaughan Williams used it to create his Seventh Symphony, *Sinfonia Antarctica*.

Despite music playing second fiddle (pun intended) to the drama, some scores have become well known in their own right, and are written by composers who have made careers out of writing for film and neglecting concert music. The scores for *Psycho* and *Cape Fear* by Bernard Hermann, *Batman* by Danny

Elfman, *The Great Escape* by Elmer Bernstein, Jerry Goldsmith's stridently modern *Planet of the Apes* and the many scores of John Williams can compete with music written for the concert platform. Many 'straight' or 'legit' composers have also been drawn to the world of film, especially in its early days. The 1938 score for *Alexander Nevsky* by the Russian composer Sergei Prokofiev is a great example of a piece that transcends the constrictions of the genre. In the 1990s the film score was performed in a concert version with the film projected behind the orchestra. This sort of meeting of the film world and the orchestral world is a mark of their mutual respect, although a more cynical view would be that orchestral musicians like film work because it pays well and film directors like orchestras because they elevate banal stories.

Because of the technical demands of film composition it has now become a separate discipline requiring pinpoint timing and an understanding of how music and image combine to create cinema. Too much scoring can overpower a scene; not enough and the scene can lack meaning. For a film score to earn the respect of classical musicians it must stand up to the same scrutiny as concert music which does not have the benefit of a moving image and must hold the audience's attention on purely musical grounds. But there are examples of pieces that have stood out from the film and had me whistling for weeks after leaving the cinema.

○ **Action:** If you like things dark and moody then Don Davies's eerie *The Matrix* from 1999 displays brilliant use of brass and John Powell's *The Bourne Identity* has a haunting bassoon solo (a large woodwind instrument) and a much-imitated string pattern or *ostinato* (short repeated phrase), although Powell's score does contain synthesisers so it's unlikely to make it into the concert hall. But how could I leave out the Arnold Schwarzenegger classic *Conan the Barbarian* by Basil Poledouris from 1982? A more pompous, melodramatic score does not exist – it ripples with pure Hollywood magic; the horns of the orchestra have never worked as hard.

○ **Shakespeare:** If you were a student of drama in the 1990s then you must have been transfixed, as I was, by Patrick Doyle's score for Kenneth Branagh's film of *Henry V*, in particular the stirring *Non nobis domine* sung on the battlefield by the composer himself.[3] Listening to this version of the Shakespeare play led me to the discovery of the music from the Olivier film of *Henry V* from 1944. This was composed by William Walton (1902–1983) whose work has the edge over the younger composer. In fact it ignited a passion for the music of Walton which took in the inimitable choral work *Belshazzar's Feast* and culminated with a performance where Sam West recited the text whilst the LSO played the music. Thrilling.

○ **Sci-fi:** Apparently it was LSO principal trumpet Maurice Murphy's first day at work when the orchestra sat in the world-famous Abbey Road studios to record the music for *Star Wars* by John Williams. If you don't know the score to *Star Wars* it begins with a blistering trumpet line which repeatedly hits the top of the trumpet's range. Maurice dispatched the part with characteristic brilliance and subsequently played on all six of the *Star Wars* movies. John Williams is one of my favourite film composers because his knowledge and love of classical music is evident in every score. Homages to the great composers can be heard everywhere: Wagner, Mahler, Strauss and particularly Holst's *The Planets Suite* in the case of *Star Wars*. If you are looking for an easy way into classical music then I suggest getting to know his many soundtracks.

I think it's the emotional scope of an orchestra as well as the fear-less playing of individuals such as Maurice Murphy that keeps film directors coming back to this traditional method of scoring a film – even when music technology offers cheaper alternatives: nothing can compete with hearing a full orchestra swell as a film reaches its emotional high point. The influence of film is as important to composers of the twentieth century as literature was in the nineteenth.

There is a commercial drive in film that simply doesn't exist in the world of 'art music'. A new commission for an orchestral piece is likely to be funded by philanthropic organisations hoping to encourage composers to innovate. A director who commissions for a film score is often hoping to add box-office numbers. This has in some cases led to what can only be described as flagrant plagiarism with rehashed versions of previously successful scores. It takes a composer of great personality and vision to create something truly original in this commercial environment, and when they do it's what I call 'classical'.

## Pieces of music that you know but don't know the title

If you watch television or listen to the radio then you might not know who wrote a piece or where it sits in the pantheon of great composers, but you will recognise it on first hearing. From the soundtrack of the BBC series *The Apprentice* (which is remarkably varied, featuring not only an atmospheric score by Dru Masters but many classical pieces by composers such as Stravinsky, Satie, and perhaps most famously its theme tune, 'Dance of the Knights' from Prokofiev's *Romeo and Juliet*) to the British Airways adverts ('The Flower Duet' from Delibes' *Lakmé*) there are countless examples of the plundering of classical music for the benefit of television. Long may it continue.

The following pieces (and those in Appendix I) are those I consider that anybody well versed in this sort of music will most probably have heard. It's the sort of stuff you're likely to hear on the radio, in the background on TV or films or played at shopping centres to prevent the local teenagers from loitering. I'm not saying that any of these pieces on their own will change your life but I believe that if you work your way through some of them then you'll have a sense of the range of classical music that is considered popular. This is first base in your relationship with music and there are at least three more bases to go.

These are the pieces that bring so many people to classical music every year. They get in through the back door on a TV advert and they stick around, bothering you until you find out what they are. That's when you succumb to the power of advertising and shell out for a 'best of' classical CD, and that isn't a bad starting point because chances are there will be something else on that CD that catches your ear.

Dip into this list. It's all available on the internet so you can try before you buy. I use a variety of sources to listen to music before settling on a purchase. Sometimes you can get lucky with YouTube; there are, for instance, videos of Glenn Gould playing the piano before his untimely death in 1982 or a very strange-sounding recording of the last castrato (look it up). There's a brilliant piece of Swedish software called Spotify, though I believe it's not available outside Europe at the moment.[4] It enables you to listen to almost any music for free (periodically you have to suffer some fairly ghastly adverts unless you pay for their premium service). If you are feeling more flush then iTunes and Amazon.co.uk or Amazon.com offer short excerpts to listen to before you download.

Or you could go to a shop. Retro. If you can find one …

## Classical big hitters

o **Carl Orff's *Carmina Burana*: This has seeped into our popular culture; 'O Fortuna' in particular has powered along behind adverts for Guinness, Old Spice, Reebok and Spicy Pringles, opened Ozzy Osbourne's stage show, and was used on Michael Jackson's 'Dangerous' tour. Recently it accompanied the entrance of Simon Cowell and the other** judges on ITV's *X Factor*. *Carmina Burana* has been used in many films, including, to name just a few:

- *Excalibur*, 1981
- *Glory*, 1989
- *Hunt for Red October*, 1990
- *The Doors*, 1991
- *Natural Born Killers*, 1994
- *The Bachelor*, 1999

- Mozart's *Eine Kleine Nachtmusik*: This piece is constantly in use on film and TV, in everything from *The Simpsons* to *X-Men 2, Batman* and *Alien, Charlie's Angels: Full Throttle, Ace Ventura: Pet Detective* … The list goes on.

- Ravel's *Boléro*: Torvill and Dean, of course, made this *the* piece to ice skate to, but *Futurama, Dr Who* and Dudley Moore (in the film *Ten*) have also been accompanied by its motoric, repeated theme.

- Prokofiev's 'Dance of the Knights' from *Romeo and Juliet*: Given that contestants have to be polite to each other even though they'd probably like to kill one another, the use of this courtly dance with murderous undertones from *Romeo and Juliet* seems an entirely appropriate choice as the theme for *The Apprentice*.

- Dvořák's Symphony No. 9 in E Minor, Op. 95, *From the New World*, Largo: Even though that small child stopped peddling up Gold Hill in Shaftesbury, Dorset, some time in the 1970s; even though he was accompanied by a brass band who were presumably (and incongruously) from the north of England; and even though they were playing music by a Czech composer who was writing while on tour in America, this piece is one of Britain's favourites. Multiple Oscar winner Ridley Scott directed this piece of ersatz nostalgia for a Hovis bread commercial and through what might have been a total mess brought the piece to the attention of the wider public.

## Other pieces you may already know – or which won't cause you much trouble if you don't

- Grieg: *Peer Gynt Suites*, 'In the Hall of the Mountain King'/'Solveig's Song'/'Morning'
- Grieg: *Lyric Pieces*, 'Wedding Day at Troldhaugen'
- Tchaikovsky: *Romeo and Juliet Fantasy Overture*
- Wagner: *Ride of the Valkyries*
- Pachelbel: Canon in D Major
- Rimsky-Korsakov, arranged by Rachmaninov: 'Flight of the Bumblebee'
- Barber: Adagio for Strings, Op. 11
- Bizet: 'Au Fond du Temple Saint' from *The Pearl Fishers*
- Massenet: 'Meditation' from *Thaïs*
- Beethoven: Symphony No. 9 in D Minor, Op. 125, 'Choral', Ode an die Freude (final movement)
- Beethoven: Symphony No. 5 in C Minor, Op. 67, first movement
- Verdi: 'Chorus of the Hebrew Slaves' *('Va', Pensiero, Sull'ali Dorate')* from *Nabucco*
- Tchaikovsky: Piano Concerto No. 1 in B Flat Minor, Op. 23
- Berlioz: 'March to the Scaffold' from *Symphonie Fantastique*
- Gershwin: *Rhapsody in Blue*, Andante (or the whole piece if you've time)
- Beethoven: Piano Sonata No. 8 in C Minor, Op. 13 ('Pathétique')
- Vivaldi: *The Four Seasons*, Op. 8, 'Spring', Allegro
- Boccherini: String Quintet in E Major, Op. 11, No. 5
- Verdi: *Messa da Requiem*, Dies Irae – Tuba Mirum (only if you are a Take That fan – it's the beginning of 'Never Forget' … only it doesn't have Robbie Williams in Verdi's version)

Hopefully you've found something which you recognise on this list. Familiarity is a useful tool with all music and I advise giving new pieces a couple of listens before giving up on them. For some more starting points for broadening your listening from the mainstream classical repertoire, see Appendix I.[5]

From here on in you may not recognise the pieces I mention or if you do then you won't have heard them on a TV advert. But just because they haven't been plucked from obscurity to be used as a theme tune or to sell cars doesn't mean they aren't worth listening to. There is so much great music that you'll already have heard … imagine how much more there is to discover.

Chapter **2**

# Why, Why, Why?

## Baggage handling

However much you stick your head in the sand, or maintain a hermit-like existence, it is very hard not to experience some classical music in your life – even if it is while waiting for your bank to answer the telephone. Subconsciously, we all build up an impression of what this world of music is like, and the very idea of 'classical' begins to gather a lot of baggage and preconceptions, what with its penguin suits, clapping regulations, and people waving sticks around.

The path to understanding is riddled with such potholes. Classical music is an activity that can trip you up with unexpected difficulty or drag you down with the weight of a piece you don't understand. Like English spelling it has its own idiosyncrasies and traditions that must simply be learnt.

That said, it may comfort you to know that there are many traditions in classical music that even some musicians don't fully understand: Why is a violin made in that particular shape? Why do opera singers do that wobbly thing? I'll deal with wobbly opera voices in Chapter 10 on singing, but this chapter aims to answer other bothersome questions. It's not an exhaustive list, but these are some of the queries that most often come my way.

## Is classical music for rich people?

Children ask this, adults ask this – everyone asks this – and I wish there was a simple answer. I strongly feel that the music is simply music and can be enjoyed by anyone – but the history of music reveals a complex relationship with money and royalty.

Classical music has relied on the sponsorship and support of benefactors throughout its history. The first examples of written music (as opposed to improvised) were paid for by the Church, and indeed the Church is a source of income for musicians to this day. By the Baroque era (late 1600s to 1750) and Classical era (1750–1800) (more of which later) the most important patronages came from royalty. The 'Sun King' Louis XIV enlisted the services of composer Jean-Baptiste Lully; Joseph Haydn had a generous sponsor in Prince Nikolaus Esterházy; and both Mozart and Beethoven received money from Joseph II, Holy Roman Emperor and Archduke of Austria.

Musicians have always tugged at the coat tails of the rich, who have in turn enjoyed the privilege of having bespoke music on tap. In the case of Lully, he was in the pocket of his patron; the music of Lully reeks of eighteenth-century regal opulence. Some of his slower dances would allow the most bloated aristocrat to saunter around the Palace of Versailles without breaking into a sweat.

During the nineteenth century the middle classes became consumers of music as never before, at first through the dissemination of sheet music to be played on instruments at home: singing songs together or, if they could afford one, around a piano. Away from the large chambers of aristocratic homes people made their own entertainment in pubs; the local musician would have been a prized member of the community.

The fashion for public concerts increased through the nineteenth century and, with the building of purpose-built venues, such as the Royal Albert Hall built in 1871, the Queen's Hall, 1893 (destroyed in the Blitz) and the Wigmore Hall, 1899, music's popularity increased. In the early twentieth century the invention of the gramophone and the wireless radio democratised classical music in a way that was impossible before; now anybody could own a recording of the complete works of Mozart *and* listen to it in their own house. This marked a dramatic change in our relationship to music.

Before these inventions it was difficult for people to hear music without going to a concert. Believe it or not, at one time people would listen to full operas down the telephone. It can't have sounded very good but the pace of invention during the twentieth century was startling: the wireless, a large radio receiving only a few stations, was an exciting window on to the world for my grandmother, who was born in a Welsh mining town in the 1920s, although her father chastised her for using it to listen to 'modern rubbish' such as Glenn Miller. Just twenty years later and my father had a record player in his home, though he had such a small collection of records in his Glasgow flat during the 1940s that as a child he would listen endlessly to the same two recordings of the tenor Beniamino Gigli. When I was a child growing up in south London in the 1970s and '80s I had a record of *Peter and the Wolf* narrated by Peter Ustinov with the Philharmonia Orchestra (recorded in 1960); my version played at 33 rpm and had to be turned over halfway (remember that?). And now I have the complete symphonies of Beethoven on my mobile phone recorded at a quality that would have stunned people even ten years ago.

So where are we now? Surely anyone can access this music? With the CD-buying public as benefactors, classical music has bifurcated into the mainstream and the specialist. More complex forms are available for those interested in musical self-improvement or expanding their knowledge (maybe that's you ...) and simpler, more accessible forms are there for those looking for a less bumpy musical ride. This can be seen clearly in the difference between BBC Radio 3 and Classic FM, where one offers in-depth analysis of a broad range of specialist works and the other caters well for a more populist palate, offering more easily digestible bite-size chunks.

Those who are more affluent can afford the tickets to see music at the more complicated end of the spectrum. At the best international venues with the finest orchestras, music is painstakingly pored over by professional musicians at the height of their powers. Gaining an introduction to the more complex forms of music tends to require an investment of three things: some musical education, time to go to concerts and the money to pay for tickets. It's little wonder that the people who attend the best concerts have these three in abundance.

66 *In Europe, when a rich woman has an affair with a conductor, they have a baby. In America, she endows an orchestra for him.* 99

EDGARD VARÈSE, composer

Today, American orchestras rely on donations from private sources. In Europe too it's more likely that a lawyer, businessman or banker with a passion for music will be the 'angel' behind a concert, since royal patronages have all but finished. These investors can be a godsend for arts organisations but the situation is not without its problems when venues require large injections of liquid cash for upgrades. When the Royal Court Theatre fell into disrepair in 1994 the Jerwood Foundation were on hand with a large amount of money, but one of their requests was that the theatre should be renamed 'The Jerwood Royal Court Theatre'. Thankfully the theatre resisted and the historic name remains above the door. It's a tightrope between getting money and not surrendering your artistic independence.

In 1999 the Cuban-American philanthropist Alberto Vilar promised £10 million towards the regeneration of the Royal

Opera House in London. Vilar was fêted as the most generous man in opera; the ROH named its Vilar Floral Hall after him and the Vilar Grand Tier at the Metropolitan Opera in New York was a testament to the influence of his chequebook. But this relationship turned sour in 2005 when he failed to make the final payments (he was rumoured to be around £5 million short, a not insubstantial sum for the opera house). A further shock was in store for the opera community when Vilar was jailed for fraud in 2008. It's easy to see how this situation arose because without these sorts of donations organisations would simply not survive. Nobody could have predicted that Vilar would turn villain. His name has long since been scrubbed off the ROH's walls and replaced with the names of other generous (and unimpeachable) organisations – the Paul Hamlyn Foundation gave its name to the Floral Hall and the Oak Foundation's vice-chair Jette Parker gave her name to the young artist programme. Though the name of Vilar has been excised, it's a salutary lesson for the arts world which walks a tightrope between artistic independence and financial dependence.

Music itself is, I believe, essentially classless, requiring no more than a pair of ears and a brain to comprehend it. However, to write or play this music professionally requires years of study at the best conservatoires. Who but the wealthy can afford to pay for the necessary sort of private tuition? Even if a child begins lessons at school there will come a point when somebody needs to buy an instrument and pay for music festival entries or youth orchestra subscriptions. It's under fairly exceptional circumstances that somebody becomes a professional classical musician without any financial support from their parents.

The more complex the music, the more expensive. A 100-piece orchestra means 100 player fees, 100 chairs to set out, 100 scores to print, 100 shirts to press, etc. In orchestral circles the pay is quite modest. It's certainly not equivalent to a professional footballer and yet the training and skill required is equivalent to that needed for brain surgery. That is what your ticket is paying for: it's not going into the coffers of plutocrats.

Until we educate everybody in the country to the same musical standard (lovely in theory but expensive in practice) and convince schools that classical music is important regardless of class (an uphill battle in some institutions) it will remain the preserve of those who are introduced to it in the correct way.

## What is a *key*?

This is straight in at the deep end, but we may as well get this out of the way. No way of explaining the key of a piece captures all of its subtleties, but that's part of the beauty of music: you can't put it into words. It's an important concept to get your head round because it's central to the development of classical music.

My father tells a story of entering a singing competition at a holiday camp in 1964.

'Do you know "Always Something There to Remind Me" by Sandie Shaw?' he asked of the resident pianist.

'Er. Yes I think so,' came the reply, although with a worrying hesitation.

The moment came and they faced the audience. Now if you know the song then you might recall that the tune begins low in Miss Shaw's voice and then builds up to the high notes of the chorus. My dad was just a few notes in when he realised the song was quite simply far too high for him (a bass-baritone) – the pianist was playing in the wrong *key*. Family legend has it that he stood on a table to try to reach the top notes; I doubt that helped.

Many famous songs build to similar perilous climaxes: songs like Bon Jovi's 'Living on a Prayer', Liverpool FC's 'You'll Never Walk Alone' and anything by Michael Jackson have busted many a larynx when sung at a karaoke bar. These songs are written in a key that is comfortable for the original performer but which may not suit lesser mortals. Also we are born with a particular voice, either high – soprano/tenor; medium – mezzo-soprano/

baritone; or low – alto/bass. There's nothing you can do to change this.

It wouldn't matter if you were only singing in the shower, but if you have foolishly agreed to perform at your friend's wedding you need to work out a way of being able to hit those high notes. Mel Brooks used to tell a story of a singer who started a song on a key note that was too high and ended with a gut-wrenching high note and a hernia. Beware – singing can damage your health. If you start a bit lower in pitch, that will allow you to hit that high note at the end of the tune (which will also be correspondingly lower). Problem is, when it comes to the wedding, how will you remember which note you have to start on? You could sing the note, find the note on the piano that sounds the same, and that will help you find the 'key'. The 'key' is the musical area where your tune lies.

## KEYS, SCHMEES

Each note on the piano has a name and that can be the name of a key. So we name C major after the note 'C' because pieces in that key *feel* related to that note. They seem to orbit around that *tonal centre* (another way of describing key) like planets orbiting the Sun. In the key of C major the note 'C' is the Sun and all the other notes are still there but in orbit. If we change to the key of G then the note 'G' becomes the Sun, and the centre of the Solar System. Keys are held together by natural forces like gravity. There are twelve keys in total named after all the notes of the scale.

But hang on, you say, there are 88 keys on a piano, not 12. Yes, but if you look at a piano keyboard it has a pattern that repeats as you go from left to right. It's a bit like a clock face, returning to the same starting point: C, D, E, F, G, A, B … then you are back to C. So there are lots of Cs on the piano, but there is only one 'key' of C.

The thing to remember is the idea of labelling the starting notes of your tune. At the risk of sounding like the late great Humph milking his metaphors on *I'm Sorry I Haven't a Clue*, your tune is like a mobile home, which needs a place to sit. Your mobile home can be moved up or down the mountain (hopefully along with the lovely Samantha). And just as in life, if you move your home, it is quite dramatic. That is called a 'key change'. If you listen to Stevie Wonder's 'I Just Called to Say I Love You', you will hear him change the key of the piece at the end.

## What is a composer?

Speaking of Stevie Wonder, why is it that he is mostly called a songwriter, or someone who writes great tunes, but Haydn is called a 'composer'? Composition is the art of organising sound in time. I'm being that vague because there are composers such as John Cage (1912–1992), who wrote a piece called 4' 33" which is entirely silent. Yes, silent – except it isn't really, because although the performer is told not to make any sound, it makes you realise that there is always some sound going on, even in a room full of people trying desperately not to cough, which I think was Cage's point. Next time you are in a 'silent' place, count the number of sounds you can hear. You'll be amazed. (In December 2010 the work reached number 21 in the pop charts as a protest purchase by people angry at Simon Cowell's *X-Factor* machine.) Another of Cage's pieces involves only metal instruments and it sounds much like my attempts at cooking. So in the end there are as many strange examples of what people define as music as there are examples of what people consider to be art.

In the traditional sense a composer is somebody who writes down notes for other people to play. Sometimes composers imagine the notes in their head and then pour them out on to paper. Mozart was said to have been able to do this, as was the French composer Ravel (1875–1937), who wrote the famous *Boléro*, until he suffered from a degeneration of his brain which tragically left him unable to put pen to paper, a condition known as agraphia. 'The opera is in my head,' he said. 'I hear it, but I will never write it down.'[1] Many people have music inside them, but it takes great discipline and skill to be able to translate that on to the page for somebody else to play and it takes years of practice to write it down in such a way that you can have it played exactly as you imagined.

Not all composers can just put it straight on to the page like that. In some cases, composers use a piano to work things out, although some composers claim this makes what they write sound like piano music – rather than, say, a flute piece. If you are writing for a flute, they say, it's better to imagine the sound of a flute playing than to listen to the sound of a piano impersonating the flute. Having little pianistic ability is not necessarily a block to becoming a composer: Irving Berlin, the great American song-writer who gave us 'White Christmas' and 'How Deep is the Ocean', was famously bad at the piano and would only play the black notes. 'The key of C,' he said, 'is only for people who study music.'[2] (You get the key of C if you play on the white notes.) He even had a piano made with a special lever to change keys.

Some composers are professional musicians, some of them are also conductors and others just do it in their spare time. There is no one rule. Composers are often consumed by their desire to write music; some are meticulous about detail, concentrating on a small output, while other composers are prolific, producing works to order. Henri Duparc (1848–1933) was so self-critical that he destroyed most of his own compositions, leaving only thirteen songs with which he was satisfied. Compare that to the output of Joseph Haydn (1732–1809) who wrote 106 symphonies.

Recent technological advances have meant that many composers now use computers to print the music physically, a process that took hours in the past. Preparing 100 parts for the musicians can now be done at the touch of a button and the computer even allows the composer to hear a version of their score as they are composing. How different from when Bach was writing his music for the weekly church services in Leipzig from 1723 to 1750. He would only have a week to compose, write, prepare parts and then rehearse an entirely new work. Imagine what a computer could have done for him! I've heard musicians complain that computers lead to a lack of rigour in the writing of scores as young composers become lazy and allow the computer to do too much of the work. I believe the same is said of university essays, many of which have been copied from the internet. Either way, we have come a long way from quills, parchment and candlewax.

As for how composers choose those notes, the techniques are almost as varied as the musicians themselves. People have used maths, chance, improvisation, philosophical schemes and systems galore to create new sounds and musical ideas. Thankfully a lot of the process remains mysterious. As film-maker and scriptwriter David Mamet once said when asked where his ideas came from, 'Oh, I just think of them.'

I'll talk about how composers write melody and harmony, along with how they structure their work, in later chapters.

## How strange, the change …

Musicians always talk about 'major and minor'. What are they? How do I know if a piece is 'minor'? Firstly there's an important distinction to be made between 'a major work' or a 'minor work' and pieces in a major or minor *key*. Major/minor has nothing to do with importance. It's about the musical character of the piece. You can have C major and C minor, just as you might have 'Gareth cheery' or 'Gareth contemplative'. Simply put, pieces in 'major keys' are more sunny and bright, those in a 'minor key' tend to be more moody and dark.

These aren't random associations but they are reinforced by the music we are used to hearing. Minor keys sound more unsettling than major keys because they contain barely perceptible dissonance (notes that clash). To the untrained ear this is hard to hear but without going into the science of harmonics (and feel free to look into this yourself) I think that's really all that is necessary to understand at this point.

- ○ Beethoven's 'Moonlight' Sonata, first movement – minor key
- ○ Bach's Brandenburg Concerto No. 3 in G Major, first movement – major key

## Who decided which instruments made up an orchestra?

Nobody sat down and planned the orchestra, and even now it's not absolutely fixed. Each time a composer writes a piece they are at liberty to use pretty much whatever instruments they like (within reason and subject to the confines of budget: those cannons in the 1812 Overture aren't cheap!) The orchestra is like a greatest hits of the instrumental world, because there have been countless instruments created in the history of music but the orchestra is a condensation of all those variations into the best modern examples.

A large modern symphony orchestra will have a certain number of musicians in its employ: on average about 60 strings, 13 woodwind, 12 brass and some percussionists. Music from earlier periods used fewer instruments; conversely, modern composers can use an extremely large number (more than 100). For large-scale works this orchestra might employ 'extras', such as a piano or harp, that aren't used by every composer in every piece, or something more exotic such as an electric guitar, saxophone or theremin (an eerie electronic instrument popular in 1940s–1960s sci-fi and mystery films such as *Spellbound* and *The Day the Earth Stood Still*).

Mahler's Symphony No. 8, 'Symphony of a Thousand', uses a huge orchestra and is only performed on special occasions. Its subtitle is due to the huge personnel required to mount a performance. This is the apotheosis of the nineteenth-century orchestra.

## SYMPHONY OF A THOUSAND

piccolo

4 flutes

4 oboes

cor anglais

4 clarinets

bass clarinet

4 bassoons

contra-bassoon

8 horns

4 trumpets

4 trombones

1 tuba

3 timpani

bass drum

cymbal

tamtam

triangle

tubular bells

glockenspiel

celeste

piano

harmonium

organ

2 harps

mandolin

strings (violins, violas, 'cellos
  and basses)

offstage 4 trumpets and
  3 trombones

3 sopranos

2 altos

tenor

baritone

bass

boys' choir

double chorus (usually more
  than 200 singers)

## There's classical music and music from the Classical 'period' … I'm confused

*The Oxford Dictionary of Music* describes the term Classical as 'vague', then goes on to list four completely different definitions. To clear things up, there is a particular musical period that we refer to as 'Classical' and there is a broad term 'classical music' which encompasses both the 'Classical period' and all of the serious music from the last thousand years.

Mozart is an example of a composer of the Classical period (note the capital letter), so he can be accurately described as a 'Classical composer'. His music conforms to classical principles of beauty and form. It's music from a time when, in art and architecture, people were looking back to 'classical antiquity' or ancient Greece for inspiration – hence the term 'classical'. To be pedantic, according to that definition Webern, Schumann, John Adams and Stravinsky cannot be described as 'classical composers'.

When I was at school, trying desperately to understand the chronology of music, my school music teacher refused to refer to any music other than that written between 1750 (the year of Bach's death) and 1897 (the year of Schubert's birth) as 'Classical'. He preferred 'serious music' as a moniker for anything outside the popular realm. This is a useful definition as far as it goes: classical music is a serious business. But what about other forms that are equally serious: jazz, folk or 'world' music, for example?

Outside the ivory towers in common parlance 'classical music' is everything that isn't jazz, pop, folk or world music. It is confusing that we use the term to mean pretty much any music written in the last thousand years. But then the term 'pop' is too generic a term to describe adequately the commercial music of the last fifty years.

If you wince at this double meaning every time you encounter it you'll end up with a sore face. Accept it and move on, is my advice.

## If it's classical does it mean it isn't popular music?

Calculating how many fans an art-form needs in order to call it 'popular' is anyone's guess, and even within classical music there is a divide between populist material and more esoteric or specialised music. Sitting in a packed Royal Albert Hall for a

Prom certainly gives off a sense of popular appeal, but how will the figures stack up against a pop music tour?

The Arts Council[3] divided the audience for musical events in the UK into broad churches[4] (classical music performance, opera or operetta, jazz, other live music event – rock and pop, soul, R&B and hip-hop, folk, country and western, etc.) and gathered audience attendance figures for 2005/2006. It concluded that opera had the smallest reach of all music: 4 per cent of the population attended at least once a year. For classical music that figure was around 9 per cent. However, even the very broad 'other' category, which encompasses pop and rock, only adds up to 26 per cent of the population, again, attending a gig at least once a year.[5]

Classical musicians tend not to crave the lifestyle that goes with mass popularity, being more dedicated to their art than to their public image. If we are going to measure by record sales or by numbers of tickets sold, then, yes, classical equals fewer sales than other forms. But there are good reasons for that: once a classical music fan has bought a recording of *Symphonie Fantastique* by Hector Berlioz they may well listen to that recording without need for another one for the next forty years. This is not the case in more popular forms which have innovation as one of the driving marketing forces.

There are clearly exceptions, where a popular appetite meets the classical world. In 1994 The Three Tenors (José Carreras, Plácido Domingo and Luciano Pavarotti) achieved a level of popular success hitherto thought impossible. Not since the great recordings of Enrico Caruso in 1902 had the operatic tenor voice been such a recording sensation. The association with football must have helped it, but achieving a Guinness world record for best-selling classical music with the *Three Tenors in Concert* CD shows that a great tune, well sung, has mass appeal even if it is classical.

But don't be too heartened; the general trend doesn't look great. A December 2010 article in the *Daily Telegraph* reported:

The classical market share has now sunk from nearly 11% in 1990 to 3.2%. According to figures drawn from the major retailers, the sector has seen sales in the last twelve-month period drop by a staggering 17.6%. This contrasts starkly with a 3.5% drop in pop recordings.

The CD market has been adversely affected by the rise of the internet and most classical fans who bought large collections of CDs in the 1990s don't feel the need to replace them with iTunes downloads. Because I'm passionate about this music, I don't care about numbers or sales as much as I care that there is enough of an audience to keep the art-form developing. People who are into classical music become obsessed by it and give time and hard-earned money to attend concerts. It's popular in my house and I hope it will be in yours too. It's not supposed to be as easy as *Coronation Street*, it's meant to be deeply rewarding.

## Why do classical players need things written down? Other musicians don't

As with every form of music there are conventions which dictate how players train and how they learn new music. The 'Western classical' approach relies on over 500 years of musical notation. This enables an orchestra to play any music that is put in front of them, even at first sight. This has obvious advantages for playing new music. Of course there are exceptions. It is unusual for opera singers to use a musical score because they are expected to act and to face the audience. The same is often true of soloists in a concerto – a kind of piece that crops up a lot in classical music (see Chapter 9 on structure for a definition).

Concertos have been around for about 400 years and involve one soloist who plays in tandem with the orchestra. The style has developed from its beginnings where the soloist was a part of the orchestra (see Handel's Concerti Grossi or Bach's Brandenburg Concertos) to the Romantic concerto which makes a feature of the virtuosity of the soloist, who is placed out in front of the orchestra, normally in a fancy outfit (see Rachmaninov's piano concertos or Bruch's violin concertos).

It is usual for the concerto soloist to play from memory (although in very complex modern works they may be seen with a score). This requires a different sort of musicianship that, although partly a bravura display of technical wizardry, is mainly a form of sustained communication with the audience. If a player is hidden behind a music stand with their head buried in the score it can make it harder to reach the audience with the performance: there is a physical barrier. Because a concerto requires much study to perfect, a soloist might tour the world playing a few pieces from memory with different orchestras, whereas the orchestra itself will play a much wider range of music.

Orchestras have two or three rehearsals before a concert and always read from a score rather than memorising; what is sometimes lost is the sense that the music has been learnt not just from memory but is somehow 'in their bones'. In some instances, due to budget restrictions, orchestras go out to play a concert on too few rehearsals and it tells in the final result – especially in new work which can take a while to become familiar. That said, during the course of a violinist's professional life they could expect to play every Beethoven, Brahms and Schubert symphony many times with many different conductors. So core repertoire will always be played without feeling that the players are hanging off the score.

The atmosphere at an early 9 a.m. rehearsal after playing a big concert the night before is always subdued, and players are not always sure what the orchestra will be playing next. They bumble in with their cappuccinos, warming up briefly before launching into the next major work. The prospect of removing the sheet music would fill most orchestral players with horror; they have become accustomed to this way of playing. Many would admit to being incapable of improvisation and reluctant to play from memory, a skill that is a requirement of so many other types of music. But few rock guitarists would be able to play a five-hour gig one night then get up the next day and rehearse an elaborately arranged musical composition they had never previously played, before jetting off on tour to play something they haven't played for several weeks. Such are the rigours of orchestral life.

## Does listening to Mozart make you more intelligent?[6]

In 1993 there was a widely reported piece of research by Rauscher, Shaw and Ky. They played a Mozart sonata to students, who subsequently showed an improved IQ test result in the area of spatio-temporal skills. For musicians and classical music advocates like me who constantly try to assert the value of classical music (especially for young people), it was as though all prayers had been answered; here at last was proof that this music was good for you. The world's press were delighted with the idea that the Sonata for Two Pianos in D-major, K. 448, could 'make you smarter'. This was the trick that every parent had been seeking, and for a number of years a lot of children were subjected to Mozart whether they liked it or not.

As is so often the case with science in the media, the facts of the study were stretched and the original findings of 1993 have since been widely challenged. Quite simply the research had never suggested that it 'made you smarter'. But the idea had made a great news story and gave rise to a whole industry of Mozart-for-kids products.

Although discredited, the 'Mozart effect' lives on in other guises, and people claim to have observed the calming effect of Mozart on people in stations, children with special needs – and cows. In Germany a study found that cows who listened to Mozart produced more milk. How much milk I'm not sure. Whether the milk was more creamy I cannot say. Behind this strange idea lies some fairly questionable science and the deification of Mozart.

Does Mozart make you cleverer? I don't think so. However, there is compelling evidence from MRI scans that playing an instrument or taking singing lessons actually changes the size of sections of your brain. (Steven Mithen took singing lessons for a year whilst writing his book *The Singing Neanderthal*; by the end of the year there were *physical* changes in his brain.)

The 'Mozart effect' is actually a massive red herring – playing any music will develop your brain, but then so will learning golf, or learning to ride a bike. The difference with music is that it is one of the most complex activities the brain can engage in and so develops the parts that other activities cannot reach on their own. For this reason it is beloved of primary school teachers and parents of young children because of the palpable effect that practical engagement with music has on the developing mind.

If it won't make you cleverer then what does Mozart do for you? It may make me sound like Oscar Wilde, but I believe it's important to have beauty in our lives. It makes us aspire to be better people. Mozart's is some of the most pleasing and mentally stimulating music ever written; it *excites* our brains into action. Beyond that I don't see the *need* to prove that it makes us cleverer. Those of us who are devotees of Mozart will always be passionate about its transformative power and those who aren't convinced will just have to live their lives devoid of Mozart's positive effects.


## Is all classical music religious?

At one time the Church was one of the few places where people would have had access to music. No other organisation has done more for the development of music. But no, it's not all religious. Composers have been moved and inspired by landscape (God-created or not), science, politics, war, philosophy, football … There's even an opera about the life of *Playboy* model Anna Nicole Smith. (I'm definitely going to that one.)

Let's be honest, there's a great deal of religious classical music and some of the most beautiful is sung by choirs. Choral music in particular is associated with cathedrals, cassocks and candles – John Rutter's carols and other religious works are immensely popular – but choirs can also sing modern pop songs, as proved by the hit TV show *Glee*. Speaking of Rutter, I am a huge fan. He has a technical expertise and a way with melody that has made him not only a composer of international note, but his harmonies have become for many (myself included) the sound of Christmas.[7]

## How can you 'understand' music? Isn't it just about emotion?

In the same way that a picture of a man running can simply mean 'man running' or be the symbol for a fire exit, music can be rich with meaning. Certain musical meanings are almost universal, and have gathered meaning through repetition. 'Happy Birthday' is widely known, and as soon as you hear the melody you know that it's someone's birthday, whatever language you speak. If you juxtapose that music with a rendition of the third movement of Chopin's Piano Sonata No. 2 (yes, you do know it, it's the Funeral March) then the meaning becomes cloudier … Did someone die on their birthday? Are there two events going on simultaneously? The music itself gives rise to potential meaning.

Much music of the nineteenth century has clear titles giving a sense of the meaning. This is known as *programme* music: Mendelssohn's *Fingal's Cave*, for instance, is an attempt in music to describe the experience of an encounter with a geographical feature; Richard Strauss's *Ein Heldenleben* ('A Hero's Life') is a wordless musical representation of an entire life. It is not literal; rather it aims to sum up the feelings of the protagonist as he progresses through life. The musical meaning is clear to the listener, as is Strauss's vision of this character. Programme music will sometimes feature musical effects designed to illustrate, for instance, the singing of birds or the babbling of a brook, but may attempt to express emotions such as joy or grief.

Of course not all music has such clear associations. We call this *absolute* music. But even in music by composers who apparently give no clue to the meaning you can deduce what the composer means, if only on an emotional level. It may have a stylistic meaning – a *scherzo* (Italian, meaning 'jokingly'), for example, is a section of music that is fast and lively. If this is followed by a *lento* (Italian for slowly) then the abrupt change will have an effect on the listener. The meaning of music is abstract and highly personal.

## Why is a violinist the 'leader' of an orchestra?

This is partly tradition and partly practical. If you think about how the violin is played, with the bow held high in the air, it's very easy for other players to see the movement of the bow and thus when the music begins. The violins usually play more music than the other sections – note for note it's not as tiring as playing a brass instrument. Moreover, you can play the violin while looking in almost any direction, and the player's face can still communicate to the other players (try doing that while playing a trombone). Look carefully and you'll see that the 'leader' uses exaggerated movements to indicate the style of playing to the entire string section. In the days before the dominance of the conductor, either a keyboard player or a violinist would have directed performances.

## Why does the orchestra tune to an oboe at the beginning of a concert?

Unless you've been to an orchestral concert you wouldn't be aware that in order to keep in tune with each other the orchestra must adjust their instruments just before the concert. This can't be done outside the concert hall because temperature can affect tuning, as instruments contract and expand with heat. The oboe provides a steady tone (normally an A) which is easier to tune to than other wind instruments. The oboe is less likely to be far out of tune when taken out of its case than other instruments. String instruments can be wildly out, so it's important for them to have a clear example of a note that the orchestra can agree on. The signal to tune the orchestra is when the leader enters and stands in front of the orchestra. The note 'A' is played and the different sections take it in turn to tune. In his Ninth Symphony Beethoven starts the work with a section which sounds very similar to the orchestra tuning up – it's a kind of 'in' joke.

## Why do some composers deliberately use unpleasant sounds? Shouldn't music be lush and beautiful?

I'll deal with the whys and wherefores of harmony in Chapter 7. The short answer is that many composers believe that the purpose of 'serious music' is not to send you to sleep but to invigorate and challenge the listener; in order to achieve this, composers have used some arresting sounds. If a piece doesn't sound lush it may be because the subject matter does not require it: should music about war or death be beautiful? Discuss.

## Is it OK to be bored by classical music? (I often am)

Chapter 12 is about surviving a concert, and I use the word surviving deliberately. I don't wish to hoodwink you into believing that all classical music is exciting and every concert is a masterpiece. I have spoken to many professional musicians who readily admit to finding certain music boring. It's OK. Seek out the music that stimulates and reject that which, after a good listen, turns out to be boring. The composer won't mind – he'll most likely be dead.

## Good point – on that subject, are all composers dead white guys?

No. But, as in many professions, women and non-Europeans struggled for recognition. At one time classical music only existed within the European world, but as the music becomes increasingly international, interesting forms of music are emerging that are influenced by 'non-Western' musics. Recording has been a help here in spreading high-quality music right around the globe.

There are many examples of music written by people who are not white Europeans: Samuel Coleridge-Taylor (not to be confused with the poet Samuel Taylor Coleridge) was a successful black English composer born in 1875 who studied at the Royal College of Music and won the support of Edward Elgar; Heitor Villa-Lobos (1887–1959), the Brazilian composer; Tan Dun (b. 1957), who writes with a distinctively Chinese voice; Astor Piazzolla (1921–1992), who elevated the Argentinean tango to a form of art music. It is no longer the preserve of a small group of white men from central Europe.

In fact there are constant efforts by the classical music world to reach out to communities who are not traditionally associated with this music. I've been involved with many such projects, and they work: I've taken Rachmaninov to African Carribean communities in Hackney; singing projects to predominantly Muslim schools in Tower Hamlets; and run composition projects at Alexandra Burke's old school in North London (I think she was there at the time but I don't remember her ...). I stand in admiration of El Sistema in Venezuela which teaches classical instruments to underprivileged children. This chimes with the dream of many classical musicians – that anybody can appreciate this wonderful music. The world famous tenor Plácido Domingo is said to have cried when he heard the Simón Bolivar Youth Orchestra of Venezuela. A handful of musicians may enjoy the prestige that comes from the exclusivity of classical music but in my experience most of us would like everyone to feel the same as we do.

Apart from composers such as Hildegard of Bingen, the twelfth-century abbess; Fanny Henschel, Felix Mendelssohn's sister; and Judith Weir, one of Britain's most successful contemporary composers[8], unfortunately most people don't realise how many female composers there are. There are also many, many composers who are not dead. It's just that it often takes a while for their music to be recognised internationally – by which time they may well be deceased.

## Who is the greatest composer?

J.S. Bach … no wait – Mozart. Hold on … Schubert. *Stop!* Stravinsky. This is impossible to answer and changes every day according to my mood. In my opinion the greatest composer is whoever is holding your attention.

## Are musical geniuses made, not born?

All music requires hard work to perfect. Even to reach a rudimentary level on an instrument takes several years of practice, and to reach a professional standard a person must start at a young age while the brain is still adaptable – I've never met a professional classical instrumentalist who started their instrument after the age of twenty. Some composers have to work harder than others at their craft. Some composers are more formal in their approach to music; others are more instinctive, but for all of them it's a craft, and that takes work.

Perfect pitch, which is the ability to recognise the name of a note without access to an instrument, is a musical gift that emerges in childhood; it often goes hand in hand with early training and other musical abilities. You'd suspect that this would only exist in a small percentage of the population; however, neuroscientist Daniel Levitin has proved (through some very innovative experiments) that in fact most people have the ability to some degree. They do not realise they have this capacity because it is not as highly developed as it would be in a musician.[9] Who knows how many Mozarts exist who never had the chance to play a piano?

It's not that perfect pitch is the mark of a musical genius but it has always been considered an ability of the most highly gifted musicians. To discover that in fact we all have the potential, given the right circumstances, to develop musical gifts does not detract from the achievements of a Bach, Beethoven or Mozart. They were born with the same mental faculties as the rest of us – they just worked harder.

In the case of Mozart, who was the son of a successful musician, he had just the right combination of circumstance and talent to start him composing. His prodigious mental gifts enabled him to complete musical tasks that others would struggle with, and sheer hard work got him there in the end. Had Mozart been raised by the local blacksmith I doubt he would have been the composer he became at the age of eight, when he wrote his first symphony – his upbringing, which by modern standards might seem like pushy parenting, enabled him to succeed. It's a lesson to all aspirational parents.

I think that the whole concept of genius does a disservice to the brilliance of our great composers. It's a nonsense that a composer can write a great symphony on inspiration alone. It takes at least ten years and thousands of repetitions to learn any new skill; becoming the architect of a great piece of classical music means you've probably discarded a lot of rubbish first, and that you've developed calluses on your hands from practising your art.

# Can a voice be made, not born?

This is another matter altogether. We are born with a voice that is uniquely our own. No amount of money or training can make a small vocal instrument into a big one or an ugly one into a beautiful one. Training can improve the sound hugely but if you fundamentally sound like a goat then there's not much that can be done about it.

# Were ye olde instrumentalists better than now?

That depends on how you define 'better'. Listening to recordings from the early twentieth century I'm struck by the difference in playing style. The ready availability of quality recordings has pushed standards higher and higher. Grade VIII used to be the standard required for admission to music college; that's no longer a guarantee. As demand for places has intensified, young players get better and better.

Unfortunately, although evidence exists in some of the reviews of the time,[10] we'll never hear Bach's unparalleled mastery of the organ, or Mozart's keyboard extemporisation. To my ear there has never been a better time to listen to music. Audio equipment is cheap and of high quality. Recordings from the last century are readily available and you can hear playing of immaculate accuracy in most modern concert halls for a reasonable amount of money.

# Why don't classical musicians improvise?

It's easy to forget that classical music used to involve a lot of improvisation. This can still be heard in certain pieces although it might not be immediately apparent that it's made up – mostly because the musician will often practise their extemporising. Soloists in music of the eighteenth century played *cadenzas* (which is Italian for cadence) towards the end of a large instrumental work. This gave the soloist a chance to show off their technical skill. As American musicologist, composer and pianist Robert Levin says: 'In the 18th century all composers were performers and virtually all performers composed. Furthermore, virtually all the music performed was new. Today's gap in popular and art music did not exist then: each involved spontaneity within a language idiomatic to the time.'[11]

Mozart was one of the first great composers to have a piano in his study, and his improvising talents were noted very early in his life.[12] In his memoirs,[13] a priest called Placidus Scharl recalls hearing the six-year-old Mozart at the keyboard:

> One had only to give him the first subject which came to mind for a fugue or an invention: he would develop it with strange variations and constantly changing passages as long as one wished; he would improvise fugally on a subject for hours, and this fantasia-playing was his greatest passion.

Organists are still very familiar with the idea of extemporisation (in his organ recitals, my old music teacher Stephen Carleston would include improvisation on a theme brought in by a member of the audience on the day). Many composers still use improvisation as a way of generating ideas – but as classical music has tended to separate the idea of the player and composer, and has become very concerned with replicating exactly what has been notated in a score, improvisation has taken a back seat – even though it is alive and well in other music, such as jazz. Twentieth-century and contemporary composers, however, have brought back the idea of chance and improvisation, and some players schooled very heavily in faithfully reproducing the 'dots' enjoy the very different kind of playing improvisation offers. In some very early music, too, the notation is only part of the story, and singers are required to decorate and elaborate on what is written down in order to bring the music to life.

# Why do orchestras (mostly) wear black?

It's cheap and doesn't show sweat. It also denotes smartness and comes from evening dress, which was the traditional wear of classical musicians for many years and still is at many concerts. At one time the audience too would have worn evening dress for concerts. Another reason is that musicians in an orchestra, as performers, are in service to the music rather than being exhibitionists who are promoting themselves, and in this sense black allows them a certain visual degree of anonymity. Some younger ensembles have attempted alternatives but generally it's hard to find something that is readily available, appears fairly neutral so as not to distract from the music and looks like the orchestra have made an effort. So I think for the time being black is here to stay.

Chapter **3**

# How to Listen

*❝ When I speak of the gifted listener, I am thinking of the non-musician primarily, of the listener who intends to retain his amateur status. It is the thought of just such a listener that excites the composer in me. ❞*

AARON COPLAND, composer

What is 'listening'? What are you supposed to be hearing and how is it possible to change the way you listen? Why is it that classical musicians can talk endlessly about the merits of one violinist over another? Does it really affect how I listen if I know that Mozart was born in 1756 or any of the myriad of apparently pointless facts that seem to surround classical music? And finally, what on earth is 'authentic performance'? Listening to classical music is not as simple as bunging on a CD and opening your ears.

## How we listen

Lesson one: there is no one correct way to listen to classical music or any other kind of music because it's an intensely personal business. That said, there are facets of the music that you may not have thought about that can direct your listening – and a little knowledge will not only give you a greater understanding but will make you sound like an expert at the bar afterwards. Most gratifying.

In some ways our tolerance for classical music can be lessened by more immediately rewarding and popular forms. As Noël Coward, with typical acerbity, once remarked: 'Extraordinary how potent cheap music is.' We are raised on a musical diet of trash; everywhere we go there is 'cheap' music in lifts, restaurants, waiting rooms, garages, shopping centres, TV adverts, the radio, telephone call centre holding music … the list is endless. This music, as Coward points out, is potently gripping and effective. To me it can be a form of torture, but more importantly I think it affects the way we listen.

**66** *Any time I travel anywhere it seems I'm forced to endure an inconsiderate person's noise. I might even normally like the song but don't really want it imposed upon me when I have, as most commuters do, other pressing matters to think about.*[1] **99**

> CHARLEY, 26-year-old commuter, complaining about mobiles playing music on buses (from Transport for London's website)

*66 We are increasingly likely to find ourselves in places with background music. No composers have thought to write for these modern spaces, which represent 30% of our musical experience. 99*

BRIAN ENO

The Polish composer Witold Lutoslawski (1913–1994) said: 'People whose sensibility is destroyed by music in trains, airports, lifts, cannot concentrate on a Beethoven quartet.' My bank has had the same music on its telephone banking service since 1997. I have heard that music so many times that I wake up singing it. There is no escape: if you want to speak to the bank then you *will* listen to this music. The title of this masterpiece of call-centre *muzak* is unknown to me. (The word muzak, incidentally, is derived from the Muzak Holdings company in the US, who specialised in ways of delivering this branch of music to public environments.) I agree with Lutoslawski that this damages our 'sensibility' towards music. It hasn't ruined my appreciation of classical music – but it clogs my ears and doesn't set me up well for a symphony. Muzak trains us to block out background music and noise, which is the opposite of what is necessary when I listen to classical music, where I require calm and quiet with open ears.

And it's not just since the invention of beatboxes in the 1980s; our cities have been noisy for a long time. The classical musician driven mad by the noise made by music from the street was brilliantly encapsulated by the engraver William Hogarth in *The Enraged Musician* (1741). In the window the musician is playing the violin, a classy instrument, while the noise of the street includes baser instruments such as drums and hunting horns. The musician's wig and attire suggest that he comes from a higher-status world than the noisy rabble outside, and he is disgusted by the appalling music of the street. I suspect part of his frustration stems from an incredulity that they don't just stop what they are doing and listen to his infinitely superior fiddling. It looks like he has no intention of listening to them even if there is a rather pretty singer in their midst.

There is a passionate campaign against 'piped music' run by an organisation called 'Pipedown – the campaign for freedom from piped music'. It's a rather small revolution, but one that matters to music lovers. We are assaulted by music at every step through our modern cities, and finding restaurants and pubs that don't play music is becoming more and more difficult. You may think that this is the whingeing of a musical snob. Does this matter to ordinary people? I think it should, because not only is it an imposition but it desensitises us to music.

If we overdose on facile forms it makes the complexities and subtleties of classical music seem laborious. The function of popular music is fundamentally different: it aims to be as immediately pleasing, as sonically gratifying and as exciting as possible, and to do all that in a very short space of time. In the time it takes to listen to a Beethoven string quartet you could have listened to well over ten different pop songs. We are used to music delivering the goods in under a minute: a pop song that doesn't get to the melodic 'hook' by this time is unlikely to be played in public. This can make it difficult for people to approach classical music because it takes more time for the music to reward the listener.

In food circles there is an acknowledgement that time is important and that fast food has a detrimental effect on our health. The slow food movement, which began in Italy, aims to redress this balance. There isn't a formal movement for 'slow music' or maybe 'slow listening', but perhaps there should be. This is not to say that all classical music is at a slow speed, merely that its creation takes more time and so does its appreciation. There is a difference between the fast-food approach – passively hearing muzak – which encourages our brains to tune out, and the slow-food approach – actively listening to classical music – which encourages us to listen more carefully. There is an enormous difference between hearing something and listening to it.

It might be that for the first few listens you will, quite simply, find some of this music boring. I am happy to admit that I have been bored in classical music concerts. I once left an opera by bombastic and grandiose French composer Hector Berlioz before the final act: it just seemed so excessively drawn out. But I have also been bored by uninteresting sport matches, dull dramas on TV and most especially by pastel landscape paintings in art galleries, although I don't stick all those interests in the bin because of that occasional boredom. The experience of being bored is often because you are in the wrong frame of mind, or the work in question simply doesn't speak to you. Don't worry, there are plenty more.

Nevertheless, one of the central themes of this book is giving things a chance. In the next chapter I'll discuss how to do the right kind of preparation so that even the most seemingly uninteresting music can tell its story and find a more receptive listener in you.

But let's get on to the music. Below I've tried to describe some different ways in which we listen to music and I'm sure you, like me, will move between these modes during any piece of classical music. Even the most practised listener can lose concentration at some point in a piece and even the musical novice may have moments of elevated listening in the presence of a truly great performance.

- o Not listening
- o Passive listening
- o Active listening
- o Creative listening
- o Comparative listening
- o Specialist listening

## Not listening

Not listening is what you do when you are thinking about how long the concert will last or how long it will take to get home. My hunch (and that's all it is) is that people will *not listen* to at least 25 per cent of a concert. It's natural, normal and perfectly acceptable. Look around you at any concert. There will be at least one person asleep, and many of the rest of them will be doing a 'this is moving me' face. This face is especially prevalent right before the interval. Adopt a comfortable position and know that it's OK to let your mind wander.

## Passive listening

This is the aural equivalent of 'taking in the view'. It's listening to the music but only hearing the surface. I find myself listening in this way when I'm engaged in another activity – typing this text, for example, with Bach's *English Suites* playing merrily in the background. It requires effort to listen to the music in a concerted way all the time, so there are bound to be times when I sit back and let the sound fall upon me. For a classical musician this feels almost naughty – surely I should be thinking a series of great and profound thoughts as I listen? No. I'm just enjoying the experience. When I eat chocolate I don't always read the ingredients and analyse what makes them combine to such indulgent effect. I simply chomp and go.

## Active listening

This is when 100 per cent of your attention is taken up with the music. I usually achieve this at the beginning of the concert and can wane after about fifteen minutes. It can take something especially interesting (a loud bit) to jolt me back into the music. At this point I will quickly put on my 'this is moving me' face.

### Creative listening

When I was a child music would constantly suggest images, as though the music played out a kaleidoscopic film in my mind. This film was different for every piece of music. I think this is the same for many people. Music suggests atmospheres, feelings or landscapes. I suppose when I was a child I did not realise that these were part of *my* response to the music; I thought they *were part* of the music. This is creative listening because it's your brain being stimulated by the music and coming up with a creative response. For many people this is part of the joy of classical music and as the repertoire is so varied you can be transported almost anywhere. For some people, and the composer Olivier Messiaen (1908–1992) was one, these connections are unavoidable. He had synaesthesia, where one sense interferes with the other. Hearing certain musical chords made him see colours.

### Comparative listening

This means that you've been to more than one concert and/or you've been listening to other pieces of classical music. It's the basis of forming an opinion – from noticing that the lead violinist was playing particularly fervently on this occasion to appreciating aspects of the composition. Anybody is capable of listening in this way as we have been consuming music all our lives and have a huge basis for comparison.

### Specialist listening

Once you've heard a piece several times you may start to notice differences between your recording and the version being performed. It might vary in any number of ways and you may feel that you can comment on these subtleties: the tenor isn't as good, the strings are more vibrant, the brass sounded louder, they played it much faster, it wasn't as emotional, etc.

# Why we listen

Music connects with us at a primal level. We have an atavistic response to rhythm because we are rhythmic creatures: our walking, our speech, our daily lives are determined by rhythm and are accompanied by the constant beat of our hearts. However, merely hearing rhythm is not enough for us to be *moved*. My washing machine is rhythmical but I want to get far away from it when it's on because it's not musical. Still, when I listen to contemporary classical music it's often the driving rhythm that I find exciting.

As well as rhythm getting under your skin, certain sounds themselves can provoke an immediate emotional reaction: my singing teacher Janice Chapman, a champion of a scientific approach to singing teaching, describes how the range of the human voice is perfectly matched to the range of our ears so that we cannot help but have a physical reaction to a highly emotive sound:

> The resonance present in the newborn child is in the 3,000 hertz area, which corresponds to the most sensitive part of the human ear. A baby's cries are 'primal sound' at its most potent as it is the only communication mode available to the newborn child, whose very survival depends upon its ability to communicate its needs when it leaves the womb. Babies practice vocalizations in utero and emerge from the womb with a highly effective vocal system ready for use.[2]

Our reaction to sounds that hit those sensitive parts of the ears are instinctive, as anybody who has listened to a baby cry will know: you simply can't ignore it, any more than you can ignore being hit on the head with a hammer.

Even minute changes in rhythm and pitch can have a huge effect on us. An excellent example of how small variations in pitch and repetitive rhythm can make compelling music can be heard in the work of Steve Reich (b. 1936). Mechanistic, repetitive and seemingly lacking in some of the traditional elements of composition (melodies in particular are entirely absent, as are familiar choices of orchestral instruments, and sometimes the harmony is very restricted as well), at first listen his music is not far from the sound of my washing machine on full cycle. His music is labelled 'Minimalist' because it uses subtle shifts in sound and texture to make us listen. Reich is deliberately making music for our time, based on the repetitive sound-world of modern cities, computers and industrial rhythms. *Music for 18 Musicians* [Sound Link 0] sounds to me like a late-night drive through half-lit and empty streets – but that's just my feeling about it.

Out of apparently meaningless repetition, music emerges. In fact, hidden within Reich's work is a classical sense of structure; the changes are meticulously planned and can be very effective through subtle variation of pitch. Composers are able to make us listen and keep us interested by varying pitch *and* rhythm. But that's not enough to keep the ear alert. If the sound quality doesn't change enough then it's like staring at a monochromatic picture – you want colour. In music we refer to colour as 'timbre'.

Timbre means tonal colour or the quality of a sound – a bit like the mix of flavours that makes up the individual taste of a wine or a particularly good cake. Our sensitivity to timbre is extremely developed. We can recognise the difference between relatively similar sounds: a champagne cork exploding and a gunshot, our own front door opening and that of our neighbour's coming through the walls, and we can often recognise people on the telephone from the first 'hello'.

Timbre is what tells you that you are listening to a flute and not a trumpet – even though they may be playing the same note. The way that an instrument starts and ends a note can also give you clues: a trumpet, for example, has that distinctive brass 'pa pa pa' or 'bbbbrr' sound before the note fully sounds, and this is very different from the breathy 'whhhoooo' onset sound made by a flute. (Professional players aim to eliminate these sounds where possible and make a feature of them where necessary.) Timbre is one of those concepts that can't really be adequately described in words, though you might say a sound is, for example, reedy, or breathy, or pure, or rasping, or bell-like [Sound Links 1 and 2].

Creating interesting timbres is part of the point of classical music. Listening to the beautiful sound of the flute can be an uplifting experience in its own right and the combination of these 'colours' can be thrilling. Some composers exploit the difference in timbre between instruments; Ravel and Debussy in particular were masters of combining orchestral sounds as a painter might combine colours. The lush effects of timbre as the sound moves from dark to light can be heard in Debussy's *La Mer* ('The Sea') and exquisite balancing of instrumental choices can be found in Ravel's *Ma Mère l'Oye* ('Mother Goose').

Timbre applies to voice as well, and in a blind test I reckon I could spot the difference between at least ten of the world's tenors: Jussi Björling, Luciano Pavarotti and Plácido Domingo have such distinctive timbres that within the space of a single note I can tell who is singing. It's the same for many experts with violins. Not only do the instruments themselves vary in sound but the playing style changes with the individual and that's what gives it away. In the days before violins were ridiculously expensive (millions of pounds for the best instruments) a player might have owned many violins and chosen the most appropriate one for the piece in question. Fritz Kreisler, a stylish early-twentieth-century virtuoso from Austria who was world-famous for his effortless playing, owned many fine instruments until he had to get rid of the famous Guarnarius del Gesù violin to settle his tax bill. Owning *two* world-class instruments is no longer financially viable even at the very top end of the profession, which can help make it easier to identify a violinist by listening to the sound of their fiddle. (Even as I write, the police are trying to track down a Stradivarius that was stolen from a player at Euston Station in London.[3] The instrument was valued at £1.2 million, the bow at £62,000. Imagine carrying something that valuable to work every day.)

How could you possibly tell one violinist from another? Actually it's simpler than you'd think and, like most things in music, practice makes perfect. First and foremost each violinist has a different personality, and that comes through clearly in the case of violin gods and goddesses such as Anne-Sophie Mutter, Jascha Heifetz or Itzhak Perlman. In addition to this the violin's sound is influenced by a number of physical factors: the type and quality of wood, the quality of the bow, the use of either metal or gut strings, the varnish used and tiny shifts in design from maker to maker. Spectrograph analysis reveals that each individual violin has an audio fingerprint unique to that instrument. The perception of these differences may be very subtle and only noticeable by professionals used to listening to violins all day long. But with practice it becomes possible to tell Maxim Vengerov from Nigel Kennedy with your eyes closed. I'm still practising.

I can't do justice to the difference between players but to my inexpert ear Anne-Sophie Mutter has a tone that gleams but then so does she when she steps on to the stage, Vengerov's playing is smoother and darker, like well-matured single malt whisky, whereas Nikolaj Znaider plays in a lyrical way that sounds almost like a singer. This is of course a waste of prose – you need to hear them to appreciate the difference. A great violinist makes us listen by varying the tone that their instrument makes; application of more pressure, vibrating their arm to create vibrato and the amount of attack with which they begin a note can alter the tonal colour. This is why it's worth checking out the same piece played by different players until you find the one that *compels* you to listen.

The difference between a good violin and a top-class violin is in the resonance. Even a child's starter violin has strings that vibrate when a bow is drawn across them which cause vibrations in the body of the violin. But a top-level violin creates more vibration and a greater range of colours. This means that a Stradivarius (the most expensive and famous violin) will make a sound that hits the ear in a more fulsome way than a cheaper and less resonant version. You can plot this resonance on a graph and prove its superiority scientifically, but the best judge is your ear, which in the presence of a live performance is able to 'feel' the difference in sound.

You may well be thinking this is like those blindfold tests where TV wine connoisseurs are hoodwinked into admiring cheap plonk and rubbishing a Château Mouton Rothschild 2005 vintage (no, I've never tasted wine that good), but honestly, there is a huge difference in the quality of sound that I believe you would be able to notice in a test. A cheap student-level violin has an abrasive, nasal quality and doesn't sound even throughout its range, whereas a truly great instrument has depth of colour, an even tone from top to bottom and, like a person with a fascinating speaking voice, the violin seems to have personality. There is a rich, creamy quality to some violins that is a million miles – and probably a million pounds – from the scratchings of a child practising on their first instrument. You'd know the difference; trust me.

## HARMONIC PENGUINS AND THE MUSIC OF BALI

While humans are fairly adept at recognising each other through the timbre of our voices, we also have the assistance of other markers, such as snazzy dressing, distinctive noses and receding hairlines. Pity the poor penguin in an Antarctic blizzard who must recognise his mate by the timbre of her squawks. In fact they do this extremely effectively by making an extraordinary two-tone sound that varies from penguin to penguin.[4] I know it's unbelievable but a penguin (unlike a human being) can make two sounds at once which are very slightly out of tune with each other. This 'out-of-tune-ness' creates what musicians call 'beats' (not to be confused with drumbeats which are entirely separate from this definition of 'beats'). Because in Western music we aim to eliminate music with 'beats', it's actually very difficult to explain, although there is the example of honky-tonk pianos.

A honky-tonk piano is created by de-tuning the three strings which are hit every time a note is played. In a normal piano these are tuned to sound as one note. A discrepancy in tuning between the different strings creates a sort of ghastly wobbly and out-of-tune noise. The effect on the British ear is fairly unpleasant, unless you like Chas and Dave. But in other musical cultures this sound is welcomed: if you've ever listened to the music of the Gamelan from the Indonesian islands of Java and Bali then you may have noticed that it sounds out of tune to your ears – many Western musicians react with shock when they first hear it. A friend of mine spent a year in Bali and on returning to England found she couldn't sing in tune because her sense of pitch had been affected by playing in a Gamelan orchestra. In Gamelan, two xylophone-like instruments sit next to each other and have almost exactly the same five notes (or seven in some cases) except that when the two instruments play together they sound marginally out of tune. This creates a shimmering effect (due to the beats created between the notes). This is the same effect as the penguin's two-tone squawking.

The advantage of these 'beats' is that they travel a long distance and can be heard through objects, clearly an advantage for the penguin trying to locate a mate on the ice. Gamelan is traditionally played outdoors and I know from personal experience that the noise can penetrate glass, steel and concrete as no other instrument can. When I worked at the LSO St Luke's, a centre for community music, the sound of the Gamelan could be heard through the acoustic glass and soundproofing, such was its resonance. The architects had put the office next to the Gamelan room and every week I'd see the support staff sitting with headphones trying to block out the relentless 'bonging'.

We perceive this difference in tuning as timbre. Anyone can tell the difference between a honky-tonk piano and a Steinway grand piano tuned for a classical recital. But the technical explanation requires an understanding of harmonics.

I have decided only to include this short explanation of harmonics as it is beyond the scope of this book. Harmonics are produced when any note is played and they resonate at frequencies higher than the fundamental, creating harmonic resonance (have I lost you yet?). Certain instruments produce sound energy at particular frequencies, which is known as formants. *Aaaaaaggghhh.* I'm going to leave it to you to research this yourself should you be interested. Just take it from me: harmonics are what make one sound different from another one. Simple.

(For a more lucid explanation of the harmonics of music see *How Music Works* by John Powell, appropriately published by Penguin!)

## Context: listening and understanding

Timbre is not the whole story of listening, because listening to classical music is helped by knowing the context in which the piece was written. Remember that music was written by human beings, people with children, wives, lovers, desires, their own victories and failures. They are fallible – even the great ones. We sometimes speak of composers as if it was only their work that mattered, but the whole person is of interest. Knowing that Bach was a devoutly religious man explains the serious nature of his composition. Knowing that Beethoven had a fiery personality tells you so much about his music, especially the furious pieces written after he became deaf. Knowing that Stravinsky could be very harsh in his criticism of other musicians tells us so much about the shifts in his own output, as if that incisive critical mind were turned in on itself, provoking him to reinvent his style.

The fact that Elgar was a rather melancholy Englishman affects the way that I listen to his Cello Concerto: the melody, the sound of the orchestra, the nostalgic quality of the music and the rather grey, melancholic emotional atmosphere all suggest to me an idealised, pastoral version of Britain that no longer exists – or may never have existed – but which, living in England, I can somehow immediately identify as English. These bits of contextual information form associations which are deeply personal and make a network of information around the music. For me they attach themselves to specific bars or harmonies like Post-it notes.

Listening doesn't happen in a vacuum and for this reason I think that it's very useful to know the rough time period in which a piece of music was written. When I don't know or can't place this period, then the 'Post-it notes' are highly personal and random, but as I get to know more about the piece then the associations can be shared with other people. For example it's nice to feel that Vivaldi's furiously energetic music makes you think of blue skies but it's much better (I think) to know that he composed in Venice and allow images of Venetian waterways to permeate the music.

*Where* you first hear a piece of music is just as important as what you know about it. Film is potent in combining powerful imagery and music, such that the two seem inseparable. Unforgettable moments for me include the use of the elegiac Barber Adagio in the film *Platoon,* the resolute *Ride of the Valkyries* in *Apocalypse Now* or the chilling juxtaposition of the sublimely civilised Aria from J.S. Bach's *Goldberg Variations* as Hannibal Lecter casually murders his jailers. It is almost impossible to forget the potent combination of images of extreme violence accompanied by music. There was an outcry in 1973 when a girl was raped whilst the perpetrators sang the song 'Singing in the Rain'. This was said to be a copycat crime following an infamous scene in Stanley Kubrick's film *A Clockwork Orange.* As a result of this and other such crimes, Kubrick withdrew the film from release in the UK. This is more than a Post-it note – it's like an indelible permanent marker.

We also have our own cultural contexts for hearing music that can change from town to town, and country to country. Hearing music from the Indian classical tradition – Ravi Shankar playing the sitar, for example – I'm aware of very few of the symbolic meanings that are attached to the music. The same for me is true of the music of the Gamelan from Bali. We recognise it as music produced by human beings; it can often have similar structures to Western music – tunes, rhythm, harmony, organisation – but it doesn't immediately have the same meaning for me as it would for someone brought up in that tradition. But if you only listened to English music then you'd be severely impoverished. The difficulty in listening to music from the Czech Republic, Russia, America, Germany, France and so on is that each country represents different attitudes and has musical styles associated with it that we may not immediately understand. That's part of the joy of classical music – each country's music 'tastes' different and has rich history to be uncovered.

## Recording has spoiled our listening

*Lieder* (German for 'songs') is a good example of music that was at one time fresh and exciting but without knowing the context it can be difficult to understand and tedious. In Vienna during the latter years of the eighteenth century and the beginning of the nineteenth there was a fashion for the salon performance which was literally chamber music, a performance in a small room (not *that* small room!). These salons differed from performances in a church or opera house because the scale of the music was smaller owing to the limited space, and it was in these salons that 'art song' or *Lieder* developed. Composers such as Schubert, Schumann and Brahms would have listened to and performed music in this context and consequently their songs are specifically written for that environment. They are often intimate, personal and tender songs about love, rejection and pain.

Sitting in the same room as a singer has a musical intimacy that many people these days never experience, living as we do in the age of the recording. Two hundred years ago there would have been no opportunity to hear music unless it was performed live. Naturally the best musicians and performers flocked to musical centres such as Vienna to share ideas and hear each other's music. Imagine the atmosphere in those *soirées*. Composers and poets would share their newly penned work, talented young musicians gathered to play the music, aristocracy mingled with artists and the possibility of hearing something fresh and of great merit was ever-present. It would have been a very dynamic way to listen; the audience were performers themselves; anybody might do a turn during the evening. It's a world away from the way we listen to the songs now – as though they are preserved and sacred. A great performer knows this and attempts to recreate the freshness that would have existed in the first performance.

Sadly there are few modern equivalents to this informal way of listening to classical music; we must buy tickets to concert halls or listen on the radio. But there are some venues that try to recreate the intimacy of those evenings, for instance the Wigmore Hall, which is small enough to create an intimate atmosphere and has a reputation for bringing together the very best musicians, who sometimes bring in historical instruments for their recitals. At the Royal Academy of Music there is an amazing room where they have all sorts of pianos dating back to the early nineteenth century. Listening to music played on the exact type of piano the composer would have owned gives you a greater understanding of why they wrote the way they did.

## Where to listen: the internet and audio technology

If you can't get to a concert hall or you are thinking about building up a library, then there are now a number of options for listening to classical music: whether you are a silver surfer or a teenager doing dodgy downloads, the internet is now making music highly accessible. Superb audio is coming to a computer near you and it's worth getting a pair of high-quality speakers hooked up to your sound card (the bit of the computer that makes the noise.) For me a decent internet connection is the ideal way to encounter music.

As a first step, if your computer can handle it and you have broadband internet access, you should be able to download Spotify. I strongly urge you to do so. Somehow it is able to give you access to almost any CD you care to listen to. There is a monthly fee for the advert-free subscription service but there is a free version which is frankly pretty good. But the reigning king of internet music is iTunes from Apple. I don't know how I lived before iTunes. It's possible to buy pretty much any music and download it instantly. The range is much greater than Spotify and if you are worried about losing your music in a computer crash then you can legally burn CD backup copies. Thanks to iTunes I have around 3,000 individual tracks stored on my mobile phone at a fairly high quality. The joy of this for me is in shuffle mode which picks tracks at random from your entire CD collection – it's a great way to rediscover music.

If you are interested in having the highest-quality audio then there is an audio format called FLAC (Free Lossless Audio Codec). Hyperion Records are now selling much of their output via the Web in FLAC. This is recorded at a higher quality than conventional formats like MP3 and WAV. If this is getting a bit geeky then let me just say this: a higher-quality file does make a difference to your listening but only if you have a decent pair of speakers. If you are listening on your kitchen radio with the fridge buzzing in the background then it's simply not worth the extra effort of seeking out higher formats. If like me you sit in a darkened room with the best speakers you can lay your hands on then *maybe* it's worth the extra money.

The most exciting development that I've seen is the Super Audio CD (SACD) which gives you 5.1 surround sound and higher quality than CD. Those still lamenting the loss of the 'warmth' of vinyl probably abhor the thought of yet another digital format. To my ears (which I like to think are pretty reliable) there's not enough difference between the CD and these newer formats to warrant the necessary expenditure unless you are an audiophile. Until the ordinary listener can hear the difference immediately and afford to buy the equipment I think that CDs and MP3s will remain the industry standard. (MP3 and other compressed formats such as M4A and OGG give quality sound for but use less space on your computer or iPod/ MP3 player. Compression is what we all do to our suitcase when coming home from holiday – we squeeze as much in as possible, and though it comes out in the same form – a shirt is still a shirt – it's probably a little crumpled. Compressed music isn't quite as vibrant as uncompressed music.)

I sincerely hope to be proved wrong in this because I would love to have the opportunity for higher and higher recording quality. The difference for me is in the *presence* of the sound. If you are used to hearing nothing but recordings of orchestras then the real thing can be surprisingly vibrant. Recording flattens the sound and seems to put it into a box or behind glass. In pop music technical wizardry makes certain sounds pop out of the texture but that doesn't work in classical music where fidelity to the natural sound is vital. Where FLAC recordings or SACD win out over MP3s and CDs is that you can hear the instruments 'in relief', there's a more palpable sense of the presence of the instruments. This brings an added depth to the sound which means you can hear through the texture – this is especially noticeable in high-density orchestral scores or choral music where there is a lot going on. At a live concert you wouldn't have a problem hearing the inner workings of the music but on MP3s especially the sound can become too full and detail gets lost – I get a sensation of too much busy-ness and noise. But if you are happy with your Roberts analogue kitchen radio from 1974 then stick with it by all means.

If you want to watch classical music then apart from patchy access on TV there are a couple of internet opportunities:

YouTube is a good way to find all sorts of hidden treasures but can be disappointing in audio quality. There's some great stuff available but you might get lost trying to find it.

The Berlin Philharmonic Orchestra are pioneering a brilliant subscription internet service which at the moment is very reasonable: for a year's subscription you can watch every concert live from the Philharmonie (their concert hall in Berlin). What is particularly exciting about this 'digital concert hall' is that it enables you to watch whatever concert you choose rather than the small number broadcast on terrestrial television – it puts you in charge of your viewing. The drawback is that you'll need a very sharp computer – and, again, quality speakers for it to be worthwhile. But this technology is coming down in price all the time and pretty soon I believe most concert halls will be offering similar services. The advantage of watching live concerts over the Web is that it can connect you with the players more directly through pre-concert talks, close-ups and general familiarity. This helps prevent that rather disengaged way of listening I mentioned earlier.

## How we listen has changed

As wonderful as it is to be able to listen to any music from almost any period of musical history, thanks to the invention of recording we now have something of a museum culture which pins down music for close examination, like a desiccated butterfly fixed to a board. Music that was once listened to in a vibrant atmosphere (taverns, salons and noisy opera houses) can now be played almost anywhere in the world on iPods, and that, I believe, cuts it off from its roots almost entirely. This can be like listening to music in a vacuum – it is rendered meaningless.

How can we have a more vital and immediate way of listening to classical music? A listening that rescues diamonds from the past and shines them up anew? Well, it's partly up to us to investigate the history and context of the music, but it's also up to the performers to create performances that bring music back to life and which convey something of the original spirit.

In the next chapter I'll look at what you can do to create a more meaningful engagement with this music.

Chapter **4**

# A Hot Date with Music

## Getting to know you, getting to know all about you …

Ever get the feeling that you are missing something? I can't tell you the number of times I've tried to read the programme notes in the half-light during the concert without knowing the title of the music I'm hearing – or worse still, I've realised what the work was about as I read the notes on the way home. This is patently not the way to do it.

Classical music benefits from repeated listening and some-times it's only by drumming a piece into your brain that you'll learn to love it. There are pieces that you'll fall for immediately, but sometimes that can mean the rewards are short-lived. Once you get beyond the 'greatest hits' of classical music, pieces will require more effort but yield more pleasure in the long run.

We've talked about music that you might already know, or at least recognise. Once you move away from the familiar it can get a little more scary. In pop music there are lyrics that can draw you in, the song may well be in a style that you know and often it has been expressly crafted to be catchy. It is more difficult to find pieces of classical music that you are going to like once you move away from the easier stuff. It simply takes time … But it's worth it.

## SHAKE, RATTLE AND ROLL

For all musicians it's a lifelong journey. The British conductor Sir Simon Rattle, who is blessed with a convivial manner and a knack for talking to the media, is currently Artistic Director and Principal Conductor of the Berlin Philharmonic, arguably the world's most prestigious orchestral job. Rattle is a man you'd think would know everything there is to know about music. Not so; his constant quest to discover new music and to learn is an inspiration to all. On his accession to the Berlin job he commented, 'This is a profession where you are always learning, always travelling and never arriving. I want that to continue.'[1] A similar sentiment was expressed by the virtuosic pianist and composer Sergei Rachmaninov: 'Music is enough for a lifetime, but a lifetime is not enough for music.'

I recently went to see Elgar's Violin Concerto performed by Nikolaj Znaider, poster-boy of the violin world, who at six foot four inches stands head and shoulders above other musicians. It's not a piece I know well, though I've heard it several times before, most notably in a deft performance by the more petite Tasmin Little. The work had always left me cold, through no fault of the musicians involved; it lacks the great melodic motifs of the 'cello concerto, which is a work I grew up listening to (Jacqueline du Pré's blistering recording, of course). That is a work that I feel welcomes the first-time listener more readily than its big sister, the violin concerto, and in du Pré's hands had a raw emotional quality and a beautiful lyricism.

So this time I was determined to get under its skin. I listened twice during the day to the measured and authoritative recording that Znaider made with Sir Colin Davis and the Staatskapelle Orchestra, Dresden. I can't say that I gave it much attention, I just put it on in the background while I went about my business. I read a little about the work on the orchestra's website before I went to the concert, and I was interested to discover that it was

100 years to the day since the world première and that Znaider was playing exactly the same violin as Fritz Kreisler played on 10 November 1910 (the one he had to give up for tax reasons). Made by renowned luthier Guarneri Del Gesù (a luthier is a string instrument maker), this violin has an astonishing tone and in the hands of Znaider, whose playing is both muscular and tender, it has an almost sugary sweetness.

The first movement was gripping, at moments frenetic with the trademark impetuousness of Elgar; I was impressed by Znaider's handling of the difficult passages; yet so far the piece was failing to pierce my heart in the way that I expected from this most famously mournful and autumnal of composers. As the work unfolded it became clear to me that it builds to an emotional climax after around thirty minutes. A casual listen in my kitchen was not equivalent to the experience of concentrating on the work in the concert hall. Finally, after about twenty minutes, there is a passage of searching tenderness where the strings of the orchestra shimmer in the background whilst the soloist soars above – but without hearing the whole work, and experiencing the climb to those emotional heights, the moment doesn't make sense.

My friend Jamie put it beautifully after the concert. 'The work has an emotional core from which the rest of the piece radiates.' When you experience those moments in the concert hall you don't care that it took an hour to get there or that you had to pay good money for your seat, because the value of that moment is beyond words, and to me beyond money.

That emotional core – a kind of golden moment in the piece – puts you in a very powerful state of mind. It is similar to what productivity gurus and self-help books call a state of 'flow'. You feel immersed. Sir Ken Robinson, an expert on education, justifies the artistic experience thus:

An aesthetic experience is one in which your senses are operating at their peak, when you're present in the current moment, when you're resonating with the excitement of 'this thing' that you're experiencing; when you're fully alive.[2]

Come to think of it, that's probably what it feels like to do a bungee jump, but if you can't do a bungee jump, go to a concert. This is the polar opposite of the way people have marketed classical music as simply 'relaxing' – it's not relaxing, it's enlivening. You may reach a state of tranquillity while listening to music, but you are not deadened by it. Classical music shouldn't really be a substitute for sleeping tablets.

Listening to the work in my kitchen had prepared me for the concert such that I knew how long the piece was, recognised much of the music and most importantly I was immersed in the sound world. I had a rough map of the layout of the music in my mind, even though I hadn't been giving it my full attention. I wasn't coming to this piece having spent all day listening to pop music – I felt ready for it.

When I start to tackle a piece of music that I don't know, there are a few stages I go through before I really feel that I *know* the work. The first stage is usually just giving it a couple of listens before I'm intrigued enough to do some background reading.

## You've got a hot date: with music

For me, developing a 'friendship' with a piece has the following stages. It's a bit like dating …

○ **Meeting the piece for the first time**
Like meeting someone in a noisy bar when you can't understand what they are saying, the first time you hear a piece of music it will be unfamiliar but may be reminiscent of other pieces in the same style or it might sound utterly meaningless.

○ **Getting to know you**

On second hearing, even the most complex piece of music becomes marginally more familiar. There may well be one or two points that you remember hearing the first time. You've got their number and you've given them that all-important second chance.

○ **Knowing the score**

By the third date something of the structure of the piece should become clearer (though the number of times you need to hear it for the piece to become familiar will depend on the length and complexity of the work). Familiarity has set in and you may be able to predict changes in the music, how many sections it is in, when we are heading for a climax, and so on. It's possible you may start to look forward to a particular moment or passage, or a certain instrumental solo. This is when the piece begins to get lodged, and you may well find moments will echo around your mind for hours after.

○ **Becoming obsessive**

You've fallen hook, line and sinker. If you're anything like me then by now you'll be listening to the piece you've fallen for at any available opportunity. You'll wake up humming it and put it on as soon as you can. Music that you know well becomes an old friend and even if you don't listen to it for twenty years it can immediately be recognised like a long-lost brother returning from overseas. But arriving at the point where you know a piece this well requires patience, time and effort. While there is some music that is instantly appealing, there is much to be gained from listening to music that has more depth; not all music surrenders its treasures on those first few listens. So stick it on repeat for a week and see how you feel then.

*○* **Seeing it live**

Things are getting serious. Now you are booking tickets to
see each other. When you see the piece live it will cement
many aspects of the work. The added visual dimension can
make sections more memorable; for instance, the use of
offstage instruments (producing a very different aural
experience than listening on a CD), perhaps the faces of the
musicians as they play emotional music strike you as
especially intense, or maybe the attire of the soloist is so
remarkable that for you it becomes forever associated with
the music.

## Memorable moments in concert

I can think of dozens of examples of this: Steven Isserlis's hair
flailing around during the Saint-Saëns Cello Concerto, the sight
of Deborah Voigt sailing on stage in a glorious frock, Ian
Bostridge clinging to the piano during the madder sections of *Die
Winterreise* and the effervescent movements of the percussion
section of the CBSO during a new work by Thomas Adès.

The list goes on and on. These moments from concerts are as
clear now as they were at the time, and being a nostalgic type I'm
always looking to experience them again ... though I know I
never can. This is my shared history with music. It's a personal,
private treasure trove.

Until you've heard a piece performed by several different
artists you don't truly know it from all sides. Many of the sounds
that we may cherish in a recording are responses by the artist to
the work and can differ from recording to recording. It's only by
listening to multiple versions that we uncover the work itself.
I'm not suggesting rushing out and buying ten versions of the
same piece, but if you fall for something then it is always interesting to listen to a different recording for comparison. Also, bear
in mind that one interpretation of the piece might seduce you,
while another leaves you cold.

## Connections between pieces

I said earlier that music can be like an old friend – a relationship that develops and matures over time. Here is a diary of my relationship with J.S. Bach. A friend once told me that he found Bach to be emotionless, mathematical and cold. I have found the complete opposite: he is ordered and precise, yes, but under that is a humanity and a reverence that I find profoundly moving. The man had twenty children and a long life by contemporary standards – to me his music oozes with the experience of living. My relationship with Bach is utterly haphazard and the result of chance musical encounters over a period of years. Without the influence of my school teachers, music teachers, friends and choirmasters I may never have developed my love of his music.

---

## BUILDING A RELATIONSHIP WITH BACH

○ **Aged 9 (1984):** Played 'Air on a G String' (based on the second movement of Bach's Orchestral Suite No. 3 in D major). Badly.

○ **Aged 13:** Heard Jacques Loussier's version of 'Air on a G String', used in the 'Happiness is a cigar called Hamlet' TV ad. Played it on the piano again – slightly better than aged 9, but still not that well.

○ **Aged 16:** Studied St Matthew Passion at school for A-Level with Mr Fairlie. Thought it was boring.

○ **Aged 18:** Saw St Matthew Passion at Barbican in London. Thought it was brilliant.

○ **Aged 20:** Sang Mass in B Minor by Bach with University Choir. Struggled with high notes.

○ **Aged 23:** Sang solo in Bach's *Magnificat*. Struggled with high notes.

○ **Aged 24:** Bought Bach's Christmas Oratorio on CD – John Eliot Gardner recording. Had it on repeat for a year.

○ **Aged 25:** Saw a Cantata BWV 82 in Christchurch Priory as part of the Monteverdi Choir's famous tour in 2000. Impressed.[3]

- *Aged 27:* Sang at a Lutheran church in the City of London and discovered that Bach studied with Buxtehude.
- *Aged 28:* Performed Buxtehude's *Membra Jesu Nostri,* Schütz's *Musikalische Exequien* and *Matthaus Passion*, pieces that Bach would almost certainly have known.
- *Aged 29:* Performed as the Evangelist in both St John and St Matthew Passion. Received some good notices but was stung by a stinking review after one very difficult performance.

*And so on …*

Bach is so well established in my life that it is impossible to imagine a world without him. It's inexplicable: there is simply something about his music that gets my brain fired up and sets my soul soaring.

When Bach was writing his great choral works he included many melodies that were written by the Protestant reformer Martin Luther (1483–1546). These 'chorales' would have been well known to Bach's contemporary audience, sung regularly in church and used in the music of Scheidt and Schütz from the previous generation of composers. Knowing that these pieces would have been immensely popular in his day, and that the audience may have sung along at times, makes me think of his music as much more of a collaboration between composer, performers and audience. It changes the way I listen to the music because knowing all this I can imagine myself as a member of his contemporary audience. In some pieces Bach used the Lutheran melodies to create intricate textures with new accompaniments [Sound Link 3].

In other places he uses the melody with a simple accompaniment. In one of the most profound moments of all choral music Bach takes a chorale melody and reharmonises it to great effect. This is the moment from the St Matthew Passion when Jesus dies [Sound Link 4].

In the context of the piece it is a moment of tranquillity followed by a dramatic section describing the splitting veil of the temple, the earth shaking and the rocks breaking apart [Sound Link 5].

Understanding the historical context as well as where this music comes within the St Matthew Passion can revolutionise the way you listen to Bach. When I was in my teens Jonathan Miller directed a production of the St Matthew Passion for BBC Television. I vividly recall watching an interview with him about the experience. His description of his own tears when listening to the aria 'Erbarme Dich' was especially poignant. Without knowing the context it's an exceptionally beautiful piece by any standards: the soaring violin emerges from a halo of strings while the voice attempts to achieve the dizzying heights of the instrumental line like Icarus reaching for the Sun. The effect is both profoundly mournful and devastatingly beautiful in equal measure, but without understanding the words and the context it might not make you cry [Sound Link 6].

Jonathan Miller described his own emotional connection with the piece and his description has stayed with me ever since. The words mean – 'Have mercy on me, God' and it's Peter's cry for forgiveness as he hears the cockerel crow and realises he's denied Jesus three times. In that moment Peter is a man coming to terms with his personal failure and lack of courage. I stand in awe of Bach's ability both to empathise with the character's failings and to use music to transform that remote moment in a 2,000-year-old book into something that can be felt by anybody whenever or wherever they hear it. Without some understanding of the piece it might leave you cold.

## Age before beauty

A friend of mine called Chris who works with computers asked me, 'Why, when I go to a classical concert, do my wife and I always feel like the youngest people there, even though I'm nearly 40?' Almost to the point of cliché, it seems that for a lot of people classical music is something they discover with age. It appears that you need to have some experience of life that comes with age before you can appreciate the beauty of some classical music. Or perhaps it is a case of rediscovery, because while listening to a piece a few times can change your perspective in the short term, over the longer term your appreciation of pieces will grow and change with time. But that's one of the exciting things about classical music: it's rich enough to develop in that way as you do.

When I was studying Shakespeare at A-Level my teacher told me that a great piece of writing 'changes' throughout your life. I looked forward to getting older so that I could experience this shift. When reading *Hamlet* as a young man I empathised with Laertes as he is given a lecture by his father, Polonius; I understood the words but they did not have any connection to my experience when I was eighteen. As I re-read them now that I grow older, it's Polonius whose perspective has become more relevant, each precept resonating with moments from my own life.

- Neither a borrower nor a lender be ...
- To thine own self be true
- Give thy thoughts no tongue,
  Nor any unproportion'd thought his act ...

It feels as though the text itself has become richer over the intervening years, though of course I know it's just because I've lived a little. Maybe one day I'll feel like King Lear? Let's hope not. Do come and say hello if you see me out and about in rags, shouting at the wind. Sadly you can't ever go back to the naïve way you once listened.

This same principle applies to music. When I first heard 'Ich Bin Der Welt Abhanden Gekommen' ('I am lost to the world') from the *Rückert Lieder* by Gustav Mahler, it seemed excessive, even syrupy. The song is a description of the poet's absorption in music. As the artist becomes seemingly more and more detached from the world, so their music becomes more and more important. In the intervening years I've got to know the piece more fully and my life has moved on: I'm now married with a child, I've lost loved ones and I've gained new and valuable friendships. More and more the song strikes me as being exquisite, almost painfully so – there's a sense of serenity and calm in the melody. However, music is also a great comforter and returning to this song brings solace in the familiar. It came on the radio only yesterday, while I was heating up my mother-in-law's leftover shepherd's pie and I stood still, my guts like jelly. (It was sung by English tenor Ben Johnson with whom I once had enormous fun singing in a particularly disastrous version of Bizet's *The Pearl Fishers*.) Partly it reassures me that people in the past have felt the same about music, but mostly it revitalises my spirit and satisfies a need in me for beauty. If you find yourself moved by this piece then it's worth listening to the fourth movement of his Fifth Symphony as well [Sound Links 7 and 8].

Pieces that affect me in this way are the ones I have known for a long time. There are pieces that I cannot bear to hear because they are either too soaked in grief or associated with moments whose loss is too painful to confront. But music can be a conduit to the past as well as a reconciler; music heals as it reminds.

## I like it, now what am I going to do?

How do you go about finding the next step on your journey of musical discovery? How can you make sense of the morass of information? How do you move beyond that one piece that you've fallen for to an understanding of its place within classical music? For me one of the joys of listening to music is in finding connections between pieces, sometimes overt quotations, sometimes the echo of a composer of the previous generation. Because composers learn by listening to each other's work, when one innovates, the rest react by either shunning the musical advance or flagrantly copying it.

You could start by buying an album of 'Greatest Classical Hits', and there are many of these available, but there is also a great satisfaction in discovering pieces for yourself. When you find a pop song you like, then you can easily find fifty more songs that have some similarities, either by the same artist or by a contemporary from the same musical area. The same is true to a limited extent with classical music, but it can be harder to trace the connections.

In the next chapter I will discuss the musical canon (music that is considered 'great' and is regularly played in concerts and on the radio). But here let's celebrate the art of discovery and the pleasure of random findings. Hang out the musical bunting.

## Some approaches

Even just finding out where a composer was born, or where and with whom they studied, can give enormous insight, though it may at first seem to be a tedious exercise in dates. Yes, it can turn into a trainspotter's paradise, but the information can make for fascinating connections. Everyone in classical music knows somebody who knows somebody else and pretty quickly you've got a connection to almost anybody.

## Read the programme

If you are already a concertgoer then it's worth getting to a concert early in order to read the programme notes in advance. Firstly it avoids you rustling them noisily during the concert but more importantly it can open the music up for you. I'll be offering a survivor's guide to concerts later in the book. Equally the sleeve notes on most CDs offer a good round-up of relevant information. This is especially true of the smaller, specialist record labels.

## Resources I simply couldn't do without

Good places to start looking for information are abundant but each will give you a slightly different slant. On TV there's a great programme called *The Choir*, presented by some guy called Gareth Malone.

Every Saturday morning I listen to a show on BBC Radio 3 called *CD Review*. It's a great way to get to know a piece of music because they play short sections of the same music from a selection of the best available recordings. If you find the chat too academic the music is always good and the repetitious nature of the show is particularly helpful in acclimatising yourself to a work. Classic FM is a great place to go to hear a wide range from the popular end of the spectrum as listed in Chapter 1 and Appendix I. The downside is that they don't always play the entire piece – rather choosing highlights, which doesn't fully prepare you for the concert experience. Radio 3 *Breakfast* and drive show *In Tune* are easily as accessible as Classic FM but again are unlikely to play a complete symphony. But these are great places to start.

I subscribe to a number of magazines of which the most useful is usually *Gramophone*. It started life as a review magazine for records but has expanded to include live concert news, Blu-ray reviews and interviews with musical luminaries. Its key selling point is that the editor handpicks a track from his favourite records each month, which used to be put on a complimentary CD. I came to Schubert this way, so many thanks to *Gramophone* for that one. Times have changed and now the tracks are available through their website. While this gives them greater scope to give away some of the best recorded music in the world every month in high-quality audio, I suspect it's left some of the less technologically savvy subscribers in the lurch, but then I'm sure they struggled with the introduction of CDs as well.

The *BBC Music Magazine*, *Gramophone's* main competitor, is in many respects similar but has the advantage of the BBC's orchestral resources, giving it the opportunity to give away *complete* recordings of classical works each month. This is an excellent way to be introduced to new works, as alongside the CD you get an interview or article giving you enough information to get started. The quality of the performances varies whereas *Gramophone* has the advantage of only choosing the very best – but then you don't get the whole work. If you are trying to build a library then *BBC Music Magazine* is probably for you. If you are looking to hear the latest inspiring recordings then it's *Gramophone.* Both these magazines cover a wide selection of music from choral through to chamber, solo instrumental to orchestral as well as opera.

While *Opera* magazine offers an excellent review section as well as advance notice of important productions the world over, its readership is more specialist, since it is limited to the operatic stage. That said, if you are planning a trip, then it's an excellent place to find out about the hottest tickets in town (or in a completely different town).

It is useful to have a couple of musical reference books as a next step after reading this book if you want to continue your musical investigations.

○ **The Rough Guide to Classical Music**
 *The Rough Guide to Classical Music* gives you an account of the major works of every composer worthy of note from the last thousand years. It's an A–Z but written with a pleasing mix of erudition and conviviality. You might find it a little overwhelmingly comprehensive unless you have an idea of where to start, but my copy is well-thumbed and great for dipping into.

○ **The Oxford Dictionary of Music** *(Michael Kennedy)*
 Although the internet can tell you many wondrous facts, not all of them are reliable. For example, at one stage my middle name was listed by Wikipedia as 'Lawrence'. It isn't

Lawrence, it's Edmund. A decent musical dictionary is a friend for life – I still use my 1994 edition although there have been updates since then. It's comprehensive, detailed but with the easy clarity you'd expect from a dictionary. If you like your facts served straight up, then this is a great addition to your bookshelves. It looks impressive too: it's got the word 'MUSIC' in large, important letters on the front.

○ **Kobbé's Opera Book** *(edited by the Earl of Harewood and Anthony Peattie)*
Top of my list is *Kobbé's Opera Book* with a mere 1,012 pages of synopses, biographical information and performance histories (when, where and who) relating to every important opera composer. It's simple to read and easy to use; works are listed under their composers. If it's in *Kobbé's* then it'll probably be worth seeing. It gives you accounts of the most important operas and accordingly gives more column inches to the big hitters such as Verdi and Mozart. There's a pocket version too which is shorter and cheaper, but looks a bit sadder on your coffee table.

## Organise your listening

There are several ways to organise your listening: by date, by theme or by school.

### Dates

Nerd alert: dates are actually more interesting than one might suspect. For instance: Handel, Bach and Scarlatti were born in the same year and Debussy, Mahler and Richard Strauss were born within four years of each other. These are very different composers: Debussy's music is impressionistic and very French; Mahler wrote big, passionate symphonies and Richard Strauss wrote some of the most beautiful vocal music of the late nineteenth century. Despite working within the same historical period they moved the history of music in different directions. This makes for interesting comparisons.

*Composers who were writing at the same time, yet whose work is totally different and might make for interesting comparisons:*[4]

- Scheidt, Schein and Schütz: all German and religious
- Henry Purcell and Dietrich Buxtehude: one English and a composer of secular operas as well as more devout religious choral works; the other a serious German composer of organ music
- Handel, Bach and Scarlatti: three composers of startling variety
- Mozart and Salieri: both great composers but the more famous one has more heart
- C.P.E. Bach and Joseph Haydn: both great innovators; Haydn's music has moments of levity
- Schumann, Mendelssohn and Wagner: Schumann's music is very much about personal experience; Mendelssohn is more outward-looking – landscapes feature regularly; Wagner is about as intense and serious as classical music gets
- Debussy, Strauss and Mahler: impressionistic, expressionistic and fantastic respectively
- Gustav Holst, Maurice Ravel and Charles Ives: English, French, American, all of them capable of brooding and finely textured music which was, for their time, experimental
- Francis Poulenc, Aaron Copland and Duke Ellington: Ellington, though a jazz composer, was influenced by French harmony and deserves as much attention as Copland for his part in American music, and his rich arrangements for jazz ensemble are especially fascinating; Poulenc must have

been aware of these harmonic advances as he has moments
of distinct jazziness

o **Ralph Vaughan Williams, Michael Tippett and Paul
Hindemith:** these are composers who, whilst flirting with
Modernism, retained a link with the sound world of the past;
Vaughan Williams, the eldest of the three, is the most
accessible

o **Edward Elgar and George Gershwin:** melancholic
autumnal leafiness versus New York sophistication

o **Steve Reich and Brian Ferneyhough:** re re re re pe pe pe ti t
it it ive ive and JUST@(£*&$ PLAIN E£&$(*!! BONKERS:::::::

o **Stockhausen and Messiaen:** Stockhausen is the
experimentalist's experimentalist; Messiaen wrote down the
notes of birdsong to include in his compositions. Both are
complex, strange and yet exciting.

## Themes

Thematic links in music could mean the same text set to music
by different composers, different attempts at describing a landscape, writing in response to war, or operas by the same librett-
ist. Here are some rich areas for exploration.

o English polyphony
o Early music from Latin America
o Settings of poems by A.E. Housman
o Music written in Vienna
o French music of the *fin de siècle*
o Songs about death (for there are plenty)
o Music about love (is there anything else worth composing?)

… and so on. You may have a particular interest in a historical
period, or a particular part of the world, or churches, or mythol-
ogy, or Impressionism. Chances are you can find a connection in
the classical world that resonates.

## -isms, schisms and schools

There are musical schools that teach music, but here I am referring to the organisation of music into stylistic groups in the same way that art is organised; Impressionism, Dadaism, etc. In some cases groups of composers create aims and rules for themselves; in other cases we gather them together posthumously because their music sounds similar, perhaps because they were writing at the same time or in the same country. Most composers can be wedged into a school of some sort ... even if it's the school of mavericks who don't fit into a school. Schools are often given the suffix '-ism' which indicates a conscious methodology, a philosophy and a style. For instance:

- **Nationalism:** Sibelius, Vaughan Williams, Copland, Smetana, Bartók
    - self-consciously nationalistic music from the late nineteenth and early twentieth centuries
    - often stirring stuff with a clear sense of pride and heritage

- **Atonalism:** Schoenberg, Varèse, Bartók, Stravinsky
    - music that abandoned traditional harmony (see later, especially Chapter 7)
    - often actually quite scary to listen to

- **Impressionism:** Ravel, Debussy
    - music that shimmers with light
    - very much about sounding exotic

- **Expressionism:** Second Viennese School of Berg, Schoenberg Webern
    - musical angst
    - pain and intensity welling up from deep within

- **Minimalism:** Terry Riley, Steve Reich, Philip Glass, John Adams, Michael Nyman, Henryk Górecki, Arvo Pärt

o using very sparse compositional material to create pieces
o sounds clean and not over-encumbered by unnecessary sentiment

Here are some recognised schools of musical thought:

o **The mighty handful, also known as 'The Five':** Balakirev, Borodin, Cui, Mussorgsky and Rimsky-Korsakov
  o Should be the name of a rock band but actually they were a group of Russian composers who aimed to create a Russian style of composition; think lush high Romantic and with a distinctly Russian flavour, often with specific reference to Russian folklore or literature.

o **German Middle Romantics:** Schumann, Brahms, Mendelssohn
  o Three of the nineteenth century's greatest melodic composers; stirring, vital and descriptive and with gorgeous harmonies, their music was heavily influenced by the literature of the time, especially in their prolific outpouring of songs.

o **First Viennese School:** three composers of the Classical period in late-eighteenth-century Vienna: Mozart, Haydn and Beethoven
  o This is the classical music that put the classical into classical, if you will; using classical principles of form they composed music that is ordered, uplifting and often sublimely beautiful.

o **Second Viennese School:** Webern, Berg, Schoenberg
  o I'll go into the whys and wherefores of Schoenberg and his associates later (in Chapters 6 and 7 on melody and harmony) but essentially they took a hammer to the whole idea of nice tunes and luscious harmonies,

breaking traditional composition apart and creating a composing system known as 'Atonalism', 'twelve-tone composing' or 'Serialism'; their music sometimes sounds as if nineteenth-century composers had woken up one morning and forgotten how to play their instruments.

- Les Six: Georges Auric (1899–1983), Louis Durey (1888–1979), Arthur Honegger (1892–1955), Darius Milhaud (1892–1974), Francis Poulenc (1899–1963), Germaine Tailleferre (1892–1983)
  - Les Six were a group of French composers trying to get away from the influences of German music and also of late-nineteenth-century Impressionism; this is distinctly French music of the twentieth century which is consciously *not* German; their music is not as overtly complex as the Second Viennese School from around the same time and is a good bet if you like French music that doesn't take itself over-seriously.

- Manchester: Harrison Birtwistle, Alexander Goehr, John Ogden and Peter Maxwell Davies
  - This group of English composers met in Manchester during the 1950s to form 'New Music Manchester'. Noisy, experimental, challenging, complex and at times plain scary, this is music to progress to long after you've tired of *Smooth Classics at Seven*; be advised that this is occasionally semi-seriously referred to amongst musicians as 'squeaky gate music' – because that's what it sometimes sounds like. But without being glib, it's very exhilarating live – especially Birtwistle whose *Last Supper* I found profoundly moving whilst acoustically stretching.

- New Complexity: Richard Barrett (UK), Aaron Cassidy (USA), James Dillon (UK), Joël-François Durand (France),

Jason Eckardt (USA), James Erber (UK), Brian Ferneyhough (UK), Michael Finnissy (UK), Claus-Steffen Mahnkopf (Germany), Roger Redgate (UK), René Wohlhauser (Switzerland)

○ Eighties term for composers dealing in extremes of tone and technique, extending all the usual parameters of playing music and taking them to their near-unplayable conclusion. Just generally a hell of a lot of notes. I'm ready to be shot down in flames or attacked by angry New Complexicists but this is 'musician's music' and is a struggle for newcomers. Aled Jones this is not. If the last group was 'squeaky gate music' then this is 'hit the gate, melt it down and reconstitute it as a Boeing 747 music'. Interestingly YouTube hits for this music are often in the low thousands or hundreds. Vivaldi's *Four Seasons* has six million hits. An unfair comparison, I know, but it tells you that you might need to graduate towards this music after some effort.

○ **Postmodernism:** Unlike the out-and-out Modernism of New Complexity there are composers writing music with a range of influences that while challenging has the advantage of sounding more familiar. The modern British composer Mark Anthony Turnage (b. 1960) writes music that is often dense and complex but throughout which you can hear moments of popular and jazz rhythms. It's also clear that he's listened to Leonard Bernstein and Hitchcock's composer, Bernard Hermann, as well as jazz trumpeter Miles Davis. This combination of modern complexity and disharmony with energetic popular rhythms is one of the hallmarks of his music [Sound Link 9].

   ○ The Scottish composer James MacMillan is also known for combining different styles of music, most notably Catholic church music and Scottish folk tunes, but with a modern twist.

o **Bel Canto:** Rossini, Donizetti, Bellini
  o *Bel Canto* is Italian, meaning 'beautiful singing'. This is an opera style that focuses on beauty of tone and vocal flexibility. Joan Sutherland, who died in 2010, and Marilyn Horne were famous exponents in recent years and made the style immensely popular. 'Casta Diva' by Bellini has recently been used in a TV advert for Jean-Paul Gaultier perfume but there are plenty more where that came from.

o **Darmstadt school:** Karlheinz Stockhausen, Pierre Boulez, Luigi Nono, Luciano Berio, Iannis Xenakis, Jean Barraque
  o A loosely connected category of 'Serial' composers who went through the Darmstadt International Summer School courses around the 1950s and '60s. Darmstadt was largely destroyed by bombing in the Second World War so it seems appropriate that these composers should have forged such radical ways of composing based on the traditions of the Second Viennese School. Boulez is a firebrand of a composer who said in the 1950s, 'It is not enough to deface the *Mona Lisa* because that does not kill the *Mona Lisa*. All the art of the past must be destroyed,' like a benign version of the Cambodian Year Zero concept, where all preceding culture must be cleared away to make way for that which is new.

o **The composers of the Fitzwilliam Virginal:** Byrd, Weelkes, Bull, Gibbons, Dowland, etc.
  o A large collection of Jacobean keyboard music, which was once thought to have belonged to Queen Elizabeth I but sadly that wasn't true. Containing just shy of 300 pieces by composers of the day, this is a treasure chest of interest.

- Sturm und Drang: some early Haydn, C.P.E. Bach, Mozart
  - Around the 1760s to '80s, some German art and music indulged in more emotional outpouring than the Enlightenment had previously sanctioned, with its emphasis on the rational. This new hot-headedness became known as 'storm and stress'.

- The Mannheim School: Johann Stamitz, Franz Xaver Richter, Carl Stamitz, Franz Ignaz Beck, Ignaz Fränzl and Christian Cannabich
  - Taken from the composers and players who passed through the doors of the Mannheim court orchestra in the late eighteenth century, giving it a sound of its own, and a penchant for sudden crescendos and 'grand' dramatic pauses in the music which gave rise to the term 'Mannheim Rocket theme' – music which at the time was thought explosive.

- Early twentieth-century English music: Vaughan Williams, Gerald Finzi, Cyril Scott, Gustav Holst, George Butterworth, Frederick Delius
  - English composers of the twentieth century who set out to create an English style of music by collecting folk music to include in their compositions (you may have heard of Cecil Sharp but he was a collector of folk songs rather than a composer). Their work is often pastoral and did not fall under the influence of their German contemporaries. It was dismissed by contemporaries as 'cowpat music' because of its self-consciously rural sound.

- The school of New American music: George Gershwin, Aaron Copland, Roger Sessions, Virgil Thomson, Samuel Barber
  - Another group pursuing a national sound. This is the sound of the Wild West and large open spaces. Copland's

style has become synonymous with the American sound and is a good starting point for getting into American music, while Gershwin's music is so strongly associated with America that it was used on the television adverts for American Airlines.

- *Rhapsody in Blue*: when George Gershwin introduced *Rhapsody in Blue* in 1924 jazz was still in its infancy. The combination of this exciting new style with the palette of orchestral colours available in the concert hall would have been a revelation at the time. Leonard Bernstein sought to combine popular music with classical music, to my ears less effectively than Gershwin. Gershwin had it all and was admired by Ravel, who refused to teach him because that would 'only make you a bad Schoenberg, and you're such a good Gershwin already'.
- *Appalachian*: listen to *Appalachian Spring* by Aaron Copland and you know that you are listening to an American composer. It's partly because his music has been endlessly imitated by film composers who wrote scores for the old Westerns, and partly because he deliberately set out to write an 'American Music'.

- **Spectral Group**: Gerard Grisey, Tristan Murail, Hugues Dufourt and others
  - Sound itself, in its amazing timbral transformations, is the real purpose of composition. Whatever schemes or systems you use to get there are of secondary importance, say the spectralists. Their music is a mixture of sound effects, atmospheres and noise-making. Plinky-plonky, whining, jangling, blowing and knocking are all appropriate adjectives. Very effective in creating entirely new and strange orchestral sound worlds, this is very much the territory of the London Sinfonietta who play music at the bleeding edge of contemporary music.

## Anything goes – do it your own way

There are ideas, places and events that composers from all periods of history have been inspired by. So you don't need to stay in one particular spot in history. The sea, for instance, has washed up lots of music in its honour:

- Beethoven, Schubert and Mendelssohn: *Calm Sea and Prosperous Voyage (Meeresstille und Glückliche Fahrt)*
- Henry Wood: *Fantasia on British Sea Songs*
- Elgar: *Sea Pictures*
- Glazunov: *The Sea*
- Vaughan Williams: *A Sea Symphony*
- Debussy: *La Mer*
- Frank Bridge: *The Sea*
- Delius: *Sea Drift*
- Benjamin Britten: 'Sea Interludes' from *Peter Grimes*

## Listening projects

Set yourself a target. Ask yourself these questions:

- What would you like to be able to appreciate but feel that you can't?
- Is there an era of history that you are interested in that might offer a good starting point for musical exploration? (Forget about the Ancient Egyptians – there's nothing written down from that period, other than a few scales.)
- Is there a piece you like by a composer who you'd like to know more about?
- Is there a composer you've heard of but have never listened to?
- Is there a piece of classical music used in a film or on television that you remember enjoying?
- Is there a particular instrument you love the sound of?

Here are some listening projects to stretch you. They move you further away into increasingly challenging repertoire. The projects are not meant to be in chronological order, and the link may seem very tenuous: but there is a thread. If you are a fan of Johann Strauss's waltzes (I'm not) then you can spend the rest of your life getting to know all of the works by his three sons. Especially the 'king of waltzes', Johann Strauss II. If you like Bach's cantatas then after working your way through around 200 of his, look into his contemporaries and predecessors, Telemann, Schütz and Buxtehude, who wrote fine cantatas too. Or once you have exhausted Mozart you might start on the music of Antonio Salieri or Vicente Martín y Soler. As suggested by the film *Amadeus*, Salieri was a lesser composer, but wrote some fine music and was a significant influence as a teacher of Beethoven and Schubert. Like their fathers, Mozart's son Franz Xaver, J.S. Bach's sons Wilhelm Friedemann and Carl Philipp Emanuel Bach were also composers and are worth a listen too.

o **Fanny Hensel née Mendelssohn** *(Felix Mendelssohn's sister)*
The story goes that when singing songs with Felix, Queen Victoria pointed to one her favourites from his collection of songs; *'Italien'* ('Italy'). He revealed to the Queen that this was in fact a song published under his name but written by the hand of his sister, Fanny.

o **Michael Haydn**
Brother of the more famous Joseph but no less worthy of a listen.

o **The Strauss brothers**
An entire dynasty of Viennese waltzers. Need I say more?

- **Alma Mahler**

  Prevented from composing by her husband, Gustav Mahler, she only completed a handful of songs. These are now gaining recognition and offer a fascinating insight into this famous *femme fatale* who so captivated Mahler.

- **The Bach boys**

  No, not a misspelling of Beach Boys. Johann Sebastian Bach had a huge family with at least two significant composers among his sons. Try C.P.E Bach's *Deposuit Potentes* from his setting of the words of the *Magnificat* (sounds like a homage to both his father and Mozart).

- **Mozart's dad**

  Leopold Mozart was 37 when his more accomplished son Wolfgang Amadeus was born. He clearly passed on his compositional gifts and the son's work bears similarities to the father's. I think we must forgive his pushiness because without it we wouldn't have had Mozart junior.

## Fin de siècle

The end of the nineteenth century was a time of tremendous upheaval and gave rise to a huge variety of music by diverse composers, such as:

- **Wagner:** more than just the composer of the Ring cycle operas; his music is full of magic and grandeur
- **Richard Strauss:** melodic, expressive and at times sumptuous
- **Mahler:** serious, mercurial, at times dark, at times uplifting
- **Debussy:** colourful, exotic and unlike anything written before
- **Ravel:** a man of melody and a master at writing for the orchestra

## Early music

If you like the simple sound of plainsong – monks or nuns chanting – then be joyous for there is a plethora of composers for you to explore. And with every passing month somebody raids the ancient libraries and makes new discoveries. I would say this is easy music to listen to – whether it holds your attention is a personal matter. After the plainsong came polyphony (multi-part singing) and there's plenty of that to set your soul a-quiver. Here are a few composers to help you start:

- Guillaume Dufay
- Josquin des Prez
- Hildegard of Bingen
- Perotin
- Tallis
- Byrd
- Taverner
- Sheppard
- Monteverdi

## Shakespeare

There is much music inspired by Shakespeare, some of it ridiculously famous and some not. The Finzi songs are my tip for a lesser-known but beautifully introspective song cycle.

- **Mendelssohn: *A Midsummer Night's Dream***
  Mendelssohn's suite (group of pieces) based on the play contains one of the most famous wedding marches of all time (although I didn't have it at my wedding); scratch beneath the surface and there are some other marvels – the Scherzo is just as tuneful, more exciting and an orchestral romp.

○ **Verdi:** *Otello, Macbeth* **and** *Falstaff*
Verdi may have created a Macbeth who sounds as Scottish
as Silvio Berlusconi but don't let that put you off; nobody
knows how to write dramatic roles like Verdi, and
Shakespeare offered the sort of subject matter that appealed
to this man of the theatre.

○ **Korngold:** *Much Ado About Nothing*
*A* hidden gem.

○ **Roger Quilter:** *Shakespeare Songs*
The first art songs I learnt when I started singing;
underrated and actually very lovely.

○ **Finzi:** *Let Us Garlands Bring*
Some of my favourite English songs, not sweet exactly but
not too tart either, like a perfect Cox apple.

○ **Vaughan Williams:** *Three Shakespeare Songs*
*A*tmospheric part songs (a song for choirs); 'Full Fathom
Five' is eerie.

○ **Shostakovich:** *Hamlet Suite*
A distinctly Russian-sounding Hamlet but hugely energetic
and dramatic as you'd expect from Shostakovich.

○ **Stravinsky:** *Three Songs from William Shakespeare*
A little more difficult as you'd expect from Stravinsky, but
these are songs to graduate towards rather than to start with.

○ **Thomas Adès:** *The Tempest*
This new opera is fabulously modern and strange; some of
the writing is very lyrical and accessible, but this is probably
like nothing you've heard before, unless you are the
adventurous type.

### A.E. Housman

A.E. Housman wrote a collection of poems call *A Shropshire Lad* in the 1890s. They became very popular in the First World War due to their nostalgic references to England as a pastoral idyll. Many composers of song have plundered the poems, including Ralph Vaughan Williams, Ivor Gurney, John Ireland and George Butterworth. My particular favourite remains the Butterworth settings (especially as recorded by Bryn Terfel and Malcolm Martineau in 1995) although the songs in *Wenlock Edge* by Vaughan Williams are also wonderful.

### Tone poems

Pieces that describe a story, landscape or person. The titles and the music combine to create images in your head and take you into another imaginative world. Here are some favourites:

- Janáček: *Taras Bulba*
- Janáček: *Sinfonietta*
- Copland: *Appalachian Spring*
- Stravinsky: *Firebird Suite*
- Smetana: *Má Vlast*
- Rimsky-Korsakov: *Scheherazade*
- Grieg: *Peer Gynt*
- Saint-Saëns: *Danse macabre*
- Sibelius: *Swan of Tuonela*

### Piano concertos

Surely the greatest instrument after the voice, the pianoforte (or piano as it is now known) has provided inspiration to many composers. Some of the greatest examples of works for soloist and orchestra (concertos) are for the piano. They are always fun to see live but it's worth checking that your seats have a view of the keyboard (sit in the left-hand side of the concert hall) if you want to see a display of fireworks.

- Grieg: Piano Concerto in A Minor, especially the second movement
- Mozart: Piano Concerto No. 23, particularly the second movement – Horowitz for me every time
- Mozart: Piano Concerto No. 21, particularly the second movement (Andante)
- Rachmaninov: Piano Concertos Nos 2 and 3
- Beethoven: Piano Concerto No. 5, 'Emperor'
- Tchaikovsky: Piano Concerto No. 1
- Shostakovich: Piano Concerto No. 2
- Bartók: Piano Concerto No. 3

## Minimalism

I'll deal with the finer points of Minimalism in the chapter on style but this is for many people the acceptable face of modern classical music, especially John Adams who is held by many to be an 'important composer' – quite an accolade for someone who broke with many of the traditions of twentieth-century composition.

- Michael Nyman: *The Piano*
- Ludovico Einaudi: *I Giorni*
- John Adams: *Short Ride in a Fast Machine*
- John Adams: *Chairman Dances*
- Nico Muhly: 'Fire Down Below' from *I Drink the Air Before Me* – gaining ground but a new addition to the pantheon of Minimalists
- Steve Reich: *Music for Eighteen Musicians*
- Philip Glass: *A Descent into the Maelström* (Philip Glass Ensemble) – I generally prefer it when he doesn't use synths or saxophones but this is an arresting sound

## Music from the movies, TV or radio shows

My favourite TV theme tune is *Black Beauty* but I don't think that counts as 'classical'. Many pieces of music are used as theme tunes from *The Minute Waltz* by Chopin for *Just a Minute* on Radio 4 and *The Wakeful Poet* by Michael Berkeley on Radio 3's *Private Passions* at the serious end of radio. *The Karelia Suite* (Sibelius) was used for ITV's long-running *This Week* current affairs programme, and I've mentioned *The Apprentice* enough already. I would suggest that you listen to the *Lord of the Rings Soundtrack* (Howard Shore). I like it because the London Philharmonic do a sterling job and it fuses some great classical singers (Renée Fleming) with pop singers (Annie Lennox) and folk instruments such as the *hardingfele* (a Norwegian violin).

### Free-association

Of course the beauty of the internet is that you could free-associate for the rest of your life and rarely find a repeat. If you view classical music as a family tree of music, taking one piece and seeing the various ways it could lead on to other music, you'll find that almost everything is related in some way. Even if the links are tangential they can lead you to make discoveries.

## Growing on you

Whatever it takes for you to feel like you are finding new music is the right course of action. As long as you are prepared to give it a fair listen and as long as you let that inform your next choice then you can hardly go wrong. Just admitting that you like classical music can be a hurdle for some people, so come on, let yourself admit it – you like this stuff.

Listening projects can be great fun but I suspect they may leave you wondering what's classical music and what isn't. In the next chapter I'm going to look at who decides whether a piece is classical or not.

Chapter **5**

# Exploding the Canon

*" The Western musical canon came about not merely by accumulation, but by opposition and subversion, both to the ruling powers on whom composers depended for their livelihoods and to other musics. "*

BRIAN FERNEYHOUGH, composer

'The canon' wasn't a term I heard until I was studying drama at university where our first course was on the 'dramatic canon'.[1] We fought our way from the Ancient Greeks to modern dramatists, covering everyone who was considered to be important on the way, and I know they do a similar trek on music courses. My tutors acknowledged that, as useful as the course was for giving an overview, there is an inherent flaw in looking at the arts in this way: in the same way as a tourist guide can never be a comprehensive description of every aspect of a city, a course about the canon will always be selective and that act of selection will omit pieces that someone else would consider essential listening. So is it an impossible task?

There are certain composers who seem to transcend argument and have earned themselves an indelible place in the pantheon of the 'great' composers. They are mostly men, and for some reason a lot of them are German or Austrian. Very few people who like classical music will say that they dislike Mozart. A few might tell you that J.S. Bach is too mathematical for their taste or that Beethoven is just a collection of scales but they will usually agree on the importance of these composers nonetheless.

We must have an idea of the canon of great composers and their works if we want to understand the history of music – it gives us a useful framework to hang things on – but it's important to remember that the list is in flux. Having said that, I doubt that anyone will nudge Mozart off the list, but if you look at how composers such as Mahler or Mendelssohn were perceived in their own time, how their reputations have risen and fallen like the stock market, then perhaps you'll be able to spot the next re-evaluation of a previous musical dark horse. This chapter aims to help you understand why the truly great composers are 'great'.

Why do fans of classical music bother watching the same orchestra play the same piece, but with a different conductor, for the fifteenth time? Why do the orchestras play these old warhorse pieces anyway? Shouldn't we just be constantly forging forth into new territory like they do in pop and to a lesser extent in jazz? Well, firstly, these pieces sell tickets and people love listening to them over and over again, for reasons I spoke about in the last chapter. But another reason for playing them is that a repertoire which the audience knows helps create a benchmark for listening – 'Did you like Sir Colin Davis's version or did you prefer Haitink's?', for example. It's also a benchmark of the craft of the musicians – 'Have you heard the LPO play it? What about the Hallé's version?' Because it takes years of practice to play these works and then a lifetime of orchestral experience to master them, they warrant hearing again and again.

There is a common misconception that an orchestra would be completely incapable of playing a symphony without a conductor, because it would all fall apart. I was speaking to an orchestral violinist recently who said that an orchestra *would* be able to play most of the core repertoire with an empty conducting podium – they know the works and they would watch each other and listen. This is unlikely to happen, but hypothetically speaking, even without a conductor there would be a London Symphony Orchestra way of playing a piece – say, for example, Brahms Symphony No. 4; there would be a Philharmonia way, a Royal Liverpool Philharmonic way, and as many different ways as there are orchestras. You'd recognise the piece, of course, but if you knew the work well you'd notice differences in the playing.

So why have a conductor if the orchestra already know how to play the great works? The answer is that some consensus needs to be reached: older players will have played the piece over 100 times in their careers with many different conductors, some of whom belong to the previous generation; the younger players will have recently emerged from conservatoires with heads full of new approaches. When that many people attempt to play together they inevitably have slightly different approaches. It's a conductor's job to unify this disparate picture and create a coherent performance – not just keeping together, but approaching things in the same musical way: louder here, quieter there, faster at the end, more vibrato, and so on. A conductor must come into rehearsal and get the version he or she wants from the orchestra; sometimes the orchestra agrees, sometimes there are fireworks. It's the alchemy of this relationship that keeps people returning to hear the same piece over and over again. 'How will it differ this time?' 'Will the magic moments be more special than before or will it work in a different way?' Just as there are myriad ways to put on a Shakespeare play, so there are many different approaches to a symphony.

For this alchemical reaction to take place, a conductor needs the catalyst of a true work of art. This is where the canon of great works becomes vital. Without a piece of music that is structurally varied enough for the conductor to be able to express a wide range of ideas or a piece that works in front of an audience, even the greatest conductor would struggle to create magic. Music of excellence has been proved to work in the concert hall and to have inbuilt resilience to a variety of interpretations by different conductors: for instance, Beethoven could be massacred by a second-rate orchestra, yet anybody could still recognise it as music of quality. The reverse is true for composers of the second division: their work requires the very best interpretation and painstaking rehearsal to bring out any inherent qualities.

I'll discuss the mysterious business of how conductors achieve their vision later in the book. But first, what are these pieces and how do we agree on what makes them 'canonical'? How does a piece become canonical in the first place? There's no simple answer because taste is a personal business. However, sometimes the initial reaction to a piece is so staggering that it marks it out as a work of importance, like it or not, the riot at the first performance of *The Rite of Spring* being the oft-quoted example. Accounts of that night vary, but there was an extreme public outcry about its primitive rhythmic drive, the violence of the dancing and a shocking narrative for a ballet of a girl dancing herself to death. (As suggested in the last chapter, listening to some of the other ballet music written at the time – and understanding what ballet more normally depicted – will help you understand the shock people must have felt.)

For a composer, there is surely no better guarantee of notoriety, with the added benefit of increasing ticket sales to people eager to see what all the fuss is about, than a riot. More recently, the conductor Michael Tilson-Thomas introduced the radically Minimalist and *painfully* repetitive *Four Organs* by Steve Reich (b. 1936) to a very conservative classical music audience in New York.

After a few minutes into Steve's piece a restlessness began to sweep through the crowd: rustlings of programs, overly loud coughs, compulsive seat shifting, gradually mixed with groans and hostile exclamations crescendoing into a true cacophony. There were at least three attempts to stop the performance by shouting it down. One woman walked down the aisle and repeatedly banged her head on the front of the stage wailing, 'Stop, stop, I confess.' The audience made so much noise that, in spite of the fact that the music was amplified, we were unable to hear one another's playing. I had to mouth numbers and shout our cues so that we could stay together. Just after the piece came to a close, there was a moment of silence followed by a veritable avalanche of boos. It was deafening. We stood up and took a bow smiling as best we could and walked off the stage. Steve was ashen, looking as lost and unhappy as a lost soul from Michelangelo's *Last Judgment*. I, on the contrary, was exhilarated. I turned to him and said, 'Steve, this is fantastic. It's the kind of thing you read about in history books, like the premiere of *Rite of Spring*. Whatever some members of the audience think about your piece, you can bet by tomorrow everyone in the United States will have heard about you and your work and will be hugely intrigued to hear it for themselves.'[2]

Other pieces have inauspicious beginnings, taking time and re-evaluation by subsequent generations before their genius is revealed. I suspect that a glimmer of the possibility of canonical immortality sustains many composers through the bleak years without commissions when their music is largely ignored. Many a Franz Kafka exists in the musical world (Kafka was unpublished and on his death asked for his life's work to be burnt; his friend rejected the idea and published to great post-humous acclaim). From their lonely garret by candlelight they mutter, 'You'll be sorry when I'm gone ...' Charles Ives, now considered a real American original, was rather overlooked in his lifetime, and he juggled composing with a successful career in insurance.

As I've already made clear, I believe the St Matthew Passion by Bach to be among the greatest works of human achievement, comparable with the Sistine Chapel or the work of Shakespeare, yet for many years it was known to few people outside Germany. First performed in 1727, it had to wait 103 years before it was finally published in 1830. The composer Felix Mendelssohn brought the work to the attention of the English, who until 1837 had not heard much of the music of J.S. Bach. Mendelssohn was introduced to Bach by his teacher, Zelter, and with cut-down (sacrilege!) performances he gradually persuaded the public. It wasn't until 1854 that the full work was performed in England. It reached a huge level of popularity in late Victorian England. As for the other works of Bach, they took longer to surface from obscurity.

Many struggled with Gustav Mahler's compositions and for his contemporary audience he was considered to be first and foremost a conductor. Mahler's music is often troubled, flitting from one style to another, but I have the sense that he was probably like that as a character: his music was grandiose by contemporary standards and the constant self-quotation, changeable sound and inward-looking nature of his music meant that it wasn't until the 1950s and '60s that champions of his music such as Leonard Bernstein and Mahler's protégé Bruno Walter began to convince the public. It can be difficult for composers who also perform, as demand for their time on the concert platform can compete with their compositional output, although this was hardly the case for Mahler who managed to write ten symphonies in his summer holidays (in different years, obviously). Symphony No. 9 went unperformed until after his death. A full-time composer would rarely write a piece of music on that scale to be left in a drawer.

However, Hector Berlioz (1803–1869) had extreme difficulty in getting his massive opera *Les Troyens* (*The Trojans*) performed because of a long-running argument with the Paris opera. Berlioz was a disappointed character who in later life railed against the musical establishment that had failed to extol the virtues of his music; there was a general feeling that his music wasn't up to scratch and so the full work wasn't performed until twenty-one years after his death. It wasn't performed in the UK until 1935, when it was put on in Glasgow. The work was the culmination of a lifetime's effort for Berlioz and I can only imagine the frustration he felt at seeing it languish unperformed.

It's not just the audience you have to please, either. Composers are very good at knifing one another in the back and scoffing at each other's efforts. So much for artistic solidarity. When the earnest young Schubert played his seminal song cycle *Winterreise* ('A Winter's Journey') to his friends they were unimpressed. His friend the composer Josef von Spaun wrote years later that 'we were quite dumbfounded by the gloomy mood of these songs', to which Schubert replied, 'I like these songs more than all the others and you will get to like them too.'[3] Spaun's recollection was written twenty years after Schubert's untimely death in 1828. It has a whiff of myth-making about it, but it illustrates perfectly that what is now taught on A-Level syllabuses and considered core repertoire for singers wasn't universally hailed immediately.

Stravinsky could be somewhat sardonic and his less than enthusiastic reaction to the work of Benjamin Britten tells us much about Stravinsky's view of his own importance. Although Britten was an excellent accompanist, he was first and foremost a composer, a fact that Stravinsky deliberately chooses to ignore when writing to a friend:

> All week here I've listened to Aunt Britten and Uncle Pears ... Britten himself makes quite a favourable impression, and he is very popular with the public. He undoubtedly has talent as a performer, especially at the piano.

This goes beyond acerbity, it's patronising and not a little homophobic. Not that Britten couldn't wield the poison pen. In his diaries he comments on conductors Sir Adrian Boult and Sir Henry Wood: 'slow, dull & ignorant', and 'an absolute vandal', respectively. Elgar? 'How I wish I could like this music.' Ralph Vaughan Williams? 'Repulses me.'

Claude Debussy, composer of Classic FM favourite *Clair de Lune,* came in for a great deal of criticism because of his musical innovations. Debussy was influenced by the Gamelan (an ensemble of traditional Balinese or Javanese instruments – see above, Chapter 3). The impressionistic atmospheres that Debussy created were considered beyond the pale for many of his contemporaries and his free use of form (his music follows its own path rather than traditional models) seemed a slap in the face of the French musical establishment. In a letter to the composer Gabriel Fauré, the sharp-tongued Camille Saint-Saëns wrote:

> I recommend you look at the pieces for two pianos, Noir et Blanc [sic], which M. Debussy has just published. It's unbelievable, and we must at all costs bar the door of the Institut against a man capable of such atrocities; they should be put next to the cubist pictures.
>
> Many greetings,
>
> C. Saint-Saëns

But Debussy was not averse to rolling his sleeves up and getting into the fray. Here he describes the music of Maurice Ravel:

> It's true that Ravel is greatly talented, but I'm annoyed by his conjurer's attitude, or one might call it that of a fakir who casts spells and makes flowers break out of chairs. Unfortunately, conjuring tricks have to be prepared, and when you've seen them the first time you're not astonished any more.[4]

One of the most famous rivalries appears to have been exaggerated. Anyone who has seen the film *Amadeus* by Peter Shaffer will remember the malevolent presence of the older composer Salieri, played by F. Murray Abraham, as he glowered at Mozart. The reality seems to have been less dramatic and there are accounts of a friendship between the two men. Yet as I listen to Salieri's music it's impossible not to feel that Mozart has the edge. There's a wit, invention and fluidity in the younger composer's work that makes Salieri's writing seem rather pedantic. The enmity between them made a great story but seems to have been dramatic licence. But it was not only competition with Salieri that threatened Mozart's superiority. Mozart is said to have had a 'piano duel' with the technically dazzling pianist and composer Muzio Clementi (1752–1832) at the request of Joseph II. Clementi impressed the audience with his undoubted skill at the keyboard but in a letter after the event Mozart said his rival had no 'taste or feeling – in short he is a mere mechanicus [robot]'. History has almost forgotten the less famous Clementi except that one of his pieces forms the basis of Phil Collins's number one hit 'A Groovy Kind of Love'. What an accolade.

As we're on the subject of musical bitchiness, other examples include:

- a poem by Schoenberg referring to Stravinsky as '*der kleine modernsky*' (the little Modernist)
- Tchaikovsky saying of Brahms 'what a giftless bastard'
- Britten being equally rude about Brahms: 'foul – I can scarcely bear to play it'.

For any composer, winning the battle and proving yourself more important than another composer is of vital importance to your longevity. Composers who have long lives might start their careers in one musical epoch and end in another. Some adapt to the changes and welcome them; others set themselves up as the keepers of important traditions and remain fixedly the same. But all young composers love to have a go at the previous generation: 'Listening to the Fifth Symphony of Ralph Vaughan Williams is like staring at a cow for forty-five minutes' (Aaron Copland).

## On the fringes and outside the canon

Why do some pieces become canonical while others don't? There is no simple answer to this question. Some make the grade and some don't. There are pieces which have been performed regularly ever since their composition. One such example is the Max Bruch (1838–1920) Violin Concerto No. 1, Op. 26, which eclipsed the rest of his output almost entirely. The piece has become a key work for any violinist.

Now let's spare a thought for an also-ran of musical history – Hermann Goetz (1840–1876) – no, I'd never heard of him either. For well over a century Goetz's long-forgotten music has remained unopened on the dusty shelves of unknown libraries. Without the modern fashion for discovering obscure repertoire there it might have remained but for the thrusting work of Hyperion Records, who have a reputation for musical excellence and a history of recording the works that other labels don't reach. In 2010 they recorded Hermann Goetz's Piano Concerto in B Flat Major, a work that despite the composer's best efforts failed to enter the canon of great works.[5]

Why should this be the case and will this new recording force the musical public to reassess Goetz's work? Listening to the piano concerto today there is much to recommend: it is melodic, expressive, well-paced and virtuosic. He reached a high level of accomplishment in composition which, although only recognised by local press in his own time, can now be appreciated by anyone who cares to listen thanks to these high-quality recordings.[6] At the time Goetz complained that he might have had more success had he been a pretty girl. It seems the world was just as fickle in the nineteenth century. Actually I think it's an interesting work (to damn it with faint praise) and worth a listen, but I'd be surprised if it became your favourite piano concerto [Sound Link 10].

Despite its being a beautiful piece in many respects it doesn't stand up to comparison with other great concerti of the same era. Brahms (1833–1897) was born seven years before Goetz, Mendelssohn was born in 1809, and their music eclipses the younger man's efforts. There's a simplicity in Brahms and Mendelssohn, whose melodies are more memorable. To create a strong melody and let that do most of the work takes a compositional confidence and talent that I think eluded Goetz, and to my ears his work sounds overstuffed with ideas. When I listen to the Mendelssohn Violin Concerto or the Bruch No. 1, I'm hooked within seconds.

If a composer writes music which sounds like a rehashing of the previous generation and doesn't sound modern or original to its initial audience, then it will most likely be relegated to dusty shelves. To gain admission to the canon a composer must be innovative and move the history of composition forward. There are many composers who lack the character to swim against the tide of musical opinion and write music that challenges the predominant style of the era in the way that Beethoven, Mahler, Wagner, Schoenberg or Debussy did. These were heroic individuals possessed of dogmatic determination and powerful self-belief, enabling them to write music which at the time attracted criticism and praise in equal measure.

## Schubert and co.

A few years ago I was working on a project to take German song (*Lieder*) into schools for the Wigmore Hall. It's never easy convincing young people to take their earphones out and listen to something by a dead composer. I was lucky because the singer who came with me to a secondary school in Kilburn, North London, was Ann Murray, DBE, one of the country's most expressive singers. Ann has a way of putting people at ease which helped the young people to feel that these songs could be worth listening to. The relationship she forms with an audience is immediate and obvious, whether it's a recital at the Wigmore, a performance at the opera house or a wet Monday morning in a school hall pungent with the smell of teenagers' deodorant. But even with this incredible talent and voice to match, Ann cannot make a great performance without a great song. Her rendition of *An den Mond* captivated the dear children who stopped chewing gum and sat open-mouthed long enough to listen to the high notes.

One of the songs I chose to focus on was the *Erlkönig* ('Erlking') by Franz Schubert (1897–1828) because of its dramatic story and relentless accompaniment. In preparing for the project I wanted to find out what it was about this famous setting of the words that was so effective so I listened to other versions of the song by different composers. *Erlkönig* by Loewe follows the dramatic structure of the poem, increasing in intensity where appropriate, but it lacks the unified simplicity of the Schubert version. It feels overly melodramatic where Schubert finds real menace and a foreboding sense of death in the relentless piano figure, which is suggestive of a frantic horse ride through a dark forest. Listening to the songs of Schubert's contemporaries, Bürde, Spohr, Loewe and Lachner, is immensely helpful if you want to understand what makes Franz Schubert one of the truly great song composers. After listening I always find myself drawn back to the greater composer: Schubert.[7]

So why is Schubert better? Well, firstly there's his facility for melody which marks out Schubert from the rest of the field. His songs have what writers of pop songs call a 'hook'. The musicologist Wilfred Mellers is popularly remembered for describing Lennon and McCartney as the greatest songwriters since Schubert, precisely for their ability to write catchy songs with hooks. I'm with Mellers here. There's very little difference between the two except that Schubert used other people's poems, which gives his work a greater breadth. 'She's Leaving Home' is as moving as 'Du bist die Ruh' ... isn't it?

Sometimes a Schubert hook is a clever and evocative piano motif – as in the depiction of the movement of water throughout *Die Schöne Müllerin* where the piano represents the literal world and the inner psychological journey of the protagonist while still appealing to the casual listener. At other times it's a turn of harmony that illuminates the words: the alternate use of major and minor (see above, Chapter 2) in the song *Ständchen* creates an unsettling yearning quality that underlines the pain of the lyrics. The repetitive melody which is repeated over the five verses becomes more poignant with each repetition. Contrast that with the more complicated version by Franz Paul Lachner (1803–1890) which has none of the strophic simplicity of the Schubert version and is consequently less convincing. (Strophic songs use a repeated tune for each verse like a pop song without a chorus.)

In the secondary schools of North London, Schubert was the clear winner – the children became genuinely excited by the macabre and fantastical story, but it was the music that drew them in first. With a truly great composer of song, the words and the music appear to be inseparable. For a musician closer examination reveals ever greater levels of subtlety which is not the case with a lesser composer and for the untrained ear there's a musical immediacy to the song.

There is also a non-musical dimension to this. Schubert died at a horribly young age from syphilis: just 32. He had been ill for some time and wrote his greatest works whilst suffering the early symptoms. You could appreciate his music without knowing this but to my mind there is an added poignancy to the music when you consider his demise – the young boy who dies in *Erlkönig* could be seen as Schubert himself with death chasing him through the dark forest, Schubert writing music as quickly as possible to escape his inevitable demise. We venerate those who die young, especially those who are extremely talented. The tragic, lovesick songs are unbearably beautiful and those which are more celebratory and energetic demonstrate how much life the young man had in him. This is as true now as it was then – think of the reaction to the death of Jimi Hendrix.

A good life story helps cement you but what confirms your place in the canon is other musicians playing your music. Almost immediately after his death, Schubert's songs were venerated, transcribed and arranged by Liszt. Through the younger composer's fascination the works were guaranteed a new audience. This process repeats and repeats until the piece is almost universally hailed as a masterpiece [Sound Link 11].

The influence of Schubert's writing can be heard in other songwriters of the nineteenth century and into the twentieth: Schumann, Wolf and Mendelssohn all owe a debt to Schubert. Roger Quilter's songs, Benjamin Britten's *Winter Words*, Vaughan Williams's *On Wenlock Edge* are all a response to Schubert's songs, though written around 100 years later.

It's hard to divorce music from its reputation. Once a composer is considered 'old-fashioned' or out of favour, it takes a complete rethink to re-establish their reputation. Rebranding a composer is the job of academics and conductors; there have been several notable examples in recent years as musicians plunder the past looking for new angles on established or forgotten reputations.

This doesn't just apply to the music of Schubert or Goetz. There are hundreds of composers who fail to capture the imagination and only a very special few who are remembered. A great composer encodes something of our shared humanity in their music. It doesn't matter whether I'm listening to music from 700 years ago or music that was written last week – what I want from music is access to another person's viewpoint, a glimpse into their world and the solace that offers. Sadly one of the side-effects of such glory is that your music becomes so ubiquitous that it can no longer have the same startling effect on audiences, who have become over-familiar and virtually immune to it so that their response to great music in general can become impassive: we can forget how difficult the composition of these masterpieces must have been if we are used to hearing nothing but the very best. I find it useful to remind myself of the mediocrity that exists because it refreshes my sense of awe at the true paragons of music.

This is a matter of taste and you might not agree with me that Schubert's music is among the most beautiful ever written (I know my old music teacher isn't a fan!). But there are certain pieces around which the rest of the classical repertoire orbits. Attitudes, tastes and playing styles change with increasing rapidity but Mozart and Beethoven remain perennially authoritative. It is a facet of the greatness of their music that with each coming age we find new things to discover about them. They stay with us, comfort us and then, in the hands of a novel interpreter, they can shock us. That is the very essence and purpose of the canon of great works.

Hopefully you now understand where to start listening, how to listen, what to listen out for and now most importantly *who* to listen to. Before you can graduate to really complex pieces it's worth going back to basics and thinking about how music is constructed at its most basic level, which I'll tackle in the second part of the book.

## Composers you should know something about

But first I think it's useful to know one or two things about each important composer. I find having a fact up your sleeve is not only useful at dinner parties but helps you remember who they all are. There are many missing: Ives and Meyerbeer, for example, but get your head round these and you'll be well on your way to expertise. This list stops in the 1960s because it's hard to say who will be the contemporary composers who stay the course. But John Adams will probably make the second edition of this book that I plan to write in my retirement.

- Bach, Johann Sebastian (1685–1750): prolific genius with a very precise style; he once walked 200 miles to attend an organ recital by Buxtehude; was renowned as an organist; married twice and had 20 children; some of his children were also composers
- Barber, Samuel (1910–1981): American composer who wrote the mega-famous Adagio for Strings; his sound is definitely American but at times dark and troubling … the American Dream gone wrong? He evaded easy definition by writing in many different styles
- Bartók, Béla (1881–1945): collected folk songs and used them in his compositions
- Beethoven, Ludwig van (1770–1827): went deaf at the end of his life; conducted the first performance of his Ninth Symphony and didn't know it was a huge success because he didn't hear the thunderous applause
- Bellini, Vincenzo (1801–1835): only lived 34 years and worked at the height of the *Bel Canto* era of opera
- Berg, Alban (1885–1935): wrote famous operas *Wozzeck* and *Lulu*; a Serialist composer (see Chapter 7); difficult
- Bizet, Georges (1838–1875): wrote great tunes; had an illegitimate son with the maid and died at 36
- Borodin, Alexander (1833–1887): Russian composer who was also a professional chemist
- Brahms, Johannes (1833–1897): had a 'did they? didn't they?' relationship with Clara Schumann after her husband's death
- Britten, Benjamin (1913–1976): he was fairly openly gay at a time when homosexuality was illegal and wrote roles such as *Peter Grimes* for his partner, the tenor Peter Pears, with whom he lived; he loved the sound of 'wrong notes' but had an equal fondness for folk songs
- Bruckner, Anton (1824–1896): wrote long symphonies and *Locus Iste*, which is a staple of all choral societies
- Buxtehude, Dietrich (c. 1637–1707): wrote music which inspired Bach

- Byrd, William (c. 1540–1623): was an English Catholic in Protestant times; pupil of Tallis; when Tallis died Byrd wrote a lovely song: 'Tallis is Dead – and Music Dies'
- Cage, John (1912–1992): more of a conceptual artist than a composer by traditional definitions
- Chopin, Frédéric (1810–1849): a wonderful pianist who wrote piano music; a cast was taken of his hands; his father was French but Chopin was brought up in Poland
- Copland, Aaron (1900–1990): his real name was Kaplan, and he became Copland when moving to America; ironically for an immigrant he went on to define an American sound
- Debussy, Claude (1862–1918): inspired by the sound of Balinese music; known as an 'Impressionist'
- Donizetti, Gaetano (1797–1848): he wrote around 60 operas, reworking the material from some to create new works; *L'Elisir d'amore* and *Lucia di Lammermoor* are his best-known works
- Dvořák, Antonín (1841–1904): took a professorship at an American university, during which time he wrote the 'New World' Symphony; he largely wrote works inspired by his Czech upbringing
- Elgar, Edward (1857–1934): had several 'muses' in the form of young ladies, wore a magnificent moustache and wrote the tune to 'Land of Hope and Glory'
- Ellington, Duke (1899–1974): a giant of jazz whose rich harmony and pianistic style have influenced the development of jazz, popular and classical music
- Fauré, Gabriel (1845–1924): famous for his Requiem, especially the 'Pie Jesu'; an organist as well as composer; I taught *Cantique de Jean Racine*, Op. 11, to the members of the Northolt School Choir in the first series of BBC2's *The Choir* because of his lush harmony; a pupil of Saint-Saëns; considered too modern for some of the musical establishment during his life but prefigures Ravel whom Fauré taught

- Gershwin, George (1898–1937): famous jazz pianist who wrote *Rhapsody in Blue* and *An American in Paris*
- Grieg, Edvard (1843–1907): A Norwegian who wrote one of the most iconic piano concerto openings in the repertoire; Debussy said his music was like 'a pink sweet filled with snow'
- Górecki, Henryk (1933–2010): wrote a symphony about the Holocaust which gained a huge popular following in the 1990s
- Handel, George Frideric (1685–1759): German who came to England and who we think of as English now; he wrote the 'Hallelujah Chorus' from the *Messiah*; born the same year as Bach
- Haydn, Joseph (1732–1809): 'Papa Haydn', 'the father of the symphony', of which he wrote over 100
- Holst, Gustav (1874–1934): writer of *The Planets* who taught at St Paul's Girl School, London
- Janáček, Leos (1854–1928): like Elgar, Janáček had a female muse, Kamila Stösslová; his fascination with women extended to his many operas featuring them as the central characters: *Jenůfa, Katya Kabanova, The Cunning Little Vixen*; he began sketching an opera of Tolstoy's *Anna Karenina* but never completed it
- Liszt, Franz (1811–1886): his hands were able to stretch wider than most pianists' due to the lack of webbing between his fingers;[8] he developed a lyrical yet virtuoso style adapting the melodies of his forebears
- Lully, Jean-Baptiste (1632–1687): French composer at the Royal Palace in Versailles; used orchestral resources as no one before and wrote many comic operas for the King
- Machaut, Guillaume de (1300–1377): a priest and composer of the fourteenth century, his music predates many musical conventions with which modern listeners are familiar so that it now sounds strangely unconventional

○ **Mahler, Gustav (1860–1911):** a tortured genius who moonlighted as a composer from his successful conducting career; Mahler expanded the notion of the symphony, using ever greater instrumental resources; he spent his last years conducting in America

○ **Mendelssohn, Felix (1809–1847):** like Handel, a favourite adopted son of England; captured the *zeitgeist* of the Victorian love of travel which can be heard in the Scottish *Fingal's Cave* and the 'Italian' Symphony; helped to make Bach famous again in the UK by conducting the first performance of the St Matthew Passion; wrote the *Wedding March*

○ **Messiaen, Olivier (1908–1992):** a major twentieth-century composer, as well as an organist and ornithologist: he believed birds to be the greatest musicians; he also had a taste for writing very complex chords which included more notes than seems normally acceptable; he wrote very complex music for the organ

○ **Monteverdi, Claudio (1567–1643):** wrote music specifically for St Mark's Cathedral in Venice that experimented with choirs in different parts of the building; widely credited as the first composer of opera as we know it today

○ **Mozart, Wolfgang Amadeus (1765–1791):** believed by some to have had Tourette's on the evidence of his scatological letters; died far too young at 35 and was buried in a pauper's grave; wrote everything from symphonies to songs; ironically he was writing a Requiem (funeral music) when he died, which was completed by his pupil

○ **Mussorgsky, Modest (1839–1881):** a Russian who struggled with alcohol addiction and consequently left works unfinished; his most famous work, *Pictures at an Exhibition*, was dedicated to a friend who had died suddenly; though originally for piano it has been orchestrated many times, most famously by Ravel

- Palestrina, Giovanni Pierluigi da (1525–1594): one of the few lay members of the Pope's own choir, he was ousted by a later pope for being married; Palestrina perfected a polyphonic style of choral music (singing in many parts)
- Prokofiev, Sergei (1891–1953): *Romeo and Juliet*, *Lieutenant Kijé* and *Peter and the Wolf* are among his best-known works; lived in the West but finally returned to the USSR, despite a hot and cold relationship with the authorities
- Puccini, Giacomo (1858–1924): the ultimate in sugar-coated, melodic opera; it's hard to escape crying at one of Puccini's tragic love stories. A major character in *Tosca* leaps from the battlements at the end of the opera (sorry for the spoiler); on certain occasions the singer has missed the safety mat – singing can be a lethal business
- Purcell, Henry (1659–1695): tragically he died young but not before he had written one of the most popular arias ever, 'Dido's Lament'; he is buried in Westminster Abbey beneath where the organ used to stand, but his career started as a boy singing in the Chapel Royal; his Funeral Sentences are stunningly beautiful
- Rachmaninov, Sergei (1873–1943): Russian pianist and composer; his Second Piano Concerto is very famous and was used in the film *Brief Encounter*; his music is lush, melodic and virtuosic; before playing his Third Concerto, he practised on a silent keyboard (no strings attached) while crossing the Atlantic
- Ravel, Maurice (1875–1937): wrote *Boléro*; had a degenerative brain condition at the end of his life; taught Vaughan Williams
- Rimsky-Korsakov, Nikolai (1844–1908): worked in the Russian Navy and composed in his spare time; he is probably best known as the composer of 'Flight of the Bumblebee' but *Scheherazade* and *Polovtsian Dances* are masterpieces of Russian music

- Rossini, Gioacchino (1792–1868): if Wagner is a serious red wine then Rossini is champagne; frothy, fast and full of sudden crescendos, his comic operas are pure entertainment; he was a famous gastronome and has many dishes named after him; not good with a deadline, he reused the overture from a different opera in *The Barber of Seville* – nobody seemed to mind, it's a great overture
- Saint-Saëns, Camille (1835–1921): although famous for his *Carnival of the Animals* it was only published posthumously because he was worried that it was too frivolous and would spoil his reputation as a serious composer; not a musician who embraced the advances of Modernism; a glorious tunesmith; his Third Symphony is well known to parents from the soundtrack to *Babe*
- Scarlatti, Domenico (1685–1757): Italian Baroque composer whose music was influential in developing Classical style
- Schoenberg, Arnold (1874–1951): moved to America from Vienna and changed the face of twentieth-century music along with Webern and Berg
- Schubert, Franz (1797–1828): wrote symphonies, songs and piano music; he carried a torch at Beethoven's funeral, but only a year later was dead himself, of syphilis, and was buried beside his idol
- Schumann, Robert (1810–1856): damaged ligaments in his own hand trying to develop his piano technique; he spent a year (1842) writing songs, many of them dedicated to Clara, his adored wife whom he married despite the strenuous objections of her father who tried to block the marriage with a court case; when playing recently written works of Chopin to his friends was heard to say, 'Hats off, gentlemen, a genius'; died of syphilis following a protracted period where his poor mental health affected his composition
- Shostakovich, Dmitri (1906–1975): another Russian composer who struggled with the Communists; Stalin objected to some of his work and Shostakovich lived his

artistic life under the scrutiny of the government; a master symphonist

o **Sibelius, Jean (1865–1957):** in 1907 he was diagnosed with throat cancer but continued to compose until the mid-1920s, after which he virtually ceased composing for the remaining thirty years of his life, and later destroyed the sketches for his unfinished Eighth Symphony; he created a style of music that became associated with rising Finnish nationalism

o **Smetana, Bedřich (1824–1884):** Smetana suffered from tinnitus, and wrote a string quartet inspired by this tragic condition for a musician

o **Stockhausen, Karlheinz (1928–2007):** one of the first major composers to use electronic instruments; you have to admire his uncompromising commitment to the avant-garde

o **Strauss, Johann II (1825–1899):** wrote many, many waltzes; some of them are played every year at the New Year's Day concert in Vienna

o **Strauss, Richard (1864–1949):** said, 'I may not be a first-rate composer, but I am a first-class second-rate composer'; big Romantic pieces for big Romantic orchestras and beautiful songs for big voices

o **Stravinsky, Igor (1882–1971):** Russian; worked with ballet impresario Diaghilev to create dramatic new ballets: *Firebird*, *Petrouchka* and his seminal work *The Rite of Spring*; Stravinsky re-invented his compositional style almost as many times as Picasso

o **Tallis, Thomas (1505–1585):** Elizabeth I gave him and Byrd the monopoly for printing music and music paper; *Spem in Alium* is written in 40 different parts and is performed with groups of singers dotted around the church

o **Tchaikovsky, Pyotr Ilyich (1840–1893):** Russian composer of ballet music such as *Swan Lake* and *The Nutcracker*; his piano and violin concertos remain ever popular along with his six major symphonies; after an unhappy marriage, he died from cholera after drinking contaminated water

- **Vaughan Williams, Ralph (1872–1958):** his music ranges from the pastoral to the symphonic and is generally accessible; he collected folk songs which often appear in his music and was also involved with the creation of the English Hymnal of 1906; though not stridently modern his music at times can be challenging – the Fourth Symphony has difficult corners; along with Elgar (who was fifteen years his senior) he created an 'English' sound
- **Verdi, Giuseppe (1813–1901):** Italian composer of operas whose name translates as 'Joe Green'; his wife and child both died while he was producing a comic opera; unsurprisingly it flopped; he became internationally famous for his grandiose style and epic narratives
- **Vivaldi, Antonio (1678–1741):** writer of *The Four Seasons* who was known as the 'red-haired priest'; taught at a girls' school in Venice
- **Wagner, Richard (1813–1883):** invented 'music-dramas'; four of them make up 'The Ring Cycle' – very Tolkien-like stories; had his own opera-house built in Bayreuth; sadly his work was adopted by the Nazi party and in his own writing he showed anti-Semitic attitudes
- **Walton, William (1902–1983):** his choral work *Belshazzar's Feast* is jazzy and immediate, featuring an extended brass section; he wrote music for films including Olivier's *Henry V*
- **Webern, Anton (1883–1945):** a pupil of Schoenberg who along with Berg advanced music in the direction of Serialism

# Part **2**
## DISCOVERING

# 6

# The Secret of Melody

> *When you know the notes to sing, you can sing most anything.*

OSCAR HAMMERSTEIN II

> **André Previn:** *You're playing all the wrong notes.*
> **Eric Morecambe:** *I'm playing all the right notes, but not necessarily in the right order.*

MORECAMBE AND WISE sketch with ANDRÉ PREVIN

Theoretically speaking, and according to the 'infinite monkey theorem', given an infinite amount of time a monkey at a type-writer could come up with the complete works of Shakespeare – so it follows, presumably, the same monkey could play the complete works of Bach on the piano given a very, very, very long time and a lot of tea (I've been playing Bach's *Goldberg Variations* for about ten years and I still sound like a monkey, so it seems very, very, very unlikely). It *is*, however, possible for anybody to create their own unique melody at the piano, because it is simply a process of selection: you just pick notes in a particular order to create something new. That is all there is to it. How then is it possible that when some people write a melody it's immediately worth millions of pounds, and when others try it sounds like a cat walking across the keyboard? For instance, think how much money Brian Eno made *per second* when he was commissioned by Microsoft to create a piece of music for their groundbreaking operating system, Windows 95.

> The thing from the agency said, 'We want a piece of music that is inspiring, universal, blah-blah, da-da-da, optimistic, futuristic, sentimental, emotional,' this whole list of adjectives, and then at the bottom it said 'and it must be 3¼ seconds long.' I thought this was so funny and an amazing thought, to actually try to make a little piece of music. It's like making a tiny little jewel.[1] [Sound Link 12]

Some composers are able to make a combination of notes into something wondrous – flirting with our expectations, surprising us with audacious choices, creating shapes and patterns that both please and excite. They can take familiar musical ideas and reinvent them so they appear to be completely original material. It is a mysterious process to anybody outside the world of music and no less miraculous for those of us on the inside.

Other composers quite deliberately pick the notes that no one else would choose. It may be an apocryphal story but my school music teacher when explaining the art of composition told us about John Cage (1912–1992) who was a keen mushroom picker. Apparently he had the idea, while out picking mushrooms, that it was impossible to select a mushroom completely at random because before you pick one you *have* to *select* it first – that act of selection, for Cage, is analogous to the act of composition.[2] Even though he realised it wasn't possible to make truly 'random' music he gave it a really good go. Cage pioneered a style called Aleatoric music or Indeterminacy – music that sounds random and without design. In some of his pieces you could imagine Cage wandering through the orchestra with his mushroom basket and picking sounds whenever they took his fancy. I must admit that I laughed uncontrollably when I first heard Cage's music – it seemed as though Cage was trying to do what the 'infinite monkeys' (see above) would manage with ease – and is that music? Cage's output divides opinion: to many people's ears it's anti-music and because it attempts to explore composition at its fundamental level it's more philosophy than music.[3] It illustrates perfectly that there is nothing left to chance in the act of selecting notes for a melody (though perhaps some ideas have had a touch of the happy accident) [Sound Links 13 and 14].

At its most basic level music is simple, which is why its appeal is so universal. I play some notes, they reverberate through the air, hit your eardrum and you perceive it as melody. Melody is a basic building block of music; what a composer does with the melody and how they stretch and adapt it is the subject of Chapter 9 ('Grand Designs').

What is this thing called 'melody'? Why do some prefer a sickly-sweet tune and others an angular, less accessible one? How does a composer create a melody? What are the processes? Does it just happen or does it involve hard work?

## Your favourite music

It's likely that when you think of your top ten favourite songs it will be the melody, another word for tune, which springs to mind immediately. When music ceases to be melodic it leaves many people behind. Music does not have to be melodic to be effective, but it has broader appeal when it is. The more 'sticky' a melody, the more commercially useful it can be, as demonstrated by the intoxicating and infuriatingly memorable music chosen for TV adverts. Who can evade the melodic 'stickiness' of Elena Kats-Chernin's *Eliza's Aria* which was used to such potent effect on the Lloyd's TV advert [Sound Link 15]. Or the frankly maddening

Nokia mobile phone theme which for years was the pariah of the concert hall – you know the one: do do *doo* do, do do *doo* do, do do *doo* do, DOOOO. For those a little older, after seeing a cloud of cigar smoke, the first four notes of *Air on a G String* by J.S. Bach as reinvented by Jacques Loussier from the Hamlet adverts still resonates after almost thirty years. The list goes on. Mmmm, Danone. Stop now.

All these melodies are created from a set of just twelve notes that make up the vast majority of Western classical pieces, and from this finite set of notes come infinite possibilities for composition. Like chess, the rules are always the same but with a different result each time. From the musically ridiculous to the musically sublime they all use the same notes but in a different order.

Imagine what a visiting Martian would make of our music. Firstly, human music is tailored to be within the human hearing range (roughly 20 to 20,000 Hertz, or cycles per second) so these aliens might not be able to hear it (if they even have ears?). If there were such a thing as 'dog music' then it's likely humans would not respond to it because dogs have a different hearing range from us. Secondly, a Martian wouldn't have absorbed the countless melodies to which we are exposed during our lives. Every time you hear a melody it is defined by its difference or similarity to other melodies that you've heard before. How many times have you heard a new piece of music and thought it sounded similar to one you already knew? Because of this musical experience almost everyone on the planet can recognise the difference between 'Happy Birthday' and the National Anthem of Uganda (at only just over thirty seconds it's better than ours in my opinion, but for a real treat listen to Turkmenistan's anthem, a mix of Hollywood schmaltz and eastern promise. I digress.).

## OCTAVES, SCALES AND DOUBLE BLACK DIAMOND SLOPES

The vast majority of Western classical music comprises just 12 notes – from C to C with sharps and flats (that's the black and white notes on the keyboard). These twelve notes repeat themselves in what we call octaves ('oct' – because their are eight white notes from one C to the C an octave above) but you don't need to know this in order to appreciate a good melody.

In some modern composition and in many non-Western forms the scale is split differently. This can sound extremely jarring to ears accustomed to the Western scale. In contemporary classical circles it is sometimes known as 'microtonal' music. If you are struggling to move beyond the nursery slopes of Vivaldi then this music could be considered the double black diamond slopes – best avoided by the novice: Brian Ferneyhough can be like climbing the north face of the Eiger after listening to a little Mozart.

This ability to hear pitch and remember it has clear evolutionary advantages. From telling the difference between animals on a hunt to communicating our needs to our families, pitch has as important a role to play as timbre, which we discussed earlier. While it isn't imperative to understand the neuroscience or physics of sound, it is worth remembering that when you 'hear' music, the process that leads you to comprehend it exists entirely inside your brain. Music is nothing more than an organised series of vibrations in the air hitting your eardrum and when you listen to amplified music what you are hearing are vibrations that result from a speaker cone moving in and out. For all its simplicity it is an incredible gift.

Melody acts like a neural tickle-stick, and we are incapable of ignoring it because there are parts of the brain that correspond directly to pitch. When we hear the notes, part of our brain gets excited. This is not a conscious process and it seems that music is alone in having this very direct connection with our brains. In his book *This Is Your Brain on Music* Daniel Levitin, a neuroscientist and former record producer, explains this link:

> If I put electrodes in your visual cortex (the part of the brain at the back of the head concerned with seeing), and I then showed you a red tomato, there is no group of neurons that will cause my electrodes to turn red. But if I put electrodes in your auditory cortex and play a pure tone in your ears at 440 Hz, there are neurons in your auditory cortex that will fire at precisely that frequency, causing the electrode to emit electrical activity at 440 Hz – for pitch, what goes into the ear comes out of the brain![4]

The Nokia tune and others like it literally get 'inside your head'. But one tone in your brain doesn't make a tune, it takes several notes in a particular order. We call the most basic ordering of notes, from bottom to top, a scale. If you think of the notes of the scale as an eight-storey building then it's relatively easy to understand how a melody works. Some tunes work by walking up and down the stairs from floor one to two to three and so on (think of 'Strangers in the Night' by Frank Sinatra) but more exciting melodies use the lift, starting on floor two, alighting on floor seven and then whizzing down to floor one to finish and so on (think of the 'Star Spangled Banner' – a notoriously difficult tune to sing because it leaps around so much). It's not the individual notes that are important but the journey between the notes: we call this journey *intervals*.

Between some floors of the building are mezzanine levels which we call *sharps* and *flats* – these are the black notes of the piano. With these extra floors we get the full Western classical scale of twelve notes as described above. You can think of sharp as being a bit higher in pitch, and flat as being a bit lower, like floor 1 and floor 1b, to continue our building analogy. That's as much as you need to understand in order to appreciate how melodies are created. That's it for the technical stuff.

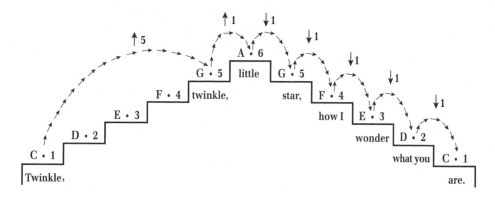

I have previously tried and failed to explain this adequately to non-musicians and it can be difficult to understand if you have never played an instrument or sung. It's equivalent to understanding cricket. People who have learned an instrument to any level will most likely have a sense that there are intervals between notes. I don't know how non-musicians perceive these intervals because I've been playing the piano since before I can remember. But I have a sense that the melody works on them in the same way. Perhaps it's more of an unconscious activity because learning to play an instrument interferes with the way you perceive music forever[5] [Sound Link 16].

Even if you don't read music you can still see the tiny, tiny steps in this extract from Rimsky-Korsakov's 'Flight of the Bumblebee':

The *Ode to Joy* from Beethoven's Ninth Symphony takes slightly bigger steps, more like a scale:

Leonard Bernstein uses a big leap at the beginning of 'Somewhere' from *West Side Story*:

Aaron Copland's *Fanfare for the Common Man* makes continuous use of intervals either four or five steps wide:

And Mozart uses lots of thirds and fourths in *Eine Kleine Nachtmusik*:

## How does melody work?

Let me put it this way. If I gave you a set of directions but didn't tell you what the destination was: go right, continue for 100 metres, turn left, go straight, second right, etc., you might not recognise those directions as the route from your house to somewhere familiar like the local train station. It's only when you start to walk the route that it becomes familiar and you can see where you are going. In fact you'd probably guess the destination before you arrived, by reading ahead or making educated guesses based on experience and likely probabilities. Along the way the route would be familiar to you and you'd follow the directions with ease and confidence because you'd walked the path before.

Listening to a melody is very similar. Within a couple of notes you'd be able to tell the difference between the National Anthem and *Eine Kleine Nachtmusik*. That's because you have, albeit unconsciously, remembered the pattern of notes (or intervals) that make up these tunes. It seems as though when they are played, your brain is able to cross-reference them with all the other tunes that you know and correctly identify the melody, like the search facility on a computer – but in reality the familiar pattern of the tune itself triggers a memory.

Composers use these patterns of notes throughout a composition and play on our expectations and what we remember of the melody. Daniel Levitin, again, explains how an appreciation of music relies on memory.

> Music works because we remember the tones we have heard and are relating them to the ones that are just now being played. Those groups of tones – phrases – might come up later in the piece in a variation or transposition that tickles our memory system at the same time it activates our emotional centers.[6]

This elegantly explains why we get a thrill from hearing a tune again and again, even within the same piece. It triggers a memory of the tune, an emotional response to the melody and also as a by-product it reminds us of the first time we heard that melody. A great composer is able to exploit this mental process by first establishing a tune and then contorting it in a variety of ways. These are some of the composer's tools: reversing the tune, slowing it down, playing it in a different key, changing the melody unexpectedly, repeating sections of the melody or turning the melody upside down. There are as many ways to change a melody to keep the listener interested as there are days in the year. It seems that some patterns of notes are more appealing than others. A great melody works on us without our realising the complexity behind its composition. To use these tools to create something that sticks in the mind takes a little luck and a lot of skill, experience and effort. John Williams (b. 1932) is famous for his Oscar-winning film scores: *Star Wars*, *Indiana Jones*, *Jurassic Park* and *Jaws* amongst many others. They are all notable for their melodic brilliance. Williams rejects the idea that a melodic composition is in any way random, putting his success down to sheer graft.

66 *Composing music is hard work. Any working composer or painter or sculptor will tell you that inspiration comes at the eighth hour of labour, rather than as a bolt out of the blue.* 99

JOHN WILLIAMS[7]

## Transforming a melody: variations on a theme

66 *A good composer does not imitate; he steals.* 99

IGOR STRAVINSKY, composer

The following three examples show the sorts of extraordinary melodic transformations it's possible for the composer to devise. Sometimes they steal ideas from other composers, or they adapt melodies, some adaptations are unrecognisable, others more overt.

The melody to 'Twinkle, Twinkle, Little Star' has been around for hundreds of years in various different guises and with differ-ent lyrics. It has endured precisely because there's not much to it. But from this simple tune much can be made, for example, Mozart's 12 Variations, K. 265 (K. 300c) [Sound Link 17].

Mozart sets out the melody and then uses it as a basis for showing off; he embellishes the melody with ornamentation, he changes the speed and puts it into a minor key. But we are always aware that it's 'Twinkle, Twinkle' that we are hearing. Mozart used this set of variations to impress the discerning aristocratic audience during the piano duel with the technically virtuosic pianist Clementi whom I mentioned in the last chapter. It was the wit and inventiveness displayed that impressed the audience – despite the simplicity of the initial material Mozart finds ever-increasing ways to dazzle.

The virtuoso pianist and composer Sergei Rachmaninov shows great ingenuity in his theme and variations. Rachmaninov's *Rhapsody on a Theme of Paganini* is a great example of how far a composer can manipulate musical material. Like a master weaver Rachmaninov transforms the material borrowed (or stolen!) from the composer-violinist Paganini for over twenty minutes. But it's in the eighteenth variation that he achieves alchemy. By turning the melody upside down he creates what appears to be an entirely new tune but is in fact merely an inversion of the original theme. This becomes a tune of overpowering romance, created from music of a more insistent character. How does this work? If I gave you a map for a walk and you turned it upside down and followed the same instructions you'd create an entirely different walk. That's what Rachmaninov achieves. This is a process that many composers use without the listener being aware. It's clever and it's almost imperceptible, except that the second version of the tune is *related* to the first. It might be reminiscent of the original in the way that you might resemble a cousin so that a stranger can't tell that you are related until it's pointed out [Sound Link 18].

The composer Andrew Lloyd Webber uses classical techniques of melodic recycling in his hugely successful musicals. His classical training is the key to his success. Like the opera composer Puccini (1858–1924) who weaves melodies throughout his works *Tosca* and *La Bohème*, to name but two, Lloyd Webber uses a handful of melodies which are then rearranged and appear several times during the play – giving the audience a chance to get to know them during the evening; this is particularly true of *Aspects of Love* and *Evita*, where 'Don't Cry for Me, Argentina' reappears in several guises. The influence of classical composers is obvious and some of his tunes bear a passing resemblance to classical tunes from the past: his song 'I Don't Know How to Love Him' has echoes of the second movement of Mendelssohn's Violin Concerto and he seems to pay tribute to a previous composer of hit tunes, Puccini, in the song 'Music of the Night' from *Phantom of the Opera* which mirrors the aria 'Quello che tacete' from *La Fanciulla del West.*

Another great example of notational manipulation (this time actual theft) is the famous 'Habanera' from Bizet's sensationally popular opera *Carmen.* This is a fabulously sexy aria – and I mean sexy literally – it seems that Bizet captures the sultry qualities of Carmen, a woman who casually uses her intense sexuality to bring about the downfall of the respectable soldier who falls for her. It is in this aria that her beguiling melody first bewitches the poor Don José. Given Bizet's rather French style, to write about a Spanish cigarette-making gypsy girl involved not only an imaginative leap but a compositional one. Any composer would quite sensibly research regional styles; many composers would attempt to write *in the style* of the country; but few would have the nerve for a flagrant rip-off.

The melody and accompaniment of the 'Habanera' (Spanish for 'dance from Havana') is lifted from the song 'El Arreglito' by the Spanish composer Sebastián Iradier. At the time the musical theft caused sniffy responses from the critics: 'Are they paying rights to Iradier for his Habanera?' asked one critic.[8] With the benefit of hindsight, 135 years later, I can forgive Bizet: to my ear, he improved on the original tune by translating it into a minor key and using a more serpent-like *chromatic** descending melody as opposed to Iradier's more chipper attempt. Poor old Iradier, destined to be forever in the shadow of Bizet. We must surely admire Bizet for stealing a popular song, improving it and using it to create one of the most performed operas of all time.

---

## *CHROMATIC

Think back to the earlier metaphor of the notes of a scale being similar to a building with eight floors plus extra mezzanine floors. Bizet's tune visits almost every floor as it winds its way downwards. This is known as a *chromaticism*, literally using all the notes of the scale. *Chroma* is the Greek for colour and a chromatic scale uses all of the 'colours' or notes. A great example of a chromatic scale used in a song can be found in Schubert's 'Gruppe aus dem Tartarus' [Sound Link 19] and in the descending melody of the theme song from *Phantom of the Opera* by Lloyd Webber.

---

Reusing a successful melody from the past must be a huge temptation for composers and it's often not a conscious activity, composers genuinely believing they have reinvented the wheel until someone points out the similarity. It's a worry for a composer because the risk of litigation is very real – especially for successful musicians. Paul McCartney is said to have dreamt the song 'Yesterday' and woke up thinking that it was someone else's tune – luckily for him (and his bank balance) it was an original.

Composers of melody are constantly striving to create something that will stick. The Germans are clever at putting two existing words together to make a new word: *Ohrwurm* is an excellent example, being a combination of 'ear' and 'worm' to mean a melody that burrows its way into your mind. I have both suffered and enjoyed this phenomenon all my life. At times I can recall great sections of music at will and enjoy allowing them to play through my mind, yet when I am over-excited, at times of great emotion or sometimes just randomly, a melody will assault me for several hours. In a really bad case it can be days. It's usually only a short section of the music that repeats and repeats. Melodies that are particularly tuneful can start to repeat themselves incessantly, finding no end and continuing even when I'm speaking.

The dubious accolade of master of the earworm I award to the Italian film composer Ennio Morricone (b. 1928). Part of his appeal is that he creates absurdly melodic compositions which combine with a distinctive use of instruments. Despite being an addict of his scores, one listen and they can bug me for days. Who can forget the whistling and electric guitar in the score for *The Good, the Bad and the Ugly* or the Jew's harp, whistle and chanting on *For a Few Dollars More*, the haunting oboe in 'Gabriel's Oboe' from *The Mission* or the eerie harmonica in 'The Man with the Harmonica' from *Once Upon a Time in the West*? Only recently did I finally rid myself of the theme from *Cinema Paradiso,* and just the act of typing its title threatens to bring it back. Help me.

In his 1949 book *Delight*, J.B. Priestley described the effect of an earworm (but without using this phrase, which has only recently been used in English). Helpfully he offers a solution.

> They would haunt me for days on end, during which I would be performing in a kind of secret ballet to their accompaniment. Their rhythm became mine. Sometimes, and this was most maddening, I would find myself endlessly pursuing the theme, now catching it, now missing it. To rid myself of this obsession there was only one thing to be done. I had to buy the music, if it existed in a piano score (and there was always the gramophone for the quartets), and then hammer out the tune for myself. This always cured me.[9]

So many times the internet has helped me out in this regard as you now can buy almost any song, almost anywhere from your mobile phone. Two summers ago I became obsessed with the Allan Sherman song 'Hello Muddah, Hello Faddah' while on holiday in Bordeaux; this summer it was the 'Floral Dance' as made famous by Sir Terry Wogan [Sound Link 20]and for a while it was Brandenburg Concerto No. 3 in G Major by J.S. Bach. Sometimes I think my brain is trying to torture me.

I think it was partly a reaction to this sort of facile melodic composition that led composers of the late nineteenth and twentieth century away from big tunes. Imagine a spectrum of tunefulness with nursery rhymes at one end, then Ennio Morricone and finally, with increasing complexity, most of classical music following – ending with some of the composers that I'll talk about next.

One man's Mantovani is another man's Mahler. There are pieces which are singable, even whistle-able, and there are pieces that are not. When we are children we learn simple songs – 'Twinkle Twinkle Little Star', for example, contains just six notes. All children's songs have a limited range of notes: 'Baa Baa Black Sheep', 'Here We Go Round the Mulberry Bush', even The Beatles' 'Octopus's Garden', to name but three. Their simplicity is beguiling, and as they are sung to us endlessly by our parents the structure of the melody is imprinted permanently on our brains. They become unforgettable. If you were to hear any of these melodies played with even one wrong note you would know immediately something was amiss. As we grow, our capacity to remember longer melodies increases. We start to appreciate more complicated music.

Briefly and reductively, the development of melody can be explained as follows. In the early nineteenth century (the Romantic period – see Chapter 8) composers such as Schumann and Wolf became increasingly expressive in their use of melody. Many composers of the late nineteenth century, such as Richard Strauss, Wagner and Mahler, rejected the 'old grey whistle test' (songs that can easily be whistled) and began to create themes that were longer, increasingly complicated and angular. To ears more used to popular forms, these advances can be a challenge.

It began innocuously enough with composers using these complicated melodies to reflect the more tortured psychological states in the literature of the era. In the nineteenth century there was much political and social upheaval combined with great advances in science; much about religion and state that had been taken for granted (or a least accepted) in the seventeenth and eighteenth century was now destabilised. This is reflected in the music: at the start of the century Beethoven was writing about God, joy and his hero, Napoleon. By the end of the century Mahler and Strauss were writing at the time of Sigmund Freud, and ideas of identity and our place within the world had shifted. Classical musicians have always written music that is about the preoccupations of the time: for years that was the Church and state. While there is still a lot of religious music being composed today, the preoccupations of 'art-music' have shifted, and that paradigm change began in the nineteenth century.

Just after the turn of the nineteenth century a change was to come in the composition of melody which effectively broke all the rules and conventions of the past 200 years. A musical revolutionary, Arnold Schoenberg (1874–1951), created a theory of composition which, to return to the earlier 'building' analogy, required the lift to call at every single floor once within the tune, and sometimes stipulated that no floor could be repeated until all had been visited. He used all twelve notes in one melody. Remember that nursery rhymes typically use around five and repeat those many times, so a twelve-note melody will be very difficult for the listener to remember. There will be more about Schoenberg, 'Serial music' and 'Atonalism' in the next chapter (Chapter 7 on harmony), because his theories had a profound impact on the way composers used harmony as well. To me these melodies are deliberately difficult, sounding like the aural equivalent to the architecture of Daniel Libeskind – angular, sharp and with a cold mathematical quality [Sound Link 21].

Schoenberg was unapologetically Modernist because he saw this musical path as inevitable. Its influence on the composers of the early twentieth century was significant. Some rejected the rather academic sound of this new angular style, others embraced it. One thing is certain: composing changed for ever. And as a result certain types of classical music began to lose popular support.

Benjamin Britten (1913–1976) was a British composer who for me embodies the melodic struggle of the twentieth century. He was a composer who loved folk songs and who could write a great tune, yet when I first heard him I couldn't help thinking that he deliberately included 'wrong notes'. (Dudley Moore's parody of the songs of Benjamin Britten using the words of 'Little Miss Muffet' satirises the difficulty many people have with this composer.) [Sound Link 22]

> I don't write a tune and think 'Oh yes, my Aunt Mary's going to like that tune very much.' On the other hand I perhaps don't write a tune that would be so complicated that Aunt Mary won't know where one's going. For instance, I can say in writing for children, at no point does one write down to them, but one tries not to give them something outside their experience. For instance, one doesn't want to write a piece for children which is so long that their attention will wander. On the other hand I don't hesitate for one moment writing music which is new to them. That, in my experience, stimulates and excites them. The artistic compromise is too risky for a composer – serious composer – to undertake.[10]

You'd be within your rights as an audience member to ask why he would want to write music that didn't appeal to his Aunt Mary. Doesn't she deserve a good tune like everyone else? Isn't popular appeal a good thing?

This is a conundrum which haunts many modern composers. For years there was a tendency to apologise for writing a hit tune. It was somehow viewed as tawdry and the business of popular musicians. Britten had what amounts to a fear of writing populist music. Here he is discussing 'the musical':

> They aim at a kind of directness, a kind of melodic simplicity, a kind of formal simplicity that I don't feel at the moment I can manage. The best musicals of many years have been those written by essentially simple people who can turn out a short melody which fits very neatly into the conventions of harmony at that moment and which is entirely dependent on that …
>
> … At the moment I am very happy with the small public that seems to like the kind of music that I like and that I want to write. You know, in fact one can only write the kind of music that one loves.[11]

I think it's hard to imagine anyone loving music that they find difficult. But the key factor here is familiarity. Britten by the time he was speaking here was in his fifties and had had a lifetime of listening to music that was difficult and angular, including some of his own.

From my initial reaction to Britten (wrong notes) I had to work hard to like his music. I've sung it on many occasions and conducted it. Until recently I had a nagging sense that he was writing 'the emperor's new clothes' – music that didn't speak directly to me or to the ordinary music lover – he was writing 'specialist classical' as it is known on Radio 3, as opposed to 'popular classical' as it is known on Classic FM. But I reached an epiphany of sorts this summer when I went to Glyndebourne Festival Opera's production of Britten's *Billy Budd.* The darkness of the story combined with the grittiness of the music in a powerful staging by Michael Grandage created moments of sheer force that pinned me to my seat. This darkly psychological opera could not have been written by Mozart because it is resolutely of the twentieth century and comes uniquely from Britten's voice. I think in that performance I made peace with Britten and finally came to terms with his music. The lack of sweetness in the melody was entirely appropriate for music about such a difficult subject: the main character Billy is treated roughly on board a ship in the eighteenth century, resulting in a murder and a subsequent hanging. Could such an opera contain nothing but hit tunes? Possibly in the hands of a different composer.

One of the most impressive moments of the opera contains one of its few memorable melodies,'This is our moment ... now we'll see action.' [Sound Link 23] As the entire ship is taken up with readying itself for battle with a French ship, every singer on stage busies himself with a different action. Britten overlays speeds and pitches of music for each group of characters: those pulling heavy ropes sing 'heave' on a slow, deep melody while the 'powder monkeys' scrabble about above; in the middle are the officers engaged in a conversational style. Triumphantly through this dense musical texture is heard 'This is our moment.' For the first few repetitions it isn't taken up by the other singers, it starts like a rumour, planting a seed in the audience's mind. At last, after a scene of frenzied theatrical action and music to match, the ensemble stands ready for a fight. For the first time everyone on stage sings in unison, their united voices joined by thundering, insistent drums beating out a warlike melody in the mode of 'Mars' from Holst's *The Planets*. To hear this in isolation doesn't do it justice, because you need to have felt the tedium of life on board the ship during the first act of the opera to become excited and energised by this moment. It stands out on the CD but it's a seismic moment in the theatre.

Britten's awareness that audiences crave a melody is the strength of this moment. After a dark, moody hour in the theatre without much melody in evidence this tune explodes with melodic surprise. Had there been more melodies in the build-up then perhaps its effect would be diminished. The resulting lack of popular appeal in some of Britten's output is as a direct result of the lack of appealing melody. I have to admire his determination to write the music that he wanted to write; he was extremely successful at it and is likely to be remembered long after many of the composers of his day have faded into obscurity, along with their popular tunes for the 'hit parade' or Broadway.

A strong melody can be incredibly powerful, as Britten realised. It can become indelibly imprinted in your mind; a faculty that many have exploited for financial gain. Melody is so intoxicating that it can quickly become associated with almost anything – for instance, I can usually remember with startling accuracy where I was when I first heard a piece, and certain tunes trigger very specific reactions. So it's not surprising that, in theatre and film, melody has the power to become quickly associated with a character. In fact it can operate as another element in an opera alongside the costume which reveals the personality of the characters on stage. It became known as the *leitmotif* (meaning a dominant and returning theme). It's not just a random association either; the melody of the *leitmotif* aims to tell you about the characteristics of the person you see on stage (heroic, villain, romantic, etc.).

If you know the brilliant score for the *Star Wars* films by John Williams you will be familiar with the concept of *leitmotif.* Each time a major character appears on screen a specific musical theme is played: the best example is Darth Vader's entrance music [Sound Link 24]. Darth Vader cannot move without the horns of the orchestra getting excited; likewise every time Luke Skywalker comes on to the screen his optimistic music pipes up, chirpily [Sound Link 25].

The same applies in *Indiana Jones, Jurassic Park* and many of his other scores. This is a technique borrowed from opera: this power was exploited by Wagner in his epic series of operas *Der Ring des Nibelungen (The Ring of the Nibelung)*. Wagner used specific tunes to identify characters through a short specific tune that belonged to them. This technique is familiar to us now but was a revolutionary idea in the nineteenth century. Wagner was a controlling man who revolutionised every aspect of opera: from the building of a new kind of theatre to the way that the notes were written and performed, Wagner oversaw every detail.

## THE RING OF TRUTH

In *The Ring of the Nibelung,* the eponymous Nibelung is a dwarf called Alberich who fashions a magical ring out of gold stolen from the maidens who swim in the river Rhine. The ring has extraordinary powers but is ultimately cursed. Death and destruction ensue. (By the way, any similarity to Tolkien is coincidental, according to Tolkien, but they certainly were inspired by similar mythologies and frankly are quite similar. To some they are pseudo-medieval bunkum with pretensions, whilst to others Wagner in particular reveals great truths about the human condition through his cast of immortals.)

The concept of attaching music to character may have been used by Richard Wagner in *The Ring* but it should be noted that he did not invent the technique but borrowed it from his benefactor, the composer Meyerbeer (1791–1864). For the record Wagner did not return Meyerbeer's kindness, attacking him with anti-Semitic vitriol in the poisonous article *Das Judenthum in der Musik* ('The Jews in Music').[12] So next time you are at a Wagner opera and are impressed by the use of recurring *leitmotifs* (and it is impressive) remember that, like Alberich stealing the gold, Wagner purloined his best idea from the man he so viciously betrayed in print. It's like the plot of a Wagner opera.

My personal view is that Wagner's *leitmotifs* are the antecedents of the modern use of melody in advertising. Every time music is used to sell an idea or a product I blame Wagner, but there's no doubting its power.

Melodic composers continue to crop up everywhere and many of them featured on the list of pieces you already know in Chapter 1 and Appendix I. From Mozart to Dvořák (pronounced DeVorZhak), Bach to Vaughan Williams and even into the twentieth century with composers like Karl Jenkins, John Adams and Ennio Morricone (rarely mentioned in the same breath) melody continues to be the chief factor in both popularity and difficulty. People's reactions to melody are entirely personal.

It's not always necessary for a melody to be saccharine to make it appealing and sometimes a melody can be too sweet for repeated listens; how many times in a week could you listen to Henry Mancini's 'Moon River'? Especially in the twentieth century, composers tried to push the idea of melody further and further, creating more and more complex forms. For many this is beyond the limits of what music should be ('I like a good tune') and for others it's daring and exciting ('I hate music that is sentimental and tuneful'). Where you sit in this debate will determine how far you want to penetrate the hinterlands of music.

From the moment we are born we are subjected to melodies as never before in our history. In our modern lives you can't move without hearing them: children's toys now enable babies to hear melodies over and over again at the touch of a button, mobile phones alert you to a call with your favourite music and shops have playlists of music that they hope will entice you to spend more money. But despite this, when we hear a new tune that we haven't heard before, we can fall in love with melody all over again.

I know a good tune when I hear one and so do you; a composer knows when he's written one too. Melody is at the heart of music that we love and it's often missing from music that we find more difficult to listen to. Composers with a gift for melody are like poets who seem to be able to summarise the whole of human existence in one pithy aphorism; it's a talent and a blessing that many musicians lack. Would that I had that gift. I started this chapter by asking what is the secret to a great melody. I hope you don't think me a fraud if I tell you that I simply don't know and if you know it then you ought to be very rich indeed.

Chapter

# The Magic of Harmony

" *Vom himmlischen Gewölbe strömt reine Harmonie zur Erde hinab ('From the celestial vault to Earth pure harmony descends')* "

HAYDN, *The Creation*

" *The ear disapproves but tolerates certain musical pieces; transfer them into the domain of our nose, and we will be forced to flee.* "

JEAN COCTEAU

## What is harmony?

- ⊘ It's not 'the backing vocal line'.
- ⊘ It's not things that sound nice together.
- ⊘ It's the progression of one chord to another.
- ⊘ It's the way the flute part interacts with the oboe part.
- ⊘ It's the glue that binds music together.

## What do I need to know about harmony?

In the days before Copernicus' ideas took hold and we still thought that the Sun revolved around the Earth, there was a popular concept that the heavens themselves were 'in harmony' and composers should try to emulate this 'music of the spheres'.

Harmony: we still use this word to describe when our life comes together, when we live peacefully with our neighbours or when our society is healthy. Humans have need of harmony just as we need the company of friends and the sustenance of food. In some senses this is the same as musical harmony – a sound that is pleasing and harmonious – but 'harmony' has a different, deeper meaning for musicians.

I should at this point tell you that not every musician fully understands harmony. If you play an instrument such as the violin or flute then it is rare for you to need to understand how different parts fit together, from a harmonic point of view. Whereas a composer must be fully in charge of this, an individual player need only play the notes. A composer is like an engine designer, putting different components together – but the carburettor doesn't need to know how the exhaust works. The one exception to this rule is organists, who are often required to improvise and must also play rich harmonies with their hands whilst playing the bass line with their feet – this usually means they are better informed about harmony than your average violinist. Many musicians never progress beyond Grade V theory (a fairly rudimentary level) and so are content to leave harmony to the experts: composers.

But it's worth trying to take you through the basics because to me it is the most fascinating aspect of music (although one of the most complex to understand for non-musicians). It can appear to be shrouded in mystery, since it is subject to complex theories and every generation of composers changes the rules. Harmony is what elevates a simple melody from the banal to the spiritual. It is learnt through hard study and yet aspects of it cannot be taught; it is a God-given talent which expresses the individuality of the composer.

I shall strive more than ever deliberately to avoid using an excess of musical terminology during this chapter. There are many shorthand words which describe harmonic effects which, although understood by musicians, can be bewildering. This book isn't aiming to get you through Grade VIII musical theory. I'm hoping to excite you about harmony and challenge you to listen to more complex harmony as you gain a sense of how it works.

There is one musical term that we can't really avoid: chords. A chord is created when three or more notes combine to make a single sound. Harmony is created when one chord is followed by another chord. Chords are difficult to describe but easily understood when heard. That is the chief difficulty in writing about harmony; anyone can hear and appreciate its effect but doing it justice with words is nearly impossible, so this could be a short chapter.

There are a few things that are worth knowing about harmony that can help to unlock certain pieces. Many of the magical moments that we are drawn to in music are an effect of harmony.

## Every chord is a step

Music is a journey. From the first note to the last we are transported, sometimes against our will, to another place. In the vast majority of music we are brought safely home to where we started with a natural sense of ending. Sometimes this ending is signalled, heralded even, with great masculine pomp – for example, in the 1812 Overture by Tchaikovsky [Sound Link 26]. At other times the descent is more gentle [Sound Links 27 and 28].

When one chord follows another chord we feel a sense of progression. A clear example of a piece that relies on the movement of one chord to another can be found in Handel's stately Sarabande (as used in the Kubrick film *Barry Lyndon*). The regular movement of just eight chords has an inexorable quality, and repetition of the pattern reinforces the effect. We begin with an emphatic minor chord, and although by the fourth chord we have moved far away we are deftly led back home by the eighth and penultimate chord in the cycle [Sound Links 29 and 30].

In this piece it's the structure of the chords that creates the musical interest. There is a melody of sorts and there is rhythmical and melodic interest in the bass line, but the essence of the piece is the movement from one chord to the next.

Musicians speak of starting in the 'home key',[1] that is the key in which the music belongs. Earlier (in Chapter 2) I compared keys to planets in the Solar System. We can also think of them as being like an area with a postcode. Each key has a letter attached to it – now this simply doesn't matter to most listeners, except where the name of the key features in the title: 'Symphony in D major', for example; it can help you to differentiate between works by name. As with a postcode there are certain boundaries within a key that the composer only crosses if convention allows.

As the music moves away from the home key, it holds a magnetic power over the listener and a degree of satisfaction is felt when we return. As the history of music advanced, composers have taken us further and further from the home key and finally in the early twentieth century destroyed the notion of key altogether, which I'll talk about later in this chapter.

## Tension and release

Even though Handel doesn't use complex chords in his Sarabande, there is an implicit tension in moving away from the first chord. If I pressed stop on your CD player (MP3/computer/ LP/45/78 or whatever) after only five chords you would have a sense of interruption. We *need* to hear the resolution. There are natural forces at work in music; it's like gravity. What goes up must come down. This inbuilt tension between one chord and the next makes me think of the periodic table of elements where elements at one end of the table, when meeting elements from the other, produce violent chemical reactions, whereas elements in the middle are more stable. Certain chords have a magnetic relationship; others react against each other.

There is a strong impulse to arrive at the home key, but on the way many different chords can be employed. The implications of this are that harmony gives the composer yet another pool of infinite possibilities, in addition to all the possibilities of melody that I discussed in the previous chapter. Any chord can be used from the 24 major and minor chords that I've already mentioned but add to this a further 12 dominant 7th chords, 12 diminished chords, 12 major 7th chords, 12 suspended 4ths, 12 augmented 5ths, 12 half-diminished chords … and a partridge in a pear tree. The list goes on and on.[2] The possibilities of harmony are limitless. When combined with infinite possibilities for melody you realise why music is a language and not a science; in the same way that language has rules and yet any speaker can create original sentences, composition means making choices, whilst observing traditions.

Of course some combinations of chords work better than others; some chord sequences can be tragic or joyful, while others don't inspire much interest in the listener at all.

Listening to the opening bass line of 'Dido's Lament' by Henry Purcell I'm struck by the inevitability of the downward journey of the harmony, which powerfully underlines the text:

> *When I am laid, am laid in earth, may my wrongs create*
> *no trouble, no trouble in thy breast …*
> *Remember me, but forget my fate.*
> [Sound Link 31]

There are some sequences of chords which have become ubiquitous. One of the most often used is most famous in its incarnation by Pachelbel. His Canon in D Major is one of the simplest yet most enduring pieces of classical music. Why should it be so popular and performed at so many weddings? I suspect part of the reason this is chosen is because it now has connotations of sophistication (*Eine Kleine Nachtmusik* has the same reputation) but I believe there is something inherently comforting about the chord sequence. It never strays too far, sticking to the most routine chords. Each subsequent chord seems to be suggested or at least perfectly prefaced by the last and that makes it very comforting.[3]

## Suspensions

Another form of harmonic tension is called 'suspension'. I've always had a bit of a thing about suspensions. They create music that seems to shimmer. How do they work and what are they? If I asked you to sing a note and to hold it for as long as possible, then I sang a different note two notes away, this would create harmony, a pleasant sound, assuming that you have a reasonable singing voice! However, if I were to move one note closer to your note, on to the adjacent note of the scale, then a *dissonance* would be created between the two notes. (Dissonance is the musical equivalent of two colours that don't go together.) That's a suspension: the sound we created would want to resolve itself away from the dissonance – either you or I would have to change note to resolve the suspension.

To give you an analogy, if you think of music as being like a twelve-lane superhighway then your note might be in the fast lane while I came speeding up to you comfortably two lanes away. If I changed lane so that my car drove next to you and we were able to stare at each other with our road rage faces on, then one of us would have to move further away by moving to a different lane – resolving the dissonance.

'Hear My Prayer, O Lord' by Henry Purcell (1659–1695) is full of the most scrumptious suspensions that often appear on the word 'crying'. He's using the suspension as a musical metaphor for sorrow [Sound Link 32].

A modern choral composer who shares my sense of joy at dissonance and suspension is Eric Whitacre (b. 1970), especially when rendered in glorious technicolor as it appears to be in *Lux Aurumque* ('Light and Gold'). The texture is resplendent with colour as the different notes collide and move away; sometimes he doesn't resolve the dissonance and lets the vibrations hang in the air. Whitacre has a refreshingly unpretentious attitude towards composing, possibly because he came to it later than most, starting singing in classical choirs in his late teens. This frees him to use the techniques and influences from popular forms of music [Sound Link 33].

Another modern composer who uses suspension is Morten Lauridsen (b. 1943). *O Magnum Mysterium* requires the most pristine singing; there can be no room for heavy use of voice, wobbly vibrato or the slightest imperfection of tuning in works of this opacity. See also *O Nata Lux.* Truly a delicious work which is rich with suspension and dripping with gorgeous harmony [Sound Link 34].

## Harmony at work: modulation

As a Londoner I think of keys like different lines on the underground. You can switch from one line to another and back again; sometimes your journey might take in three or more lines. Sometimes the interchange is very complex, sometimes it's a hop across the platform. Changing keys during a piece of music is sometimes called *modulation* and sometimes simply *a key change.* Now I'm not just talking about the moment when Westlife stand up from their stools and the music goes up a gear (Westlife are a pop boy band – purveyors of the uplifting ballad and demi-gods of the pop keychange). I'm talking about musical shifts that can be profoundly beautiful and truly unexpected.

Before the Classical era, music tended to stay within one key for a whole piece or movement of a piece. Although Bach and composers before him would move through different keys there is always a sense of where the home key lies and he *always* returns at the end [Sound Link 35].

By the time we get to Mozart, composers were *modulating* to different keys for whole sections of the music before returning to the home key. In his Piano Sonata No. 16 in C Major, K. 545, after two minutes in the home key Mozart repeats the main theme in a new, higher key [Sound Link 36].

## WHAT IS K?

K. 545 is a cataloguing number named after the man who catalogued Mozart's work, Köchel. Most composers have a numbering system so that you can keep track. Sometimes this might be Opus 1, for example ('opus' is Latin for 'work').

And then Mozart alternates major and minor keys for different sections in the second movement of the same piece [Sound Link 37].

Schubert made even greater use of major/minor in the penultimate song of *Die Schöne Müllerin* and introduced some glorious chords to the composer's palette. The golden syrup voice of Fritz Wunderlich draws out all the harmonic interest of Schubert with amazing emotional and lyrical potency [Sound Link 38].

The heartrending folkloric opening yields to the optimistic voice of the stream which Schubert puts into the major key. The tragic young lad, represented by the minor key, throws himself into the stream. As he does so his minor motif is transformed into the major. It may sound tame as a transition to modern ears but in a musically more monochromatic world this was an adventurous shift.

But compare that with the wondrous modulation in the Agnus Dei from the Requiem by Gabriel Fauré (1845–1924) and you realise how much is possible with a simple modulation. About three-quarters of the way through he modulates quite far away from the original key and it's a moment that has always made the hairs on the back of my neck stand on end [Sound Link 39].

Another spine-tingling moment from an earlier song (1842) comes from one of my all-time favourite songs: 'Widmung' by Robert Schumann (1810–1856 … syphilis again, I'm afraid).[4] In the song he makes a glorious feature of the key change.

> *You my soul, you my heart,*
> *you my bliss, oh you my pain,*
> *You are my world, in which I live;*
> *you are my heaven, in which I'm floating,*
> *Oh you, my grave, into which*
> *I forever cast my grief.* [Here comes the key change]
> *You are rest, you are peace,*
> *you are bestowed upon me from heaven.*
> *That you love me makes me worthy;*
> *your glance transfigures me;*
> *you raise me lovingly above myself,*
> *my good spirit, my better self!*

On the words 'you are rest' Schumann pulls an audacious modulation which marks the song out from the humdrum. In that change of musical character Schumann creates a moment of intimacy that makes this one of the most beautiful love songs ever written. Fact.

Where composers of the early nineteenth century might make a feature of just one small modulation within a work, Wagner pioneered the use of many keys within one piece: completed in 1845, Wagner's *Tannhäuser* Overture moves through many keys with a constant sense of upward motion. At this point in musical history there was still a sense of a tonal centre – it doesn't sound *dis*cordant. There are melodies throughout but they simply move from one area to another. I wouldn't imagine anybody would find the music of *Tannhäuser* difficult; it might not be your cup of tea but it's a long way from being as inaccessible as some of the music that followed.

'O du mein Holder Abendstern' (usually translated as 'Song of the Evening Star') is one of Wagner's most sumptuous uses of harmony; it is also one of his most conventional arias, having the structure of a song. It is measured and repeats its fabulous melodic hook several times. I cannot recommend this aria highly enough for someone coming to Wagner for the first time. On the other hand, from the same opera 'Inbrunst im Herzen' pushes harmony in the direction of Wagner's later work: the dramatic Wagner that has become synonymous with his name, the world of hats with horns on and massive ladies screaming. Here there is such tenderness in his use of harmony that you can almost forget that Wagner's reputation is one of the most troubling in all music history (see below, Chapters 5 and 6, and note 46). [Sound Link 40]

Not all of Wagner's œuvre is as accessible as this little diamond. As rival opera composer Gioacchino Rossini put it: 'Wagner is a composer who has beautiful moments but awful quarter hours.'


## Dissonance

As the subject matter became more and more about subjective experience, as opposed to universal themes of religion and state that preoccupied the previous generations, so the music of the nineteenth century became increasingly more complicated from a harmonic point of view. This was the time of expressionism – plays like *A Dream Play* by August Strindberg written in 1902 and art by Munch reflect a growing preoccupation with the psyche. The music of the psyche demanded a new harmonic language. This is the world of Sigmund Freud and Carl Jung. Mahler once said, 'I don't choose what I compose. It chooses me', revealing that music for him came from the psyche – it is deeply personal and it comes as no surprise to discover that he underwent treatment with Freud. His music is as inward-looking as any I can think of, for example his Seventh Symphony, which from a harmonic point of view is one of the most uncertain and neurotic openings in all of Mahler [Sound Link 41].

The piece starts on what we call a 'minor' chord but with an added note which gives the impression of having no allegiance to a particular key (the extra note is a sixth, if you're interested). Mahler uses that chord to destabilise the sense of key such that it's not until several minutes in that we know where we are.

By the early part of the twentieth century the traditional allegiance to a tonal centre (and the notion of a home key) began to break down. A fairly brutal example is from one of the century's great lyrical composers: Richard Strauss ('Morgen' from *Four Last Songs* is a beautiful example of his melodic credentials) [Sound Link 42].

His score for the opera *Elektra*, however, seems to me to be at the limits of the tonal system. At times chords pile on top of each other to create dissonant polychords, melodies have strange contours and keys irritate each other. That said, the piece is a theatrical masterpiece and the intensity of the drama[5] requires music that is this complex. Like Britten's *Billy Budd* (see Chapter 6) it's not the sort of music to listen to in excerpt form; it demands immersion in the full theatrical experience [Sound Link 43].

Conventional relationships between keys had become elastic. Listening to music from this *fin de siècle* period, the late symphonies of Mahler (1860–1911), the harmonic language of Debussy (1862–1918) or Richard Strauss (1864–1949) who between them point the way to the more complex harmony of the twentieth century, it's obvious that we are no longer in the early nineteenth century of Schubert and Beethoven where tentative changes of key were used to fairly subtle effect.

Since music must develop or stagnate, composers after Strauss, Mahler and Wagner were left with one inevitable but treacherous musical pathway.

## Atonalism

If you picked this book up because you were interested in getting to know classical music then we may well be at the frontiers of what you find acceptable, but there's no need to be afraid. Arnold Schoenberg (1874–1951) is regarded by many as the man responsible for developments which took music into the realms of academic exercise and staunchly away from what is popular. Those who studied with him (Berg and Webern amongst others) became disciples of his infamous approach. My composer friend Catherine reacted so violently to the extremes of Atonalism that she trained her dog to bark when she mentioned Berg or Webern; he's a guard dog at the gates of tonality.

Schönberg (he dropped the umlaut 'ö' when he moved to America) was born in Vienna, home to Johann Strauss II, composer of all those cosy waltzes they show on New Year's Day television. There the similarities end. Arnold Schoenberg took harmony to its inevitable conclusion. Despite his early compositions showing[6] hints of Mahler and Strauss he took a strident path later in his career which would help to change music forever. Pieces such as *Verklärte Nacht* (1899) [Sound Link 44] and *Gurrelieder* (completed 1911) [Sound Link 45] are both intense yet beautiful and most definitely *tonal*. The opening of *Gurrelieder* sounds like Wagner and if that sounds to you like an advert then I recommend checking this piece out. It's lush, late Romantic but with a dark expression at its heart that is typically Schoenberg. The melodic line in 'Nun dämpft die Dämm'rung jeden Ton Von Meer und Land' ('Now twilight mutes every sound on land and sea') is ravishingly beautiful and could almost be from a twentieth-century film score. The harmony moves around at will before arriving at some mesmerising chords on the words *Ruh' aus, mein Sinn, ruh' aus!* ('Rest my senses, rest!') To me this one line alone makes the whole piece worth while listening to and the work confirms Schoenberg's reputation as being amongst the greats of the last Romantic composers.

From then on his work took a turn towards what he termed Atonalism, that is, music that doesn't have a tonal centre; it's essentially homeless, questing around in a no man's land of different keys. This part of his output can be unsettling as a result. In 1909 he wrote *Drei Klavierstücke*, Op. 11 ('Three Piano Pieces') [Sound Link 46].

From there Schoenberg created a theory called Serialism which was taken up by many composers after him. It's simple to explain: try making up a telephone number that uses all of the buttons without ever repeating one until they've all been pressed. Schoenberg did that with the notes of a musical scale. That's what Schoenberg called a *tone row*. He would create melodies using all twelve notes of the chromatic scale – to return to the analogy of a building used in the last chapter, it's like visiting every single floor in one melody. To the unseasoned listener it's hard to find something in a tone row to hold on to: both melody and harmony course wildly around, and all that remain of the idioms of the nineteenth century are the rhythms and structures; this is music for the twentieth century. It became the soundtrack to two world wars, and hearing it now summons up images of grim documentaries about the atrocities of the Holocaust.

If you struggle with the idea of listening to music that has such complex harmony then remember that without Schoenberg there would be no horror movie scores, no edgy Modernism, no Bernard Hermann, Cliff Eidelman, Gerry Goldsmith, who all use the sometimes cold language of Serialism in their film scores [Sound Link 47].

Listen to Bartók's *Music for Strings, Percussion and Celesta*, Sz. 106, BB 114. Without knowing that it was used in the Stanley Kubrick film *The Shining* it can sound totally sparse and alien, but in the context of that movie the piece works beautifully even if it is rather unsettling [Sound Link 48]. Kubrick was the director who made impeccable music choices, none more successfully than in *2001: A Space Odyssey*. Here he used some of Ligeti's most terrifying works, combining them with momentous images of space [Sound Links 49 and 50].

If you are looking for music that is disturbing, challenging and a world away from chintzy Strauss waltzes, then Serialism offers you the antidote to syrupy melody and sickly-sweet harmony. John Rutter's Christmas carols this is not; I could not imagine Aled Jones singing any work by Berg, Webern or Boulez (other high priests of Modernism). This is the specialist end of specialist music and operates in something of an ivory tower.

Boulez (b. 1925) and Stockhausen (1928–2007) are both composers whose output is uncompromisingly modern and who belong to a small but influential group of high Modernists. If you don't like their music I don't think they'd care – I suspect they aren't going to change their music to suit your needs. So there. This isn't snobbery or them feeling that they are elevated – I once met Pierre Boulez in the queue for coffee at the Barbican Centre and he was utterly charming – but this is the kind of music they *like*. Go figure [Sound Link 51].

Tolerance for dissonance varies from person to person. I've spent a lot of time writing music with children and it strikes me how much they crave consonance (sounds that go well together), avoiding difficult intervals and preferring that which is musically immediate (hence most children's songs are harmonically very simple). For some this desire for instant harmonic gratification never leaves us – and to some extent I include myself in that.

Many people simply can't understand why anybody would want to listen to music that is not 'tuneful'. So why are musicians passionate about this music that alienates many people? I believe that as musicians we build up tolerance to avant-garde forms of music through repeated exposure.

The first example I remember of this was when I was at school. I remember vividly being forced to listen to *The Rite of Spring* by Stravinsky, when I was just twelve years old. The 'great composers' records had clearly been bequeathed to the school some time after the dark ages and the school record player was laughably outdated when compared with the Sony Walkman that was standard issue for kids of my generation. It was played to me by a locum music teacher who gingerly placed a well-used needle on to the scratched LP. We were given little by way of context, other than being told there was a riot at its first performance. There was very nearly a riot in our classroom. Frankly I thought it was a ridiculous piece. I had enjoyed listening to the *Firebird* a few weeks before but this aural onslaught was just beyond me [Sound Link 52].

Years later I revisited the work and was amazed at how different I found it. The experience of seeing it live conducted by Pierre Boulez with the LSO helped a great deal (a phenomenon I'll discuss in Chapter 11) but fundamentally my taste had changed. I'd grown accustomed to Shostakovich, Strauss, even Berg, and so can you. The piece is so dynamic, constantly changing and unpredictable. Stravinsky developed a technique where he'd put jarring sections of music next to each other and change without warning. It sounds like nothing that came before it and its influence can be felt in much of the music that followed. I love to imagine how daring his harmonic and rhythmical innovations must have sounded at the time.

I've had similar journeys with a number of twentieth-century composers who at first appear impenetrable but who yield for me after several listens. If you are feeling adventurous, poke your nose into: Brian Ferneyhough, whose work is determinedly complex; Mark Anthony Turnage, who synthesises contemporary jazz, modern classical music and rock influences; and James MacMillan's orchestral works, which have a real darkness and bite to them. All these composers are living and working today.

You may have detected a running argument that I'm having with myself about the merits of complexity in harmony. At times I find myself craving dissonance, actively enjoying it. I know that sounds perverse but there is so much pleasing harmony available from every mobile-phone jingle to the pop tunes played in a late-night taxi that sometimes I want the bitter taste of

Modernism – I want to have my sensibilities shaken. But most days I'm happy with Mozart.

Whilst the composers mentioned below have continued along the Modernist path cleared by Schoenberg, one of the impacts of the Serialists was to give composers permission to experiment with the way they compose. We now find ourselves in the post-modern era where pretty much anything goes.

○ **Charles Ives (1874–1954)**
Created 'polytonal' music which involves musicians playing in two keys at that same time (in his youth he was an organist who for his own amusement would play the hymns in a different key from the one the audience was singing – imagine the looks from the congregation!). Listen to his *Variations on America* which to British ears will sound extremely familiar as it's the same tune as our national anthem.

○ **Igor Stravinsky**
Retreated from his uncompromising position that caused the riot at *The Rite of Spring* [Sound Link 53] to look back to music of a much earlier era which became known as *Neoclassicism*. If all this talk of Cage and Schoenberg has been hurting your head then may I suggest the balm of *Pulcinella* by Stravinsky. It's a completely accessible work in every respect. It's hard to imagine they are the works of the same composer. In fact they aren't: Stravinsky 'borrowed' material from composers of the past and put his stamp on their work. A bold move for any composer [Sound Link 54].

○ **Olivier Messiaen (1908–1992)**
Was a composer who took a very different approach to writing music. He was a very serious ornithologist and would listen attentively to the sound of birdsong, writing it

down in musical notation and including it in his composition. The rule book had really been thrown out and composers were able to devise whatever system of composition they fancied [Sound Link 55].

*O* **Edgard Varèse (1883–1965)**
Abandoned traditional orchestral instruments entirely and began to work in electronic sound. Some of his more experimental work is barely harmonic at all – there's hardly any pitch involved and it certainly bears no relation to Mozart or Bach. His piece *Poème Electronique* challenges the listener and begs the question – is this music? For many (especially electronic composers) this marked a whole new avenue of musical exploration using technology to make sound, which has become more and more exciting with the advent of computers. This piece sounds rather dated now. It was written in 1958 and I can imagine the reaction of the audience was one of shock – but I'm certain it sounded 'new' to them. Listening to it now, it sounds like an episode of *Dr Who* from the Tom Baker era [Sound Link 56].

## The backlash begins – Minimalism

By the 1960s there had been so much harmonic innovation that it seemed almost inevitable that a backlash would come. The first notable composers to reject the complexity of twentieth-century music were Philip Glass (b. 1937), Terry Riley (b. 1935) and Steve Reich (b. 1936), among others, who created music that was harmonically very simple. The result was a whole new direction in music. It's called Minimalism because it uses small musical elements repeated with only small changes in harmony at specific points. Some of their experiments sound like just that – experiments – and don't really feel as though they belong in the concert hall [Sound Link 57].

The composer John Adams (b. 1947) came to the forefront a little later in the 1980s and was one of the first composers to synthesise the Minimalist school with the mainstream orchestral sound [Sound Link 58]. John Adams is outspoken in his antipathy towards music that is born out of Schoenberg's ideology:

66 *Schoenberg also represented to me something twisted and contorted. He was the first composer to assume the role of high-priest, a creative mind whose entire life ran unfailingly against the grain of society, almost as if he had chosen the role of irritant. Despite my respect for and even intimidation by the persona of Schoenberg, I felt it only honest to acknowledge that I profoundly disliked the sound of twelve-tone music. His aesthetic was to me an overripening of 19th century Individualism, one in which the composer was a god of sorts, to which the listener would come as if to a sacramental altar. It was with Schoenberg that the 'agony of modern music' had been born, and it was no secret that the audience for classical music during the twentieth century was rapidly shrinking, in no small part because of the aural ugliness of so much of the new work being written.* 99

JOHN ADAMS, composer [Sound Link 59]

John Adams didn't invent Minimalism but he made it popular in the concert hall. He is without question a distinctive composer who writes music that is arresting without being over-complex. His influence can now be felt everywhere from adverts to film scores. When Adams changes key you really feel it – he makes great use of simple materials and for me that's a return to the traditional craft of the composer, though his music sounds far from traditional.

And that's where we've got to. There are constant developments in music and I know I've left many out. I've tried to give you the main influences on harmonic development. But it's OK: there is loveliness out there for you in abundance. Without question it's the luxurious harmony that keeps me coming back for more. A composer who understands harmony and can manipulate it effectively is one that you'll want to hear again and again.

In Chapter 6 on melody, I discussed Benjamin Britten's love of 'wrong notes' but it would not be fair to him if I left you with that impression of this diverse composer. Many of his pieces feature the sounds of boys' choirs, from the fairies in *Midsummer Night's Dream* to the boy treble in *The Turn of the Screw*; Britten knew how to write for their voices and loved the sound that they made. The celestial sound of boys' voices singing together in church music has a tradition going back hundreds of years in Britain, for example Winchester Cathedral's Quiristers have been singing for 600 years (clearly dating back to the time before standardised spelling of 'chorister'). The sound of the cathedral and the harmonies found there seems to soften even the most discordant composer.

Britten's *Hymn to Saint Cecilia*, *Ceremony of Carols* and the sublime *Hymn to the Virgin* show Britten's profound understanding of conventional harmony and his ability to write music that appeals to a broader audience [Sound Link 60]. 'This Little Babe' from his *Ceremony of Carols* is a rollicking ride but contains a brilliant musical device – a three-part echo. The tune is repeated several times with different groups of singers starting slightly out of sync with each other. The effect is stunning and harmonically not a challenge for the listener [Sound Link 61].

Another composer whose harmonic choral work belies his orchestral Modernism is James MacMillan (b. 1959). This

Scottish composer is one of my favourites working today. His orchestral music is percussive, dark and probing whilst his choral music is easier for the first-time listener, owing much to the influence of the plainsong he heard during his Catholic upbringing. A few years ago I had the pleasure of working on an education project to take his St John Passion (the Easter story from the Gospel according to St John) into an inner-city secondary school. MacMillan writes from a very personal standpoint and his deeply felt religious faith informs much of his work. The staunch nature of his views and the sincerity of his music impressed the teenagers who were from a wide variety of religious backgrounds despite the difference in age and education that stood between them and the composer. There have been many attempts to set the text of the St John Gospel, though most of them were several hundred years ago – Bach and Schütz for example. MacMillan brought it into the twenty-first century with music that acknowledges the past and yet sounds audaciously modern [Sound Link 62].

Choral music is awash with lush harmony and in some ways the human voice offers the best platform for really beautiful harmony. Sir John Tavener is perhaps best know for his *Song for Athene* which so memorably accompanied the procession leaving Westminster Abbey following the funeral of Princess Diana in 1997. I was struck by that piece more than any other aspect of the ceremony (although Lynn Dawson did a cracking job of the Libera Me from Verdi's Requiem, as I remember). Tavener is a member of the Russian Orthodox Church and his harmony shows the clear influence of their style of chant. *Song for Athene* caught the public imagination with its plangent, repeated 'alleluias' and moderate melodic angularity. It seemed to catch the general mood of tragedy around her death. The sight of her cortège – as the sombre, dulcet minor chords gave way to the fulsome, hopeful and glorious major finale as her coffin left the building – was a moment of musical and historical poignancy [Sound Link 63].

But my favourite piece of Tavener's is *The Lamb,* written in 1982 for his nephew's third birthday. A nice present indeed. He uses the harmonic equivalent of mirroring where, as one part moves up, another moves an equal distance down. The effect is stunning and an entirely appropriate setting of the William Blake poem [Sound Link 64].

It's encouraging to find more and more composers working outside the Eurocentric tradition: Tan Dun combines elements of Chinese composition and instruments with Western orchestral textures to create a very pleasing sound world. His film scores for *Crouching Tiger, Hidden Dragon*, *The Hero* and *The Banquet* fuse the sometimes over-syrupy sound of Hollywood with cool elegance gleaned from his Chinese roots, but his more experimental works for the concert hall owe much to European avant-garde composers. In *Water Passion after St Matthew* Tan Dun creates an eerie sound world from diverse elements: splashing water, Western classical singers, monks intoning, Tibetan percussion. His orchestration includes violin, 'cello, and most radically a sound engineer manipulating a Yamaha A-3000 sound sampler. What excites me about Tan Dun is that he shows influences from some of the most difficult compositional styles of the twentieth century yet writes music that is coherent and accessible. His writing for strings, in particular the 'cello, is particularly idiosyncratic [Sound Link 65]. Despite writing for string orchestra and piano his work retains a Chinese character [Sound Link 66].

## Harmony and change

> *The way of the Creative works through change and transformation, so that each thing receives its true nature and destiny and comes into permanent accord with the Great Harmony: this is what furthers and what perseveres.*

ALEXANDER POPE

As mentioned in Chapter 5 on the musical canon, telling the story of music involves choosing emblematic pieces and building a narrative around them. For every piece which fits this steady progression, from Baroque to Classical to Romantic to Modernism, there are pieces that stick out as anomalies. C.P.E. Bach, for example, feels neither Baroque nor truly Classical. Early Beethoven sounds like late Mozart and yet late Beethoven defined the beginnings of the Romantic era. But some general principles can be drawn from this complex picture.

Harmony reached a level of complexity in the twentieth century that challenges the casual listener but there is still music being written that is harmonic, lush, beautiful and sounds *right*. Just knowing that difficult music is *supposed* to be difficult, that it doesn't make compromises for its audience, can make it easier to listen to. Give yourself time for the hard stuff. Listen in context – find out *why* the composer might have written like that. You might only hear it as an academic exercise but it's better than writing it off because you don't understand.

I find it very hard to tell which pieces that are being written now will be around in 200 years but I do find it exciting to listen to new music. It's partly because it speaks very directly to me and precisely because it doesn't sound like a museum piece. Harmony and music are constantly changing and always will.

It's partly about fashion and partly about reflecting the time that we live in. As we leave the twentieth century behind us, music being written now is less and less about the preoccupations of our parents' time: nationalism, fascism and war. Modern composers are taking account of our increasingly global world and producing music that is less angry and embraces non-Western forms of harmony (Tan Dun, for example). You may never understand exactly *how* they do it without studying for a music degree but what you can do is feel the effects of harmonic development and marvel at their infinite splendour.

# 8

# Style and the Orchestra

> ❝ *Fashion is a form of ugliness so intolerable that we have to alter it every six months.* ❞

OSCAR WILDE

## Puttin' on the style

> *She's puttin' on the agony*
> *Puttin' on the style*
> *That's what all the young folks*
> *Are doing all the while*
> *And as I look around me*
> *I sometimes have to smile*
> *Seeing all the young folks*
> *Puttin' on the style*
> George P. Wright/Norman Cazden
> sung by Lonnie Donegan

My taste has evolved as I've got older. When I told my mother-in-law that I was buying a Rococo mirror for our house she couldn't believe it: 'Surely you'd like something more modern?' It's true that for many years I'd been into plain white walls and empty surfaced Minimalism; now I like things that are old-fashioned and of good quality. Taste changes in the blink of an eye, as anyone who purchased a shell suit will know; classical music is no exception, although in music the fashions and tastes can take longer to change. The inherent value of the music often remains long after musicians have moved on to the next big thing.

For a long time the harpsichord was the instrument *du jour.* Its rhythmic clacking could be heard throughout the seventeenth and eighteenth centuries, but the smoother-operating pianoforte (or the piano as we now know it) arrived on the scene from around 1700, and that gradually became the must-have instrument. The piano was the iPod/iPhone/iPad of its day. Here was an instrument that you could have *in your house* and make music *yourself!* It was a revolution. Then somebody invented the wireless and messed it up for the piano. As with all innovation, there are those who welcome it and those who look back ruefully. How many times have I heard that vinyl has a warmer sound than CDs? And now it looks as though CDs are coming to an end. You didn't know? I'm afraid it's true: keep up.

How can we hope to stay on top of all the changes in style that music has been through in the last 500 or so years? Even once you have a sense of where composers come in the story of music, there are all sorts of composers whose stylistic anomalies don't quite fit. People become anxious about classical music because they can't tell Beethoven from Mozart and if you know a classical music nerd (me, for example) then you may have encountered that ability they have to deduce a composer's name after hearing about ten seconds of music. How is that possible? There are a few tell-tale signs which can help you narrow it down. This chapter should help.

Even though they may sound similar to other composers of their generation, most composers have a distinctive sound which is so individual that it could not be mistaken for anyone else's work. For example Handel and Bach are both composers of the Baroque period (more of which later) and yet you'd never get them mixed up if you knew that Handel wrote in English and Italian whereas Bach wrote in German. That's an easy way to play spot the difference (irritatingly on occasions both composers wrote in Latin, which might cause you problems). As composers they have a completely different sound to their harmony. There are moments which sound similar but if you listened to the whole of *The Messiah* by Handel and then the whole of the Mass in B Minor by Bach, you'd have a pretty good idea of how they differ.

You can learn to hear the difference between a big modern orchestra and a smaller earlier one in a matter of minutes. Once you know the key developments in the orchestra it's easy to attribute them to musical period. And once you've got the periods in your mind then it's simply a matter of grouping all of the major composers from that era together and then you'll feel that you *know* about music. I'll deal with the musical periods later in this chapter but first let's talk about development of the orchestra because understanding the make-up of orchestras will help you to understand the styles of music they play.

In the beginning men (and women) hit things (and probably each other) with sticks to make music. At some point (although exactly when is hotly contested) they started blowing through hollowed-out animal bones and making proto-flutes. In 2009 a bone flute around 35,000 years old was discovered in Germany. Perhaps this is why the Germans have so many great composers – they had a head start.

There are accounts of music in texts going back thousands of years and many examples in the Bible but it's in the last 500 years that the orchestral instruments as we know them have developed. But why *these* instruments? Why not the thousands of others that are no longer in use? What of the shofar, the lyre and the crumhorn? Some instruments have succeeded in gaining longevity and others have failed. The modern orchestra contains versions of instruments that have existed in Europe in one form or another for hundreds of years. Their sound and method of playing have existed in our culture for centuries.

The orchestra as we know it today became formalised around the seventeenth century for reasons of taste, fashion and availability of musicians. This was during the height of the Baroque era when the epicentre of fashion was the court of Louis XIV. It was there that moves towards the modern orchestra were pioneered by the French composer Jean Baptiste Lully (1632–1687). Louis XIV was famous for his opulent taste, as the Palace of Versailles testifies; he favoured operatic spectaculars requiring large instrumental forces. In 1653 Lully, aged just twenty years, was appointed head of music at Versailles, surely the plum job for any musician. Lully began bringing together the cavalry musicians with the resident string band. Before this there was no orchestra as we conceive it today; instead there were only 'ad hoc' bands. As *The Grove Dictionary of Music* explains:

> When in 1664 Lully pulled together these and additional forces for a multi-day entertainment at Versailles called *Les plaisirs de l'isle enchantée*, he used them in typical pre-orchestral fashion: consorts of like instruments, in costume, joined together on an ad hoc basis (Lemaître, 1991). Ten years later, when Lully produced his opera *Alceste* as well as Molière and Charpentier's *comédie-ballet Le malade imaginaire*, at a similar entertainment, he organized his instrumental forces very differently. [...] Lully's ensemble with doubled strings, oboes and bassoon provided an important model of orchestral scoring to several generations of French, English and German composers.[1]

The idea of a regular band comprised of different instrument groups quickly spread throughout Europe as other heads of state decided they wanted what King Louis had.[2]

Bach also employed large orchestral forces for his grand works: the St Matthew Passion of 1727 is written for double orchestra. In those days that meant predominantly strings, which have always been the most important section, mostly because of their innate musical flexibility; they can do soft, long, short, loud, melody, harmony – the lot. There would also have been an accompanying instrument such as harpsichord, lute (like a strangely shaped guitar), theorbo (like an overgrown guitar) or organ along with a bass instrument like the double bass or the bassoon. These were collectively known as the *basso continuo,* meaning the bass line that ran *continuously* through the piece. This is a key feature of music from the Baroque era. Over the top of the basso continuo Bach could call on flutes, oboes, trumpets and drums along with other contemporary instruments which are no longer in use such as the oboe d'amore (big brother to the modern oboe) and the viola da gamba (played like a 'cello and with frets like a guitar). These were often added in significant sections of the work where Bach either used solo instruments to accompany a singer (a practice known as *obligato)* or brought all the forces together for a really big shindig at the end.

The orchestra that we have today resembles Bach and Lully's orchestras in essence but not in formation. It wasn't until the time of Mozart and Haydn in the eighteenth century that the 'Classical' orchestra developed, and it's that configuration that we have inherited. The reasons for this are again to do with musical fashion. Instrumental music had become increasingly important in the royal courts of Europe and large-scale works for the newly devised configuration became known as the *symphony,* which literally means 'sounding together'. I will discuss the structure of the symphony and how it works in Chapter 9.

The 'symphonic' strings of the late Classical period were played in four parts: first violins, second violins and violas, alongside 'cellos and double basses, which played the same line. Flutes and oboes could be played by the same player in the Baroque era (a similar practice can be found in modern musical pit bands where budgets are tight: a flautist might be expected to play another instrument such as the saxophone during the evening). By the time Beethoven was writing his symphonies, almost 100 years after Bach, the expectation of audiences was for a larger sound in instrumental writing so that Beethoven's Symphony No. 2, for example, calls for larger forces: two flutes, two oboes, two clarinets and two bassoons. In addition to this larger wind section he asks for two horns, two trumpets and timpani. This larger orchestra and its ebullient sound gave Beethoven the means to push the dynamic range of the orchestra in music which tested the technical virtuosity of the players. The Romantic orchestra was born.

Through the nineteenth century the loud bits got louder. Music was infused with passion, with words by poets like Goethe or Schiller requiring ever greater resources from the composition. One of the defining sounds of the Romantic orchestra was the addition of the trombone, used only in special cases during the eighteenth century. Beethoven first used the instrument in his Fifth Symphony (that's the one that goes da-da-da DAAA, da-da-da DAAA) but he was not the first to do so; that honour belongs to the little-known Swedish composer Joachim Nikolas Eggert (1779–1813) who is now warmly remembered by history as the man who beat Beethoven to the use of the trombone in a symphony by several months. The trombone, the tuba and more and more horns were added to an ever-increasing string section. The instruments themselves were refined: more buttons were added to the oboe to make it easier to play complicated music. The percussion became weightier with exotic instruments as composers began to quest for innovation.

As with most things in the modern world there are no hard and fast rules about what instruments you might expect in a modern orchestra. Large pieces will doubtless include all of the instruments mentioned above in varying numbers. But composers are free with their interpretation of 'the orchestra' and often write for interestingly shaped ensembles. One of the craziest pieces I've ever seen was Peter Maxwell Davies's *Songs for a Mad King* written in 1969 and based on the madness of King George III, or perhaps just a madman who believes that he's George the III; it's hard to tell. It's described by his music publisher as a 'neo-expressionistic music theatre' piece but it's performed in the concert hall. During the work the mad king tries to teach birds to sing. The wind instruments are supposed to play from within giant bird cages. You get the idea: mad, but brilliantly zany. It's scored for the followed unconventional ensemble:

> Flute, piccolo, clarinet, railway whistle, snare drum, two suspended cymbals, foot cymbal, two woodblocks, bassdrum, chains, ratchet, tom-tom, tam-tam, tambourine, rototoms, toy bird-calls, 2 temple bells, wind chimes, crotales, sleigh bells, glockenspiel, steel bars, crow, didjeridu, pianoforte, harpsichord, dulcimer, violin, 'cello

What would Mozart have made of that? I suspect that Mozart would have delighted in the modern orchestra and written music for whatever forces were available to him. As a thought experiment try to imagine how Mozart would have written a piece featuring pedal-timpani, an electric guitar and temple blocks ...

## Sections of the orchestra

The key features of an orchestra have always been and remain the following groups:

- o strings
- o woodwind
- o brass
- o percussion

Numbers in each section vary widely, depending on the music they are playing. Early orchestras were smaller, having few brass instruments and a handful of woodwind. In modern orchestras the personnel can be large in every section. The sections are divided by the technique used to get a sound out of them.

### Strings

Drawing a bow of horse hair across a string which is under tension creates movement and vibration in the body of the violin. The body works as a sound box, amplifying the sound. This applies to the violins, viola (slightly larger than a violin), violoncello or 'cello as it is commonly known (larger still) and double bass[3] (massive and difficult to move around without help; double bass players tend to be tall and strong). There are early examples of bowed string instruments from as far afield as China from the seventh century but the lush sound that we associate with our modern concert halls is the result of the incredible craftsmanship that developed from the sixteenth century, and arrived at what is known as a 'golden age' from 1650 to 1750, most famously with Stradivarius (1644–1737). Although there are many other makers whose instruments are worth millions of pounds, for example Guarneri and Amati, it's a 'Strad' that attracts the big spenders. The popularity of the violin, its size and the fabulous nineteenth-century repertoire for the instrument have led to intense commodification of the best violins. Violinists struggle to buy instruments which cost more than their houses unless they are lucky enough to be loaned a great instrument by a philanthropist. Most of the best violins are now in the hands of private collectors. Shame.

When I first worked at the LSO I was in Dagenham for a schools workshop alongside a 'cellist. She made a particularly fantastic sound but then so did most of the LSO players that I worked with so I thought nothing of it. Later on we all went for a drink on Dagenham High Street. It was Friday night and the bar was getting pretty busy. A somewhat inebriated local spotted her large 'cello case and demanded of my colleague how much her 'guitar' was worth. Cool as ice she replied, 'Oh a couple of hundred pounds; it's a student model.' The man shuffled away uninterested.

It wasn't until we were safely on the tube home that she revealed that the instrument had been loaned to her by one of the

London music colleges. It was almost 300 years old and worth several hundred thousand pounds, if not millions. I don't think I'd have had the nerve to play it. Of course this is what the violins were made for, not to be stuck in a glass case, though it's a risky business taking a violin worth around £2 million out on tour, as violinist David Garrett found out to his cost. He fell over after a concert and caused £60,000 worth of damage to his 1772 Guadagnini, worth a cool £500,000. Happily a London violin dealer stepped in to loan him the San Lorenzo Stradivarius, but this came with a three-man security detail.[4]

In terms of numbers, if you go to see the Orchestra of the Age of Enlightenment, a 'period instrument' band, you might expect to see a small group of violins and violas, three or four 'cellos and only one or two double basses, because they play music of the Baroque and Classical periods, whereas at a modern orchestra, say for example the Royal Philharmonic Orchestra, there will be around ten first violins, ten second violins, ten violas, ten 'cellos and about eight double basses which make a significantly more robust sound. These larger string sections are appropriate for Romantic and modern pieces.

### Woodwind

With the exception of the flute, these might more accurately be called 'reed' instruments because the sound is produced by blowing into a reed. The reed is found growing naturally, which makes the woodwind section only marginally more complicated than blowing a piece of grass between your hands to make the sound of a duck, though they are a lot more expensive. The flute and its little sister, the piccolo, are metal instruments through which you blow. You have to blow in a particular way (like making a sound with a milk bottle) or else it sounds like a draughty window. They are called 'woodwind' because the original flutes were made of wood.

Reed instruments have a very long history: the Ancient Greeks had an instrument (called the *Aulos*) and in the first millennium the Arab world had a version called the *Surnāy*. These were similar to the modern oboe in that they had a double reed (two bits of reed through which air passes, causing vibrations) as opposed to the clarinet which has a single reed. Before the oboe and clarinet developed all the shiny silver buttons, they were much harder to play in tune; indeed some period orchestras have a slightly 'earthy' tuning because the instruments are a bit temperamental. The addition of these mechanics makes it easier to close off the holes using a button rather than the less effective finger with which it's hard to make an airtight covering over the finger holes.[5]

Players agonise over their reeds. As they are a natural material and since they spend most of their time stuck in the wet mouth of the player, they decay quickly. A favourite reed may only last for a few concerts so players learn how to make their own, using sharp blades and shaping tools. You can often see them at the back of a rehearsal shaving a few nanometres off their latest reed. When a reed goes wrong it is consigned to the dustbin. A reed must be properly wet and warm, which is why oboe players endlessly suck them before concerts.

Modern orchestras have two flutes, two oboes, two clarinets and two bassoons. At the top and the bottom of the woodwind section there may in addition be a piccolo (a very small and high-pitched flute) and a contra-bassoon (a large and deep-pitched bassoon). There are other instruments which come somewhere in the middle but aren't used in every concert: the *cor anglais* – a sort of large oboe with a crooked neck; and the *bass clarinet* – a big brother to the usual clarinet.

### Brass
A favourite trick of the orchestral trumpeter when demonstrating the instrument is to use a piece of hosepipe, a kitchen funnel and their mouth to play well-known trumpet tunes. That you are able to get a trumpet-like sound from a garden hose does not devalue the members of the brass family. All these instruments

require incredibly athletic control of the facial muscles to create a sound. The vibration is set up in the lips and the tube and funnel merely amplify and intensify the soundwaves. Using high-quality metals with very exact dimensions, modern instruments make a very steady sound. The origins of all the brass family are in instruments like the *shofar* (a ram's horn used in Jewish New Year celebrations).

If you've ever see a horn or trumpet player empty their instrument you may have noticed drops of water fall on to the floor. Children seem to be obsessed with the idea that it's spit, but it's not. The result of blowing hot breath through a cold metal instrument is that it creates a lot of condensation. Moisture collects inside the pipes of the instruments and must be released, usually on to the shoes of the player next to you, otherwise you run the risk of making embarrassing gurgling noises during your solo.

Modern orchestras have a minimum of two to three trumpets, the same number of trombones and usually only one tuba. There can be many horns for large works but you'd expect to see at least four at most concerts. The instrument used to be known as the French horn but is now more simply referred to as the horn.

## Percussion

The piano is officially a member of the percussion section because although it has strings it is the action of a hammer hitting the string that creates the sound. This qualifies it for the 'hitting' section of the orchestra. Anything that can be hit has been used by modern composers, from car suspension springs to glasses filled with water, but traditionally the main percussion instruments were timpani and cymbals. The percussion section is where the most innovation has happened in the last 200 years: tam tams (a large gong) from Asia, castanets from Spain, the vibraphone from America and so on. It's through clever use of the percussion section and by making interesting choices that a composer can create very personal sound worlds.

The development of the orchestra is inexplicably bound up with the development of classical singing, even though the human voice doesn't qualify as an orchestral instrument.

## Singing styles

The pop voice that we are used to hearing on the radio grew out of the technical advances in microphone and recording technology. The volume that most pop singers achieve without a microphone is negligible, but of course you never get to hear them with the naked ear unless you happen to have them over for lunch. What we have grown accustomed to is artificially amplified voices, so the sound of the natural human voice now seems slightly peculiar.

To me this is the vocal equivalent of fast food. Opera and classical singing is like organic produce: no artificiality. Any size of voice can be heard with a microphone but it takes a special singer to be heard over an orchestra in a live concert where there can be no cheating, pitch correction, auto-tune, compression, EQ, vocoder or any of the dozens of electronic enhancements that are commonplace in popular music. It always strikes me as interesting that people are obsessed with the lack of integrity associated with artificial enhancements in sport, where anyone caught using performance-enhancing drugs is banned, yet in music many people like the sound of heavily processed singing. For me it's the difference between a piece of antique wood furniture and a bit of plywood from Ikea. It's a question of quality.

A major influence on singing is the prevalent style of instrumental playing. For example, Bach writes music for the voice which makes almost no concessions to the singer's need to breathe but which mimics the lines of the orchestra. Bach's vocal lines are often long, with many embellishments. This requires a flexible voice but doesn't need to be huge, since the Baroque orchestra is relatively small.

So how did the classical voice become so large? Two thousand years ago, performing in a Greek amphitheatre, you'd have needed a stentorian voice to be heard above the clamour of the crowd. Since all singers use their natural vocal apparatus to be heard (diaphragm, lungs, larynx) I suspect in a Greek amphitheatre the performers would have been as vocally active and nearly as enormous as today's opera singers. The origins of our modern singing style are based in the resonant acoustics of cathedrals which inspired the choral tradition in the early part of the second millennium. But with the need for more dramatic and characterful interpretation in the new style of opera, singers had to compete with a larger orchestra. Training styles and repertoire adapted to create bigger and louder styles of singing to fill the increasingly popular opera houses.

By the time we get to Mozart writing *The Magic Flute* in 1791, the voice is being pushed to greater extremes of range – both pitch and volume. Two excellent examples are the Queen of the Night's aria 'Der Hölle Rache', where the unearthly high notes suggest a very definitely fantastical character and sounds almost indistinguishable from those of a flute and during the soprano solo in the Kyrie of Mozart's unfinished Mass in C Minor he begins by writing scales for the singer and then demands extreme low notes followed by much higher ones. The effect, which is both dramatic and flamboyant, would not have been attempted in Bach's music just fifty years before [Sound Link 67].

As demand for opera increased, and the buildings became larger and larger, so instruments had to be louder to fill the space. As people began to sing louder to be heard over the instruments, the music began to push their vocal limits. What ensued was a vocal arms-race with its apotheosis in the music of Richard Wagner (1813–1883) which demands enormous stamina, vast range and sheer volume. Wagner's larger-than-life characters need large voices to fill them.

As with all innovation, over a period these developments became the norm. By the time Wagner was writing huge vocal music at the end of the nineteenth century singers needed to have built up their voices to athletic standards just to be heard over the increasingly massive orchestra. Regulars at the opera would seldom recommend listening to recordings of singing through the tiny speakers of your television. The experience of hearing 'that voice' live is totally different from hearing it recorded or through microphones. Don't knock it until you've tried it.

Because of the demands put on singers it is a highly specialised business. A singer will learn a small number of roles that suit their voice; this is known as their *fach* (German for 'subject'). This means that they'll wait until their voice is big enough for a role and try not to sing it too early. Rolando Villazón got into vocal difficulty recently and took a long break from singing as a result of singing roles that didn't suit him. I was at a performance of *Les Contes d'Hoffmann* ('The Tales of Hoffmann') that he gave a few years ago when he was just hitting the international scene. He showed himself to be a superb actor and sang impeccably. I was dismayed, as I'm sure Villazón was, when things started to go wrong for him: he started to sound strained where before it had been effortless. I heard him about five years later singing Verdi and there were many signs of vocal stress: he popped and cracked at the top of his range, not what the opera audience is hoping for when they buy a ticket. His recent return to form singing the music of Handel is a relief, because unlike David Garrett's broken violin a broken voice is hard to fix.

Without need of a scientific explanation you can easily hear the 'ping' in the recordings of the voice of Luciano Pavarotti (1935–2007), an Italian tenor with a ringing quality to his instrument. Whatever note he sang, there was always that characteristic shine to the voice and it's that 'ping' that cuts through the orchestra – no matter how large. He may have been famous as the 'King of the high Cs' due to his ability to sing very high notes with apparent ease, but it was his particular resonance that made his voice a commercial prospect; it was both effective in the opera house and utterly distinctive on record. So how did he do it? How do opera stars get their voices over the massive sound of the orchestra? Well, a really top-quality classical singer has an abundance of 'ping'; this is what's called resonance. A singer is trained to add certain frequencies of sound – rather like you can with the tone controls on your hi-fi. If you emphasise the frequencies that our hearing is especially sensitive to, you can produce a sound that will cut through and always be heard, even if there is a lot of other sound being made around it. (That's why we can always hear a baby crying: it contains lots of those frequencies.)

## Understanding the different musical eras: composer overlap

It's a tantalising thought to imagine what Mozart might have written had he lived beyond 35. How many innovations would he have initiated? Beethoven was born just fourteen years later than Mozart but living to the age of 57 gave him the chance to lead the developments in music that began the Romantic era. Although J.S. Bach continued to write music in the same style throughout his life, his son, C.P.E. Bach, moved with the times and was alive during Mozart's life. If Mozart had lived as long as Joseph Haydn he'd have outlived Schubert and may well have grown into a Romantic composer. Beethoven was taught by Haydn and was steeped in the 'Classical' era, yet when he died Schumann, Mendelssohn and Wagner were all in their teens. Robert Schumann died at 46 from syphilis and Felix Mendelssohn died from a brain haemorrhage at just 38, yet Richard Wagner achieved 70 years. Wagner therefore overlaps with Mahler, Schoenberg and Richard Strauss. By living that little bit longer Wagner was part of the musical developments of the end of the nineteenth century even though he was born in an earlier musical epoch.

Think what you will but I insist on having my CD collection in alphabetical order by the name of composer. I know some people do it by record label (more colourful that way but ultimately useless). Some do it by name of composition and many people divide it by era. We love to categorise music and there is a plethora of terms in popular music the meaning of which is patently clear to aficionados but utterly obscure to the outside world (indie, rock, grime, dancehall, electronica, reggae, hiphop, MOR or bashment anyone?) The same applies to 'classical' music (though as we've discussed before that term is problematic).

Given this morass of composers and styles it's understandable that we try to clear things up by fitting composers into definitions of musical style: Renaissance, Baroque, Classical, Romantic, Serialist, Modernist, Minimalist. These are extremely helpful labels. The history of music is like a great river with each composer coming in as a tributary at different points along the way, each affecting the sounds in minute ways, some changing the course altogether. But remember they are merely labels and some composers have aspects of different eras – Beethoven for example began as a Classical composer but ended as a Romantic one.

If you have no concept of where different composers fit into the history of music, you'll be glad to hear that it can be split into about six easily identifiable periods. Each period has features that can be spotted by the most inexpert of listeners. It's not vital to know about this but a general sense of how we got to the sound that we are used to today can really help to identify music. One of the biggest differences between the musical styles and the easiest to spot is in the use of different sizes of musical ensemble: from a small collection of singers to a full symphony orchestra.

*Before 1900 things are roughly organised as follows:*
- Early music/Medieval (1000–1400s)
- Renaissance (1400s–1600)
- Baroque (1600–1750)
- Classical (1750–1800)
- Romantic (1800–1900)

As with literature and art, in the twentieth century things became more complicated and music took several different paths. There was a greater emphasis on being original and conspicuously different.

*The twentieth century*
- *O* Modernism
- *O* Second Viennese School
- *O* Nationalism
- *O* Neo-Classicism
- *O* Minimalism
- *O* New Complexity

## How to identify

You are in the car and on to the radio comes a piece of music you cannot identify. Getting the right composer takes practice; it might be easier first to ascertain when it was written. This simple guide should help. I've always loved playing 'guess the composer'. And ever since my A-Level music history lessons I've enjoyed spotting musical features and trying to attribute them to the correct era. It might seem like a dry activity, and while you are welcome to skip to the next chapter I think it's worth spending time getting to know the key features of each subdivision to help you navigate.

## EARLY MUSIC/MEDIEVAL (1000–1400s)

What you are likely to hear of it on the radio is almost exclusively vocal. The music rarely changes keys – in fact they didn't have the concept of keys. You might hear some harmony and a little decoration. The religious vocal music is in the language of Latin.

*Easy features to spot:*
- Long-held 'drone' notes as a bass line
- A strong, improvisatory vocal line
- Usually recorded in a cathedral acoustic
- A little haunting because of its simplicity
- Any accompaniment is likely to be simple drums, basic 'nasal-sounding' wind instruments or scratchy strings

*More subtle features:*
- Recorders which are made of wood, unlike the plastic primary school variety
- Simple string instruments which sound much thinner than their modern equivalent
- Many 'schools' of polyphony, which sang religious music, but also a growing and vibrant secular music from troubadours and itinerant musicians

*Features requiring homework:*
- Modal writing – that is, similar to scales, but using different patterns of notes and intervals; there are eight of these so-called 'church' modes; this gives a distinctly medieval flavour
- Gregorian and pre-Gregorian chant

*You could try:*
- **Hildegard of Bingen:** Antiphons
- **Francesco Landini:** Ballatas and Songs
- **Guillaume de Machaut:** Ballades

*Performing ensembles:*
- Anonymous 4
- The Dufay Collective
- The Hilliard Ensemble

## RENAISSANCE (1400s–1600)

Playing and singing characterised by a 'straight' sound without vibrato; overall a smoother and more homogenised sound; you are likely to hear small instrumental groups or small vocal ensembles.

*Easy features to spot:*
- Dance rhythms
- The lute (an instrument like the guitar)
- The increasing elaboration of polyphonic choral music – many parts singing interweaving lines
- Venetian Renaissance choral music pioneered the use of multiple choirs placed in different locations around the church; this is known as *antiphonal* writing

*More subtle features:*
- Introduction of 'accidentals' or chromatic notes
- A greater feeling of a flow of chords, or harmony
- Increased use of imitation between the musical parts
- Towards the end of the Renaissance there was a reaction against all this complex harmony and music where the words were obscured, and a new style emerged, *monody* (singing alone). The earliest operas began at the end of this period and they were all written for one voice singing at a time
- Madrigals – secular songs for choirs

*Features requiring homework:*
- The Pavan, Galliard and Courante were dance forms prevalent in instrumental writing

*You could try:*
- Josquin des Prez
- Carlo Gesualdo: Madrigals
- Thomas Tallis: *Spem in alium*
- Giovanni Pierluigi da Palestrina: *Missa Papae Marcelli*

- *Byrd*: Mass for 5 voices
- *John Dowland*: Lute Songs

*Performing ensembles:*
- Stile Antico
- The Sixteen
- I Fagiolini

## BAROQUE (1600–1750)

Decoration is one of the hallmarks of the Baroque era. In music that means florid vocal lines and instrumental writing.

*Easy features to spot:*
- Use of the harpsichord or organ
- Florid ornamentation of the melody
- Dancelike rhythms
- A feeling of perpetual motion
- Works include vocal music for the church, small instrumental ensembles or solo instruments; secular music is now more common

*More subtle features:*
- Playing and singing characterised by a 'straight' sound without vibrato
- Natural horns and trumpets (these have a characteristically inexact sound)
- Limited use of timpani (usually a maximum of two notes)
- Use of ABA form, for example in *Da Capo* arias – and other forms such as binary and fugue
- Modes are now replaced with the major/minor key system
- Lots of different musical forms (e.g. binary, fugue)
- Music notated but designed to include improvisation

*Features requiring homework:*
- Fugues
- Some instruments no longer in common use (Oboe d'amore, Oboe da Caccia, Viola da Gamba)
- The basso continuo (figured bass)

*Exemplar pieces/composers:*
- **Antonio Vivaldi:** Concerto for Two Trumpets, *Four Seasons*
- **J.S. Bach:** Goldberg Variations; organ music; church music; instrumental music
- **George Frideric Handel:** *Water Music*; *Fireworks Music*; *Messiah*; operas
- **Domenico Scarlatti:** keyboard sonatas
- **Claudio Monteverdi:** *Vespers*
- **Henry Purcell:** *Dido and Aeneas, The Fairy Queen*, anthems

*Performing ensembles:*
- The Monteverdi Choir
- The English Concert
- Ton Koopman and the Amsterdam Baroque Orchestra
- Collegium Vocale Ghent

# CLASSICAL (1750–1800)

Music of the Classical period is ordered and aims to please without becoming overly expressive. The orchestra, whilst bigger than in the Baroque period, still contains few brass and woodwind instruments.

*Easy features to spot:*
- Themes are less florid than in Baroque music
- Broader range of subject matter, especially in opera
- Orchestra is now larger and includes clarinets

- Opera now has choruses, overtures, recitative and arias
- Music sounds structured, organised and elegant, adhering to the principles of the Enlightenment: rationality and a belief in the importance of the arts
- The harpsichord is used less and less and is eventually replaced by the piano

*More subtle features:*
- Clearly defined sections within the music that conform to a 'classical' structure, i.e. influenced by classical antiquity
- Greater variety and contrast within pieces than previously, both musically and emotionally
- Shorter melodies than in Baroque examples, very clearly defined phrases
- Some virtuosic showmanship, but within the context of a piece

*Features requiring homework:*
- Use of multiple themes and development of those themes
- Use of key change to define sections of music
- Sonata form

*You could try …*
- **Mozart:** Symphony No. 41, *The Magic Flute* … just about anything
- **Haydn:** String Quartets, Symphony No. 94, Symphony No. 45, 'Farewell', *Creation*, Mass in D Minor
- **Beethoven:** Piano Sonata in C Minor, Op. 13, 'Pathétique'

*Performing ensembles:*
- Orchestra of the Age of Enlightenment

# ROMANTIC (1800–1900)

The inner workings of the heart pour out in this music, throwing caution to the wind – the music was often written for large forces of players and singers as the orchestra grew. Composers were often more overtly inspired by art and literature. The drama and romance of this music has been so plundered by film music, etc., that it is quite easy to recognise.

*Easy features to spot:*
- Lush harmony and heartfelt, lyrical tunes
- Strident writing in the fast movements
- A larger orchestra but limited use of percussion
- Key changes more prevalent, and lots of rich discords but with a clear tonal centre
- A very large dynamic range

*More subtle features:*
- A more personal and emotional sound less in thrall to musical structure and design
- The invention of the valve opens up and enlarges the brass section
- Programme music becomes more popular – a story told in music
- Extreme instrumental virtuosity

*Features requiring homework:*
- A rise in musical nationalism in the arts brings out local signatures, and the use of folk forms and rhythms
- Grand musical structures

*You could try:*
- Bizet: *Carmen*
- Dvořák: Symphony No. 9, 'From the New World'
- Schubert: 'Death and the Maiden' String Quartet
- Tchaikovsky: Piano Concerto No. 1
- Berlioz: *Symphonie Fantastique*

- Chopin: Nocturnes and Études
- Schumann: Symphonies
- Wagner: *Tristan and Isolde*
- Tchaikovsky: Symphony No. 6, 'Pathétique'
- Mendelssohn: Octet
- Brahms: Violin Concerto
- Schubert: Symphony No. 8, 'Unfinished'
- Dvořák: Piano Quintet
- Verdi: *La Traviata*

*Performing ensembles:*
- London Symphony Orchestra,
- Philharmonia, Royal Opera House

## TWENTIETH CENTURY ... AND ON ...

There is greater diversity in the music of the twentieth century than ever before, but for all that diversity the music can usually be identified as coming from that era. There are composers who deliberately pastiche the music of different centuries but they are the exception rather than the rule. We don't have much critical distance from the music of this century, of course, so who knows how it will eventually be summed up.

*Easy features to spot:*
- Use of extreme dissonance
- Unusual pairings of instruments
- Lack of melody
- Dark sounding
- May sound like music of previous generations but with a modern twist
- Exotic percussion instruments, or instruments grabbed from other kinds of music, e.g. saxophone

- The use of tape, electronic or other synthesised sounds
- Highly energetic performance

*More subtle features:*
- Investigation of extremes: Minimalism and Maximalism – barely any notes through to bewildering numbers of notes
- Rhythmically unpredictable and 'uncountable'

*Features requiring homework:*
- Use of composition systems
- Extremes of range in instrumental playing
- Unorthodox methods of playing

*You could try:*
- Igor Stravinsky: *The Rite of Spring*
- Benjamin Britten: *War Requiem*
- Charles Ives: *The Unanswered Question*
- Ralph Vaughan Williams: *Fantasia on a Theme of Thomas Tallis*
- Edward Elgar: Cello Concerto
- Edgard Varèse: *Ionisation*
- Béla Bartók: Music for Strings, Percussion and Celesta
- Dimitri Shostakovich: Symphony No. 5
- Aaron Copland: *Appalachian Spring*
- Sergei Prokofiev: Violin Sonata No. 1
- Olivier Messiaen: Turangalîla Symphony
- Pierre Boulez: *Le Marteau sans maître*
- Iannis Xenakis: *Metastaseis*
- Karlheinz Stockhausen: *Kontakte*
- Luciano Berio: Sinfonia
- Steve Reich: Music for 18 Musicians
- György Ligeti: *Le Grand Macabre*
- Oliver Knussen: *Where the Wild Things Are*
- John Adams: *Nixon in China*

- Thomas Adès: *Asyla*
- Mark-Anthony Turnage: *Blood on the Floor*

*Performing ensembles:*
- London Sinfonietta
- Britten Sinfonia
- Birmingham Contemporary Music Group

## Authentic performance

This isn't a style but it is such an important movement in music that I think it deserves a place in this chapter. With performances that took place before the invention of recording, it is impossible to hear the music exactly as it was received by audiences at the time. But with an act of imagination and a little knowledge we can try putting ourselves in their place. Following my studies at the Royal Academy of Music I spent a glorious week singing in a German abbey at Neresheim. The building is a masterpiece by Baroque architect Johann Balthasar Neumann, built in the latter part of the eighteenth century. Entering the gloriously white, opulent abbey, I was struck by how extreme the contrast would have been between the atmosphere of this building and how different it must have been from the lives of ordinary local people. Imagine if your daily diet of music was hearing farmers sing as they tilled the field, entering the abbey on a Sunday to hear the reverberant intoning of the monks – or the effect of hearing harmony on the great organ on people who had no musical skill themselves and little education. It must have seemed celestial. I had a small sense of this effect talking with the monks there, whose daily musical diet consists of plainsong. Our small choir brought harmony to their worship, and the effect on the monks was noticeable. The simplicity of their lives enabled them to have a perspective on our music that is hard to replicate in the modern world. Music that makes little sense in the modern world sounds utterly appropriate in buildings such as this abbey.

To appreciate fully the music of previous generations in modern times it helps if you attempt to divest yourself of modern life and listen to the music in the buildings for which it was written. But for the music to really spring out of the past it needs to be played in the style and on the instruments of the time in which it was written. Traditional ways of playing classical music have changed since the time they were written: what sounds passionate and intense in one generation can sound overburdened and weighty to the next. In the 1960s and '70s a new movement began, known variously as 'historically informed', 'authentic performance' or 'period performance'. This was a game changer.

Where did this change come from? Before the Authentic Performance movement, conductors would play the core repertoire of works – symphonies, etc. – in pretty much whatever manner had been handed down to them by the previous generation. There was a 'Chinese whisper' effect when playing music that was 200 years old.

The great orchestral conductors of the 1950s approached Baroque music with the same grandeur and sonorous largesse as they approached the music from two generations later – the Romantic era. Tempos were slower to allow the music to saturate a large acoustic, the vocal style was rich and operatic, and the instrumental sound was as burnished as an old mahogany chest. As a useful comparison listen to Otto Klemperer's 1989 recording of the opening movement of Bach's St Matthew Passion. It weighs in at an impressive 11.46 minutes. The first version I ever heard was Karl Richter's and I was knocked sideways by John Eliot Gardiner's version (recorded in the same year) which I heard about five years later, as he'd not only chopped three minutes off but he treated Bach like dance music (much more historically appropriate) rather than like something from a mausoleum. Here's a comparison chart:

| | |
|---|---|
| Otto Klemperer | 11.46 |
| Karl Richter | 9.52 |
| Sir David Willcocks | 8.34 |
| Leonard Bernstein | 7.46 |
| Franz Brüggen | 7.36 |
| John Eliot Gardiner | 6.59 |
| Philippe Herreweghe | 6.58 |
| Nikolaus Harnoncourt | 6.40 |

That is a range of almost five minutes' difference in one movement. Applied to the entire work it makes a bum-numbing difference. Conductors of period instrument bands like Gardiner, Herreweghe and Harnoncourt have a lightness and speed that have now become the norm. This has a dramatic effect on how we listen to music because if you hear a very heavy and slow version of a piece that was intended to be lighter and faster, then you are being given the wrong impression entirely.

With a breath of fresh air, young radical conductors from the 1960s onwards dug about in the history books and looked in the cupboard under the stairs for evidence of how 'early' music would have been played. What emerged was a light, energetic and crucially more authentic approach. Philippe Herreweghe, John Eliot Gardiner, Andrew Parrott, Trevor Pinnock, Harry Christophers and their ilk created a new academically and historically informed performance style that revolutionised the way we perform and listen to music. Suddenly we were hearing works that had previously sounded laborious and dull in a completely new way. The aim of the movement is simple: to create a performance that is as close as possible to what the composer would have heard and imagined. The execution of that aim is more complicated. Using contemporary descriptions or drawings of concerts, original instruments dating from the period and a will, as John Eliot Gardiner puts it, to 'fresh-mint' the music, these conductors and their period-instrument orchestras offered an important new perspective and a way for us to listen with fresh ears.

As people started to listen to Baroque music in entirely new ways, conductors and orchestras turned their attention to the music of other periods. In 1994 I remember being very excited about John Eliot Gardiner's approach to Beethoven's Symphony No. 9. As part of a *South Bank Show*, he related it to French revolutionary songs, used original instruments and generally brought a vigorous freshness to the whole enterprise in his 1994 Archiv recording. Sir Roger Norrington is another British conductor who applies techniques honed in the early music scene to repertoire traditionally the preserve of larger orchestras. In his 2005 recording of Beethoven's Piano Concerto No. 5 in E Flat Major, Norrington and the London Classical Players achieve a lightness of touch that owes much to the string technique of Baroque bands. This attempts to get back to the original Beethoven before he was rudely romanticised. To my ear it sounds closer to Mozart than previous interpretations. The recording I grew up with was Sir Georg Solti and the Chicago Symphony Orchestra with Vladimir Ashkenazy at the piano. Though I love this passionate rendition, from the perspective of the Norrington performance Solti's feels overfull of romantic fervour (albeit impeccably executed).

This new approach of academically informed performance could seem like the efforts of a worthily intentioned museum curator, if a balance is not struck between a desire to be attentive to history and the imperative to make something that works in front of an audience. There has been a relaxation of the strictures of historical performance in recent years, which acknowledges that we can never fully recreate the sound of the past and that not everything modern does a disservice to the composer's intentions.

# CH-CH-CH-CH-CH-CH-CH-CHANGES ...

One of the ways in which music has been revitalised was the reintroduction of improvisation to the concert platform. Music of the last 200 years is written down and so leaves little room for embellishment by the performer. Today violinists working in Baroque music like Daniel Hope, Rachel Podger and Andrew Manze use improvisation to decorate the music that is written on the page. They use their intimate knowledge of the era to keep their extemporising appropriate but it's closer to the way a jazz or rock musician might play than many people would suspect. They reconstruct work where the score might leave room for improvisation, and where the composer expected embellishment by the performer. Even as late as Mozart, performers were encouraged to improvise.

Another important difference is in the use of violin bows from the Baroque era. These are shorter and lighter, with a different tension in the hair that is pulled across the string. This gives greater speed and agility but sacrifices volume and tone. Period instrument bands therefore sound substantially lighter than modern alternatives.

The period music movement affected choirs as well. Scholars looking at contemporary sources have been able to deduce the numbers involved, but what is more subtle is how to sing the notes themselves. By the 1950s the choral society was at the end of a glorious period that began around 100 years before. Choral societies had become bigger and bigger to match the size of the modern orchestra and concert hall: an extreme example is the double chorus needed for Mahler's Eighth Symphony, 'Symphony of a Thousand'; the twentieth-century orchestral chorus at its most robust, it takes about 300 singers to compete with the massive orchestra. The period movement created a need for much small ensembles such as the Monteverdi Choir, the Tallis Scholars and The Sixteen because a smaller ensemble can be heard over a Baroque orchestra. Of necessity with a smaller choir comes a lighter style of singing, which results in faster speeds and a greater flexibility.

# 9

# Grand Designs:
# The Structure of Music

*" It is not hard to compose, but what is fabulously hard is to leave the superfluous notes under the table. "*

JOHANNES BRAHMS

## Taking time

Going for a walk has a structure: you arrive at the car park, put your walking boots on, walk for an hour, take a break, eat a glorious pub lunch and finally end up, exhausted and ruddy-cheeked, back at the car. Eating a meal has a structure: starter, main course and dessert – perhaps an *amuse bouche* if you are eating in a fancy restaurant. Music is the same: all music has structure. Sometimes this structure is overt, with the piece split into clear sections, like a Beethoven symphony with three clear gaps which tell you precisely when it's finished. In other works it can be harder to discern.

It is useful to have a grasp of the *broad* structure of the music you listen to. Knowing whether or not it's a tone poem, a symphony, a concerto, a theme and variations or a set of songs, knowing how long the piece will last, when the fast bits come and how many sections there are, will help you to accommodate the music and, most usefully, tell you when to applaud.

When you listen to music on shuffle or switch the radio on midstream, it can hurl you into the middle of a work, like the Starship *Enterprise* dropping out of warp drive and arriving in an unexpected galaxy. This can throw up surprises and in this way you can happen upon little gems. But this is a 'pop' way of listening to music and doesn't give you an appreciation of the whole piece as the composer conceived it. Who cares? You may well ask … Can we really take a socking forty minutes out of our busy modern lives to dedicate to a piece of music when we could just skip to the good bit and have done with it? I acknowledge that there isn't always time for a full symphony but I want to explore why it might be worth setting aside more than fifteen minutes for concerted listening.

Works of the nineteenth century were written for a very different era where instant musical gratification wasn't readily available. In those days if you were lucky enough to get to a concert then it might be the only music you heard all week, unless you played it yourself. You'd want value for money. Today we are musically over-indulged; our ears are fat with music, so it can be hard to appreciate music from leaner times. When I sit through a piece of music that is substantial (say more than twenty minutes long) I get a sense that I've achieved something; I've endured the whole work and now I'm free to let it run through my mind or forget it forever – my choice. Sometimes it's only in the dying moments of the piece that I appreciate what's gone before.

Picking appealing sections from a larger piece, as they are wont to do on Classic FM – let's say, for example only, 'The Aquarium' from *Carnival of the Animals* by Camille Saint-Saëns – there is a danger that you might overdose on the more sugary sections and miss the nourishing parts; the main course that sets up the dessert. Haven't you got time for 'The Elephant', one of the greatest tunes for double bass in the repertoire? What about

'The Kangaroo' which only bounces along for thirty seconds? Or 'Fossils', which ingeniously contains musical references to several 'musical fossils', 'Twinkle Twinkle Little Star' and 'Una Voce Poco Fa' from the *Barber of Seville* by Rossini being the most obvious? But above all, how could you miss 'The Swan'? It's utterly enchanting and as accurate a depiction of the graceful movement of a swan as I can imagine in music. You could easily miss the greater point by taking chunks out of the piece: it's a procession of animals. Cutting the work up in bits is what a Radio 3 producer described to me as 'bleeding chunks'. You don't get a sense of the complete menagerie as imagined by Saint-Saëns. It's through listening to the whole work that you encounter the composer's vision as opposed to just sampling one of his vignettes.

This happens to classical music all the time, in films, in adverts and on the radio – there is little time for the build-up so the highlights must suffice. This is a great way to become familiar with music but the more advanced listener cultivates a monk-like stillness through a work waiting for the good bits. Classical music is all about the experience. Some of the experience will be arduous and some will be simple and appealing. The patient listener learns to wait for those moments. Composers are aware of the attention span of the audience they are writing for (it's considerably shorter in modern times than in previous generations) and will vary the material accordingly.

I do not say this out of snobbishness. I dip in and out of pieces all the time. I drive my wife potty by listening to thirty seconds before I think of another piece of music I'd like to hear and I hit skip on my iPod. However, the experience of plunging into a large-scale work is infinitely more satisfying than dipping your toe in the water, and understanding the structure can take away some of the pain.

The precise structure of music is often obscure to the listener and can baffle all but the most determined scholars. At the highest levels of academic study the relationship of the grand structure to the compositional material is of the utmost fascination yet to the casual listener it may not be immediately apparent. So what is to be gained from knowing a sonata from a sonatina?

When you don't know what you are listening to, it can be like the Isner *vs* Mahut tennis match in 2010 that went to 183 games in the final set – endless. Sitting in a concert hall feeling perilously close to a breakdown during an unexpectedly long concert was summed up pithily by Colin, a friend of mine, describing watching his mother-in-law perform Handel's *Messiah* with her local amateur choir. Badly bitten before by tedious concerts, Colin came prepared; he looked at the lyrics (properly called the *libretto)* before the concert. Colin was overjoyed to see that the work appeared mercifully short. The first choral movement he noted contained few words: 'And the glory of the Lord shall be revealed, and all flesh shall see it together, for the mouth of the Lord hath spoken it.'

*This will be a short concert*, he thought.

Imagine Colin's horror when the choir repeated the words about ten times.

*Oh God. It's never going to end.*

I love to imagine the mental arithmetic that Colin then undertook as he furiously extrapolated this new ratio of lyric to length for 53 parts of *The Messiah*, realising that an 8.30 p.m. finish was a pipedream and he'd be lucky to get a pint in before last orders.

As Stravinsky said: 'Too many pieces of music finish too long after the end.'

## The 10-second rule

There's no doubting that some pieces seem to go on forever and if you've never heard them before it can be hard to take. Why should it be that some music gets straight into our brains and sticks there whilst other pieces take longer to get to know? The structure of the piece is at the heart of its stickability. A current theory[1] is that memorable melodies last roughly as long as your sense of the present and anything longer begins to use your short-term memory. It takes between 10 and 30 seconds for a moment to feel like 'the past'. Try tapping your leg and wait 10 seconds for the moment to become 'historical'. Before that transition it feels as if you are still in the same time-frame as the leg tap, but afterwards it is forever in the past. By the time you've read the next paragraph this sentence will seem like it's in the past. Not very far in the past but definitely not 'now'.

In music, once 10 seconds have elapsed you may feel like you are entering a new section. Try it. Listen to almost any piece you can find and after around 10 seconds you'll perceive that some of the music is 'in the past' and you are now listening to new music in the present tense. After another 10 seconds the process repeats itself and so on until the end of the piece. This teasing of the short-term memory happens all the time in classical music. Our consciousness is a constantly evolving present tense (unless we are very drunk) and music offers us a way of dividing time. It leads us through time and brings us into new moments. But it does this in a highly organised way; life is rarely so beautifully arranged, unless you are Nigella Lawson. Each moment of melody leads to the next; these moments may string together to form a much larger melody. To appreciate this longer melody we need to use our short-term memory. The joy of listening to well-ordered music is in the return of pleasant melodies and moments. A good composer knows just how much tolerance we have for innovation and when we need to be reminded of the tune.

In the Classical period, composers used the 'sonata' form which perfectly exploits this ability of our brains to remember short musical phrases. Take a well-known example such as the first movement of *Eine Kleine Nachtmusik*. In the first two minutes of the piece Mozart changes the sound of the music roughly every 10 seconds. That means by the time you get to a minute or so into the piece you've heard five or six 'bits' of music. In that time you can remember most of what's gone before using a mixture of your sense of the present (the music that is playing now and has just played) and your short-term memory (the music from about a minute ago). People who don't have a memory (as a result of brain injuries, for example) will find this sort of structure a complete anathema (for an account of the difficulty some people have with music following brain trauma see Oliver Sacks's book *Musicophilia*).

By the time we get two minutes in, your brain can't quite keep all the material in mind and for me that's the point of submersion – where you feel like you are in the middle of the music. This first section is called the 'exposition' – an expounding of the main ideas of the piece. It's at this point that Mozart repeats the whole thing so you get to hear the first two minutes again. Now you are really using your short-term memory because you are hearing the same music – only this time you've heard it before, so your brain (like it or not) is following along, predicting what comes next – that's a very different sensation from the first time you heard it. After this repeat Mozart uses a brilliant technique of the Classical period – he develops the original material, which is known as the 'development' section. You've now heard the basic ideas set out twice and now you are hearing them again, subtly transformed. Finally Mozart repeats some of the music from the beginning of the movement to finish, known as a recapitulation. This is about as perfect a music structure as has ever been invented. It works for the first-time listener but it also works when you listen to the piece over and over again. It's a useful rhetorical technique too – make your point, repeat it emphatically, discuss it and then repeat it once more just to make sure everybody understood.

I'm not saying that you need to understand every piece of music in this way; the composer should be in charge of the structure to prevent you from getting bored. How long you can go before hearing something familiar is a very personal thing. If I don't hear something repeated in the first five minutes of music (that's to say there's nothing but *new* music for a full five minutes) then I get lost; that's way too complex for me. I need to have something to help me locate myself within the piece.

In the same way that architects use repetition and variation of forms in buildings so that they make sense – for example a regular number of windows, doors of the same height in formal arrangement, corridors based on a coherent floor-plan – composers rely on a similar sense of structure. Randomness in both music and architecture is confusing. Goethe said that architecture is 'frozen music' and I agree – a composer builds up a composition from small elements into a large structure just as an architect who starts with a single brick can create palaces and cathedrals.

At a deep level it's fabulously satisfying to hear music that repeats and it plays on our sense of time passing. Music is notes suspended in time. When the melody repeats it is like having a time machine that returns to previous versions of our self. From this new perspective we are given the chance to look back on ourselves. That is how classical music offers us the possibility of very deep reflection. Enough philosophy.

## How to compose in a large structure

How does a composer go about creating a piece of music that is an hour long? How do they plan their work? Composing is a laborious process and a piece of music lasting a few minutes might be months in gestation, but this is the work that a composer loves. Many of them are academic types who love study, the quiet life of reflection and time to get their thoughts on to paper.

> **❝** *I was born out of due time in the sense that by temperament and talent I should have been more suited for the life of a small Bach, living in anonymity and composing regularly for an established service and for God.* **❞**

IGOR STRAVINSKY

Bach's life as a composer might in one sense sound idyllic and he was lucky to have the patronage of the Church and regular employment. But in another sense composers of his day were only as good as their last piece.

In the past composers had existing forms of music with conventions they could adhere to or work against. In the nineteenth century a composer would have written a symphony as a statement of their musical personality, for without writing a symphony how could you be taken seriously as a serious composer? However, for a twenty-first-century composer all bets are off. Today's composers can write in any style. So how do they go from a small idea for a tune to writing a full-blown symphony?

In Chapter 6 I explained some of the ways in which composers could transform melodies by inverting, stretching, playing them backwards, chopping them up and generally abusing them. These techniques allow composers to use compositional material sparingly. Very broadly speaking, a good composition doesn't need a new tune every ten seconds; repetition of the initial material and appropriate development of that material over the course of the piece is enough to keep an audience satisfied. Following that, a composer needs some sort of high point in the piece where the music peaks and then possibly an end section like a summary. The American composer Samuel Barber (1910–1981) wrote a beautiful string quartet which he then adapted into the Adagio for Strings (it's the piece from the end of the film *Platoon* and I taught it to the singers of South Oxhey in the third series of *The Choir: Unsung Town*). Part of its success as a piece of music is due to its simple structure. It has a twisting, simple melody which repeats a few times before building to a series of climactic chords followed by silence and then a tailpiece which reminds us of the original tune.

As with any art-form it is both the structure and the material that produces the effect; one cannot be separated from the other. The establishment of a theme or musical idea and its subsequent development and modification throughout a piece is what keeps a listener attentive (even Colin listening to the *Messiah*). The moments of magic are both harmonically *and* structurally significant. For instance Mendelssohn's Italian Symphony is a work that has a toe-tapping main theme that gets wheeled out several times through the first movement. But when the main theme returns at the end after a Romantic middle section in a minor key, Mendelssohn first softens the music before finally cranking up the tension and hitting us with a powerful recapitulation of the theme. This is a Classical technique in the hands of a Romantic composer. Just hearing the theme once is not enough – you need to listen to the whole movement.

My favourite pieces have a moment where the music overwhelms my senses; this is often about two-thirds of the way through. There are structurally significant moments in all great music where it feels as though the micro is related to the macro, the particular moment is related to the general structure. Traditionally a composer creates small units of music which are then deployed throughout the superstructure to create a unified whole. Generally they aim to do this in a way that is *organic,* so that the structure has become subsumed by the content. This may sound rather esoteric but actually it's quite obvious when you encounter a work that *doesn't* work structurally, we don't usually hear these pieces on the radio because they are deemed to be lesser works. Put simply, they are boring.

In the same way as it's hard to define how a composer creates original melodies, it's very hard to say how a composer goes from that initial inspiration to a work that is as large as a symphony. Leaning on established forms is one way of doing it; repetition is another way of stringing out material, but it's the work of a genius that manages to structure a work so that it seems to have a touch of the divine.

## COMPOSERS ON COMPOSING

" *There's nothing remarkable about it. All one has to do is hit the right keys at the right time and the instrument plays itself.* "

JOHANN SEBASTIAN BACH

" *Without craftsmanship, inspiration is a mere reed shaken in the wind.* "

JOHANNES BRAHMS

" *Simplicity is the final achievement. After one has played a vast quantity of notes and more notes, it is simplicity that emerges as the crowning reward of art.* "

FRÉDÉRIC CHOPIN

" *Whether I was in my body or out of my body as I wrote it I know not. God knows.* "

GEORGE FRIDERIC HANDEL

" *Neither a lofty degree of intelligence nor imagination nor both together go to the making of genius. Love, love, love, that is the soul of genius.* "

WOLFGANG AMADEUS MOZART

66 *I sit down to the piano regularly at nine o'clock in the morning and Mesdames les Muses have learned to be on time for that rendezvous.* 99

PYOTR ILYICH TCHAIKOVSKY

66 *Music is the one incorporeal entrance into the higher world of knowledge which comprehends mankind but which mankind cannot comprehend.* 99

LUDWIG VAN BEETHOVEN,
*quoted by Bettina von Arnin, letter to Goethe, 1810*

66 *People compose for many reasons: to become immortal; because the pianoforte happens to be open; because they want to become a millionaire; because of the praise of friends; because they have looked into a pair of beautiful eyes; for no reason whatsoever.* 99

ROBERT SCHUMANN

66 *What is best in music is not to be found within the notes.* 99

GUSTAV MAHLER

66 *If a composer could say what he had to say in words he would not bother trying to say it in music.* 99

GUSTAV MAHLER

66 *He roused my admiration when I was young; he caused me to despair when I reached maturity; he is now the comfort of my old age.* 99

GIOACHINO ROSSINI
*of Mozart*

66 *All the good music has already been written by people with wigs and stuff.* 99

FRANK ZAPPA

> **❝** *I can't understand why people are frightened of new ideas. I'm frightened of the old ones.* **❞**
>
> JOHN CAGE

## Musical structures

Discerning the precise form of a piece of music was at one time fairly straightforward. Musicians knew how to play a sarabande, chaconne, gigue or minuet from their musical studies. They would then write something in a similar vein. It's the same process that many pop musicians follow – they listen to successful examples and base their 'new' work loosely upon them. That's why a lot of pop songs sound the same. Ahem.

Of course composers of the twentieth century play tricks, turn forms on their heads and general mess about until a sarabande isn't a sarabande any more (a sarabande is a type of slow dance). But there are certain musical forms which are worth knowing about. To list every form in which music is written would make this a musical dictionary, for there are hundreds, but in exposing yourself to classical music you are likely to encounter the following major forms:

### Concerto
With its zenith during the nineteenth century when flamboyant technical virtuosity was the fashion, the concerto is a piece for orchestra and solo instrument. This can be any instrument of the orchestra but the greatest examples are for violin, piano, flute, trumpet and horn. The double bass tends not to have as many concerti written for it because of its general musical inflexibility – it's always going to be a low instrument. The same is true of the tuba. (I await the letters from disgruntled fans of the Vaughan Williams Tuba Concerto – surely an exception rather than the

rule?) And while I'm about it, although it's not a concerto, I can't help mentioning Malcolm Arnold's *A Grand, Grand Overture for 3 Vacuum Cleaners, 1 Floor Polisher, 4 Rifles and Orchestra* (written for the 1956 Hoffnung Music Festival) [Sound Link 68].

The interest of a concerto lies in the soloist's ability and musical personality which are clearly foregrounded, not the case in an orchestral solo. During a concerto the soloist stands (or sits) at the front of the orchestra, dressed up with extra sparkles for a lady and an especially crisp white shirt for the gents to denote the significant musical effort they are going to. The interaction between the soloist and the orchestra is also of interest: at times the orchestra is merely backdrop whilst at other times it takes over and gives the soloist a rest before the next furiously difficult section. (I've seen many strings broken during concertos.)

Technical ability and artistic merit is valued highly in this form. Solo violinists like Anne-Sophie Mutter, Maxim Vengerov, Tasmin Little and Hilary Hahn will specialise in a small number of concertos and play them all over the world. Just learning one concerto can be the work of years; although some may be relatively easy, others have fearsome reputations. Those written by virtuoso performers such as Rachmaninov, Liszt and Chopin are amongst the most technically challenging from the Romantic repertoire as they were written to demonstrate the composers' skill at playing their instrument.

It helps if the soloist is nice to look at. I know it shouldn't, but it does.

### Piano concertos

- Beethoven: Piano Concerto No. 5 'Emperor'
- Mozart: Piano Concerto No. 21 – made famous by the film *Elvira Madigan*
- Grieg: Piano Concerto
- Rachmaninov: Third Piano Concerto – made famous by the film *Shine*

o **Gershwin:** after writing *Rhapsody in Blue* for piano and orchestra, Gershwin wrote his piano concerto which straddles the worlds of jazz and classical concertos

o **Shostakovich:** Piano Concerto No. 2 – hugely energetic and full of biting sarcasm

o **Stravinsky:** Concerto for Piano and Wind Instruments – more challenging

o **Britten:** Piano Concerto

## Violin concertos

The violin concerto is one of the most popular musical forms. The following list comprises the really *big* violin concertos that should be on your shelves, but there are others – Bach, Mozart, Barber, Korngold, Britten, Sibelius, to name but a few.

o **Vivaldi:** as made super-famous by Nigel Kennedy (so popular he recorded it twice, once with the English Chamber Orchestra in 1989 and again in 2003 with the Berlin Philharmonic Orchestra)

o **Mendelssohn:** one of the most accessible and melodic of all the violin concerti

o **Elgar:** a brooding masterpiece

o **Beethoven:** the first movement contains a distinctive repeated note which sounds audacious for the time it was written; to my mind this is Beethoven at his best

o **Tchaikovsky:** a virtuosic *tour de force* with a plangent central movement – one of the greats, if not the greatest work for the instrument from the nineteenth century

o **Bruch:** his First Violin Concerto is a work of enduring popularity and intense emotion

o **Brahms:** strident, passionate and showy, this is not my favourite concerto and I'd rank it somewhere below the other big Romantic violin concertos on melodic interest, but nevertheless the third and final movement makes up for it in energetic style

○ **Walton:** Original and, along with his viola concerto, worth exploring after you've tired of the rest of this list (if that's possible)

### Medium fast – slow – fast

Like a solid meal, much music is tripartite. We call each musical 'course' a *movement*. This is because each section has a different speed or feel, it *moves* differently, hence movement. For a beautiful example of works with three movements in perfect balance listen to Bach's Brandenburg Concerto No. 4 in G, BWV1049. Its three movements are:

| I. | Allegro (a lively speed) |
|------|---------------------------|
| II. | Andante (walking pace) |
| III. | Presto (fast) |

There is to me something eminently satisfactory about this pattern. Composers have used it in a variety of ways and even when a work has five movements the extra two merely support this classic beginning, middle and end structure.

## A–B–A

Not a misspelling of the Swedish pop group; this is a very common musical structure. The first section 'A' being established, the composer tests out new material 'B' before a return to the first section. This was all the rage in the Baroque era when singers would embellish the vocal line on the repeat. Most Handel operas contain A–B–A arias known as 'Da Capo' arias. *Da Capo* means 'from the beginning' (literally, 'from the head').

'Lascia Ch'io Pianga' from Handel's *Rinaldo* is a good example of this. In the film *Farinelli* about the famous castrato singer of Handel's era (look it up in a dictionary, I can't bring myself to define it here) the powerful effect of the embellishments in the repeat appears to completely unsettle Mr Handel who sweats profusely and has to remove his wig; such is the power of Farinelli's performance. As well as a viciously long high note, it's the effect of the musical structure that apparently overcomes the audience – music we have already heard sung up an octave and with greater emotional intensity than the first time. It's a bit hammy but it makes the point – this is a very successful musical structure.

### Ritornello

An earlier form than the sonata, the *ritornello* establishes the first theme, then we have a new section, then the first theme is repeated, then a new section, followed by the first theme again and so on. This can go on for as long as you like. The term *ritornello* means 'little return'. Obviously it is highly repetitive as the main theme 'returns' and 'returns', but this is mitigated by the new material sandwiched in between.

### Symphony

Symphony means 'sounds together', which is not a very helpful title at all and hardly suggests what you may be in for. In Handel's *Messiah* there is a rather pastoral section entitled 'Sinfonia' which gives us the seventeenth-century meaning of the word: back then it was merely a musical interlude or an overture. By the time of Mozart, Haydn and Beethoven it had become a formal structure that has remained the benchmark for composers ever since.

Traditionally the symphony is split into four movements or sections. The first is most likely to be the longest, followed by three less substantial sections. Either the second or the third will be slower than the first section, and one of them may well be a lighter piece called a *scherzo* (a musical joke – more frivolous in character). The final movement is nearly always faster and grander in scope. In later symphonies the final movement draws together the ideas of the preceding movements, sometimes using repetition of musical ideas.

- There are as many exceptions to this structure as there are symphonies.
- Many people have written ludicrously long symphonies, but fear not, you are unlikely to hear them. It's the musical equivalent of running the marathon in fancy dress, a nice idea in theory but hard work in practice.
- The longest symphonies are by the late Romantic composers, with Mahler's Third Symphony running to over ninety minutes. But it's unlikely to be paired with another piece so although this can be a bum-number it's full of variety and you'll be out in time for the last train.

## Chamber music

Music has always involved much solitary practice and the pleasure for a musician in finally being allowed out to play music with other people can be overwhelming, especially if, as the stereotype goes, they were kept in with the curtains closed by cruel parents intent on musical success whilst the other children skipped gaily and played conkers. My piano teacher organised chamber concerts for her students and it was there that I made my first public recitals. Chamber music is for small spaces, rooms in houses, museums, churches and small recital halls.

There are many configurations in chamber music:

- Solo instrument and piano (almost any instrument or voice)
- Piano duo (two pianos)
- Piano trio (violin, piano and 'cello)
- String quartet (two violins, viola and 'cello)
- Wind quintet (flute, oboe, clarinet, horn and bassoon)
- Brass quintet (two trumpets, horn, trombone and tuba)
- Septets, octets, etc., in various combinations
- Nonet (flute, oboe, clarinet, horn, bassoon, violin, viola, 'cello, double bass)

From salons of the nineteenth century to the intimate stage of the Wigmore Hall, chamber music offers a chance to focus on a small group of performers playing together. Good intonation (a musical word for tuning), tight ensemble playing (doing things together) and interesting interpretation (making good choices about how to play the music) are essential in a chamber performance. Players will form groups that stay together for years, developing an on-stage rapport (though off-stage tempers and egos may rule). It's a great example of musical teamwork: there is no conductor to make the decisions.

### Song cycle

A song cycle is a selection of songs linked by narrative or theme. This is a particular tradition of 'art song' as opposed to the more popular variety. There are two other countries with such a strong tradition that we use their words for song in those languages: *Lieder* (German) and *Mélodie* (French).

A good place to start is with Franz Schubert (1797–1828). Schubert wrote complex intertwining narrative song cycles which stand as great examples of the genre, such as *Die Schöne Müllerin*, in which an effete young man sets out on a journey of discovery, becomes an itinerant worker, falls in love with the boss's daughter, is passed over in favour of a handsome hunter and promptly throws himself into a watery grave, but not before singing about how upset he is. In *Winterreise* a young man sets out on a journey of discovery *following* the break-up of a relationship and walks bleakly out into the snow. The final song has a touch of the grim reaper about it. In the wrong hands this is the self-regarding Romantic nonsense that turns people off; the lyrics are of the pseudo-bucolic stuff that was fashionable at the time. But Schubert makes us care for the protagonists and creates music of beauty and simplicity that develops along their paths. The simplicity of the story is part of its appeal and the music and lyrics are beautifully balanced.

If Schubert is not expressive enough for your taste then I recommend *Dichterliebe* by Robert Schumann, Op. 48. It translates as 'the poet's love' and is the archetypal Romantic song cycle, featuring outpourings of grief and joy as well as much wandering through the flowers looking mournful.

Balance between the keyboard and the singer is part of the appeal of a recital of song. Watching the carefully planned interaction between a great exponent of song and their accompanist is akin to watching two tennis giants battle it out on centre court. But it's a partnership where neither is more important.

Where Schubert created integrated cycles, later composers grouped their songs more thematically and narratives become more fractured. Schumann tackled single narratives whilst Brahms and Wolf tend to collect together pieces by one poet. In twentieth-century song more often than not it's merely a selection of interconnected songs rather than a simple narrative. But the end is the same. You are watching two performers tell stories, present moods and create harmonious music.

Among the song cycle's greatest exponents:

- Brahms
- Henze (if you like things adventurous)
- Mahler
- Poulenc
- Schubert
- Schumann
- Vaughan Williams
- Wagner
- Wolf

### String quartet

If your only experience of the string quartet is in George Martin's brilliant arrangement on The Beatles' 'Eleanor Rigby' then you are in for a treat. The string quartet is a form in which there is huge variety. From Haydn to Ligeti many composers have used the limited instrumental palette as a canvas for experimentation.

The quartet comprises two violins, a viola and a 'cello. Whilst in the orchestra the first violin is called 'the leader', and as such is in a position of musical authority, this is not the case in a string quartet. At its ideal it's a democratic unity where each individual player contributes to a homogeneous sound. The repertoire is challenging: Beethoven especially pushed the string quartet during the latter part of his life; there is a great deal of personal fury to be heard in some of the 'late quartets', in particular No. 14 in C Sharp Minor, Op. 131, about which Schubert is said to have commented, 'After this, what is left for us to write?' Beethoven was deaf at the time of writing and he seems to have poured all of his experience and passion into a piece for just four musicians. There is a painful intensity and intimacy in these pieces.

There are many experimental twentieth-century string quartets but nothing makes me chuckle quite as much as that of radical composer Karlheinz Stockhausen (1928–2007). His piece Helikopter String Quartet requires that each member of the string quartet play in a helicopter in flight. A *different* helicopter for each player. The piece is not performed that often [Sound Link 69].

Other exponents of the string quartet:

- Mozart
- Schubert
- Haydn
- Bartók (adventurous)
- Shostakovich (dynamic)
- Elliot Carter (difficult)

### Theme and variations

As discussed in Chapter 6, Rachmaninov and Mozart both created sublime examples of 'theme and variations'. This is a popular exercise for composers: taking a simple musical idea or 'theme' and developing it through a series of 'variations' as the name would suggest.

### The sonata and 'sonata form'

There is a small confusion to be cleared up here. If you go to see a concert with a pianist playing solo works by Mozart or Beethoven it will most likely be *a sonata*. This means that it'll be a work with a number of movements, usually three or more. Now here's the confusion: it's possible that the first movement of the piece will adhere to a structure called *sonata form*. This is an established set of rules about how to write the first movement of a sonata.

All simple so far except that other forms of music, most notably the symphony, started to borrow the formal structure of sonata form and adapt it for full orchestra instead of the usual solo instrument. This is not *a* sonata but merely *in the form of a* sonata. Simple. So what is sonata form? Imagine the structure of a business meeting; they often have standard features: an agenda, approval of the minutes, any other business, date of the next meeting and so on. Sonata form is a structure just like that. Except that it relies on changes of key to work its magic.

The features of the sonata form are exposition, development and recapitulation (these are principles which are used in many forms of music but in sonata form there is a formal discipline to be studied and perfected).

- ○ **Exposition:** the composer sets out his stall and lets you hear the main themes
- ○ **Development:** the composer breathes new life into the themes, introduces new ones and crucially modulates (moves) to a different key (see Chapter 2 for more information about keys); this section builds in intensity towards the inevitable return to the ...
- ○ **Recapitulation:** the composer revisits the main theme in the original key.

There are many variations and adaptations to this form, definitions of which take up shelves of musical libraries. The key feature is the recapitulation – it's a brilliant word to bandy about at parties and very useful at concerts.

## Programme music and tone poems

When listening to music we are often left to make of it what we will. Programme music is the composer's attempt to direct our listening by explaining the artistic meaning of the piece through a title or text. In some cases the music is a literal attempt to represent something outside the realm of music: trees, birds, the sea, etc. In more complex Romantic examples it might represent a narrative, climbing a mountain or the journey of the soul through life; these works are known as *tone poems,* and are pieces on a symphonic scale but which have a non-musical dimension. Absolute music is the opposite, the composer rejects extra-musical definitions and writes purely abstract music. Some good examples of programme music are:

- Vivaldi: *The Four Seasons*
- Mussorgsky: *Pictures at an Exhibition*
- Debussy: *La Mer*
- Sibelius: *Finlandia*
- Mahler: Symphony No. 2, 'Resurrection'
- Richard Strauss: *Alpine Symphony*

## Opera

This is pretty simple and I think most people understand that opera is a play which is sung. The crucial distinction between an opera and a musical theatre piece is that opera usually has a full orchestra and almost never uses microphones. Musical theatre often uses amplification and pop vocal techniques which are absent in opera houses.

Opera is usually based on epic stories. The plots and characters are larger than life and the music is written to match the sense of drama. It is total theatre which at its best engages the audience emotionally, intellectually, musically and visually. If you are unlucky enough to see a bad one then it's four hours of the proverbial 'fat lady' screaming.

The development of opera in the last 400 years has left a legacy of music of stunning variety and potency. From the works of Monteverdi, through Mozart to Verdi, Rossini, Wagner and Strauss the world of opera has become an art-form in its own right. Many composers fear the writing of opera because of the demands placed on the composer and some write only one and never return to the genre. The demands of the theatre require music that supports the story and fills an entire evening of entertainment, much more work than writing one short piece for orchestra.

When opera is good it grips you by the throat and shakes you. Frank Skinner spoke of his surprising level of excitement at an opera in an interview on Radio Four's *Desert Island Discs* in 2010:

> I've got an office that I write in, and it's very close to the Royal Opera House in Covent Garden. I didn't know anything about opera, but I thought, as they're neighbours, I ought to go down and see what they're doing. So I went and saw *The Magic Flute*. I didn't get one of these 200 quid tickets – I paid 20 quid and sat in the upper amphitheatre.
>
> It started off and I was a bit bored, then this woman, the Queen of the Night, comes on and does this aria. I don't think I even knew the word aria at the time. She did things with the human voice that I couldn't believe were actually leaving another human being, and I realised I listened to the whole thing with my mouth open, I mean it completely blew me away.

## Oratorio

The oratorio was fashionable in London during the time Handel was living there. He stopped writing Italian operas with which he had much success and moved on to this new form which attracted healthy audiences.

An oratorio is a religious text or story set to music. In the hands of Handel, who had experience of dramatising operas through music, the oratorio is like an unstaged opera. Stories of Jeptha, Solomon, Saul, Deborah and Esther from the Bible were set to music. This proved extremely popular with the public. His most famous work, *The Messiah,* used text from the Bible to chronicle the life of Jesus and gave rise to some of his most beautiful writing. It was first performed in Dublin in 1742 but during the nineteenth-century choral boom it was performed up and down the country by choral societies (although strangely for many years it was in a re-orchestration by Mozart). It is still popular with choirs today and you are never more than a bus ride away from a performance.

## Cantata

A cantata is also a sung work (from the Latin *cantare* – to sing), usually religious in nature. They are fairly short, not on the same scale as an oratorio, and centre around one or more soloists. They will have a number of movements and may involve a choir (especially in the works of J.S. Bach). Despite the religious theme, they are poetic explorations of the Gospel rather than settings of religious texts.

## Recitative/aria/chorus

Opera, oratorio and cantatas all feature a form of singing called *recitative.* This means singing in the rhythm of speech as opposed to music that has a constant pulse; it has a sparse accompaniment, usually harpsichord and 'cello. It literally means 'recitation' and the small number of instruments allow the text to come over clearly: vital in storytelling. Once the important information has been communicated there is time for reflection on the action which often takes the form of an *aria,* a solo vocal piece. The aria will have richer accompaniment than the recitative and isn't in speech rhythms. This may be followed by a chorus, which is when the choir sings.

# Part 3

# PERFORMING
# AND SURVIVING

# Chapter 10

# The Singers not the Songs

> " *The soul of man is audible, not visible.* "

HENRY WADSWORTH LONGFELLOW

## Singing

If you've had your eyes sown shut for the last five years you might be unaware of *The X-Factor*, a popular and gladiatorial television talent show featuring a brutally honest judge in the form of Simon Cowell. People often ask me if I like *The X Factor*. As a musician and educator I do have certain misgivings about how it promotes the notion that instant fame and glory are available simply by opening your mouth to give a mangled rendition of 'Hero' by Mariah Carey. I have a very real sense of distaste as we are encouraged to laugh at people who, for reasons of mental health or disability, are unable to put on a performance which matches the standards set by previous musical luminaries Leona Lewis, Steve Brookstein and that short Scottish one whose name escapes me.

However, I must admit that I do derive a certain guilty pleasure when watching people's performances being savaged by Cowell. In order to improve as any kind of singer you have to take on criticism from every side and be prepared to bounce back. I think it's because I have been through the grinder myself that I love to watch other people suffer the same torment. Studying singing was without doubt the hardest thing I've ever done. Every day I would bound into the Royal Academy full of hope, and then I'd have my performance picked over by musical coaches, pianists, singing teachers, opera dialogue coaches and a plethora of highly critical but brilliant individuals. It was exhausting: we sang for hours every day and in several different languages. We forced down a plate of cold chips before rehearsing opera scenes into the night. I went home shattered. What's more, I paid for the privilege. These were some of the happiest experiences of my life: I was challenged, I improved, I gained the respect of my peers and tutors (I hope!) and was rewarded for my efforts. I'd do it all again tomorrow but I'm not sure I'd go on *The X Factor*.

Most of my friends who are classical singers eschew the instant route to success and continue their ongoing, self-evaluative learning for their entire careers – always acquiring new pieces, always going to teachers to help them improve. It's a skill honed over years, not weeks, in the privacy of a practice room, not under the glare of a TV camera. My friend Catherine Hopper (a mezzo-soprano) studied three years for a music degree, then spent a year studying in Germany, followed by two years on the postgraduate course at the Royal Academy of Music, followed by two years on their opera course. After that she spent a final year at the National Opera Studio. That's nine years of study after school, which is fairly standard for classical singers. Not to say that she's finished studying: she will need to learn the major roles that she hopes to perform throughout her career – a difficult task in itself – though in my mind she's already peaked; she sang at my wedding. In comparison to that degree of scrutiny, a couple of harsh words from Simon Cowell seems like nothing.

Classical singing is not the same as other types of singing because it's not meant to be listened to through a microphone, it's designed to fill large spaces and have a visceral effect on the listener. It's expressive, bold and varied. Whilst pop singers must have 'pleasing' voices which communicate well on CD, opera singers must fill a range of roles, playing everything from villain to hero during their career. They must sing song cycles which run the gamut of human emotion for which they need athletic technique – operas are long and physically demanding – and a gut full of life experience.

Many opera singers begin their lives as choristers before their instrument develops sufficiently to fill an opera house. Choral singing is a very different discipline. Where an opera singer is encouraged to develop individual qualities in their voice, a choral singer must blend with the rest of the choir. Professional choristers, like orchestral musicians, must be ready to sight-read music from any era and perform it to a very high standard. There are a small number of highly talented professional choral singers in the country who flit from one choir to another and if you look carefully you can spot members of one choir moonlighting in another. It can be a hand-to-mouth existence for many, but few go into singing for the money, they do it mostly for the love of the music. This is a love which develops at an early age – many start singing as probationers (on a short trial period) at around eight.

Cathedral choirs are mostly composed of boys, though girls are gaining ground, notably in Wells Cathedral under the tutelage of Master of the Choristers, Matthew Owens. The boys' choir of Wells Cathedral recently celebrated its 1100th – yes, 1100th – birthday; boys first sang there in 909. The girls' choir is a recent innovation: 1994. You have to admire the progressiveness! The boys' choir has been endowed with money and sponsorship for some years and is therefore financially secure, whereas the girls' choir hasn't had time to build up a source of funds, so if you are a feminist who wants to support girls' choral singing you know where to send the cheque.

Recently I was asked to compose a song for a York Cathedral chorister, Isabel Suckling, who had recently signed a record deal with Decca – she was the first girl chorister to do so. Though she hasn't yet reached the popularity of former boy choristers Aled Jones (famous for 'Walking in the Air') and Anthony Way (who recorded 'O for the Wings of a Dove' in the 1990s), there's no question that the idea that girls can sing is gaining ground in traditional choral circles. It's ironic really that it can be so hard to get boys to sing in this country (I speak from bitter experience) and yet the sound of their voices is so cherished. I believe there is a difference between boys' and girls' voices: speaking *very* generally, boys' choirs have a cut-glass, ringing quality while girls' choirs are often smoother. I believe I could tell the difference in a blind test, before you ask. For me the reason that listening to boys sing is so especially poignant is because that sound is so finite. Once they have reached puberty the game is up.

One man who knows about the effect of this change on his pupils is Ralph Allwood, precentor at Eton College, which means that he is in charge of music in the act of worship. A few years ago he invited me to Eton to see a stunning performance of Bach's *Magnificat* performed by Eton's star choristers and conducted by one of the students. Amongst them was a cherubic boy who sang the sublime '*Quia respexit humilitatem*' ('For He hath regarded the lowliness of His handmaiden'). He sang it with an almost adult assurance, an impossibly solid technique and the sort of tone that makes grown men weep (well, this grown man anyway).

A couple of months later I was on the phone to Ralph and mentioned this wonderful performance, whereupon he related this story. The night before our conversation they'd had a regular rehearsal for the chapel choir. The boy in question had sung well but Ralph noticed a few unusual gravelly noises in the sound. After the rehearsal he casually mentioned to the boy, 'I think your voice might be beginning to change.' The thirteen-year-old boy shrugged and looked away. A few minutes later Ralph saw him standing in the corner, tears rolling silently down his face.

Whilst for many, growing up is a moment to look forward to (that first shave or a first trip with Dad to the pub), for choristers it's the last time they will ever sing the tune. They are fêted as the soloists for years and it's all over in a couple of gurgles. It's stories like this that lend a mystical significance to boys' singing. Girls on the other hand continue and grow in strength, arriving at vocal maturity in their late teens. I remember so clearly being able to sing a top 'A' in the soprano range with ease. I remember so clearly the day I couldn't.

Boys' careers are curtailed as hormones cause their vocal cords to expand rapidly. Voices do not break, I hasten to add – they merely grow bigger, resulting in those embarrassing squeaks until the young man learns to control his new instrument months or sometimes years later. Until that fateful day for the choristers of these choirs, it's a musical education *par excellence*. It's a daily diet of singing, vocal training and often access to an excellent private education; it can be a ticket into a wonderful world. Some finish singing aged around 12 or 13 as their voices start to descend but benefit from the discipline learnt in choirs as they pursue alternative careers, but many continue as music professionals as a direct result of this musical head start.

For example, my friend Tim Carleston (son of my aforementioned music teacher) has sung choral music all his life and from the humble beginnings as a boy at St Peter's Church in Bournemouth (and singing alongside me in school choir every day) he has won a highly prized position of lay-clerk at St George's, Windsor Castle. Not only does he get to sing the most beautiful music from a seat in the 'Quire' (an archaic word for choir stalls) which was completed in 1484, but he gets to live *in* Windsor Castle, although not actually with the Queen. Knowing his temperament, and the temperament of many choristers like him, this cloistered life suits him perfectly. Being in a cathedral-style choir like this is about singing to the best of your ability but putting your voice at the service of worship. That means blending with the other singers to create a sound that seems celestial because no individual could create it. It is the definition of Utopia.

And then they all go down the hill to Windsor for a pint and a Sunday roast.

## Inside the choir

All this talk of choirs may make you wonder how they actually function. The most common form is known as SATB – that's an acronym for soprano/alto/tenor/bass, which are the four major voice types. Numbers of singers vary from around twelve in really small choral ensembles who are usually very confident, to 150 in the large choral societies. In between there is a whole rainbow of different choirs: barbershop, folk, glee clubs, jazz choir, gospel, women's barbershop, children's choir, youth choir; anything is possible. Many choirs are now singing a wider range of music than ever before but I'll restrict myself here to talking about classical choirs.

Before Christmas in 2010 for their annual festive concert I joined the tenor section of the Voce Chamber Choir, a youthful, zesty outfit run by a brilliantly vivacious conductor called Suzi Digby (Lady Eatwell), OBE. The singers are amateur but most of them have sung in high-quality youth choirs or church choirs for most of their lives and some were choral scholars at university. The standard is high. Since it was Christmas Suzi had chosen a range of festive music from 'In Dulci Jubilo' by Samuel Scheidt (1587–1654) to 'White Christmas' by Irving Berlin (1888–1989), written in 1940.

We began to sing and within about an hour of rehearsals I felt part of the team and by the third week I was helping with handing out the music like I'd been there all my life – it's a friendly choir. But even with these committed, auditioned singers it was still necessary for Suzi to crack the whip during rehearsal and that's because, no matter what level people sing at, they enjoy the social experience. One singer was passing chocolates round, several were extremely keen to finish bang on 9 p.m. to guarantee them time for a pint in the pub and, as in most choirs, several relationships had formed. There are leaders who encourage everyone to knuckle down, there are the keen ticket sellers (one had sold 35 tickets to her friends and family), there are the serious singers, the jokers and those who are there for the fun: it's a microcosm of society.

In rehearsal we struggled with the style of a jazzy Christmas number, looked pained as we messed up a difficult modern composition for the third week running, and busted our larynxes aiming for the high notes, just as every other choir in the country – that's what rehearsals are like. Gradually the pieces came into focus. From our tentative read-through in the first week, it was starting to sound like music. As a member of the tenor section I became aware of how my part fitted together with the other singers. Come the concert, we sounded pretty good, if I say so myself, and the audience obviously enjoyed it too. From the opening solo of 'Once in Royal David's City' I had a thrill of excitement at singing in a choir for the first time in five years – I've been exclusively conducting them during that time. Singing is totally different from conducting and much better than watching.

Suzi's obvious delight with us was immensely rewarding and I was reminded of the times when members of my own choirs ask me eagerly after every performance, 'Are you proud of us?' and 'Did we do well?' I genuinely wanted to please my conductor, and this is a common part of the experience of singing in a choir. Happily, after this concert there was a tremendous feeling of a job well done. There'd been some very sensitive music-making, some truly beautiful moments and I found the whole experience very moving. And afterwards we all tucked into a well-earned mince pie and a shockingly alcoholic mulled wine as the lights of Mayfair twinkled outside. Now that for me is Christmas, and Christmas isn't Christmas without a choir.

## Operatic singing

*Natural amplification: the secret of operatic vocal mastery*
In the Voce Chamber Choir, as with most choirs, vocal purity is prized because that is the style of singing that helps reveal the intricacies of choral harmonies. If one person's voice is bigger than another's then this precious blend cannot be achieved. After hearing the still, even tone of choral singing it can seem a shock to hear the more fulsome tone of the classical opera singer. How did this enormous, boisterous style develop?

Opera was invented before microphones and it was popular enough to require major international houses to be built with seats for thousands of people. A good opera singer uses the natural resonance of the voice to be heard over an orchestra. How is this possible? Well, there is an almost magical attribute of the voice called 'the singer's formant' which is an acoustic property allowing the voice to 'cut through like a hot knife in butter', to use my singing teacher's expression; it's that twangy sound that opera singers have. Whilst an orchestra might be very loud at certain frequencies, the opera singer creates sound energy at frequencies above the level of the instruments. Remember, I'm not talking about volume – although it is perhaps perceived as 'louder' than the other instruments. If you're struggling to understand this three-dimensional concept of loudness then put it this way: it's the aural equivalent of somebody wearing pastel shades and putting on a DayGlo hat. You don't notice the softer-coloured shades because they don't interfere with your vision in the way that something fluorescent does. The hat reflects light at different frequencies just as different instruments emit different frequencies of sound. As human beings our brains and ears are perfectly set up to respond to the frequency of the human voice even when there is other noise around; think of trying to hold a conversation in a nightclub or a busy high street.

In order for an opera singer to achieve this magical effect and be heard over a full orchestra they must have very precise control over their larynx, which must be in a very particular position. Get it wrong and you won't be heard. It takes years of practice to achieve true mastery of this ability, and to hear a high-quality operatic voice live is to understand why they simply do not need a microphone.

### Wobbly opera voices and tight-throated pop singers

The singer's 'vibrato' is a hotly debated aspect of singing. It is often caricatured, and can be off-putting for an audience when it is extreme. However, the voice is not the only instrument that 'wobbles': strings, woodwind and brass all have a little vibrato in their sound. When a baby is highly distressed and making a plaintive cry there is a slight vibrato to the sound. This is because vibrato is a natural facet of the human voice: in trying to achieve the 'singer's formant' (see above) the vocal tract and airways will be in perfect alignment and this naturally produces vibrato.

Although we have come to think of the 'wobbly opera voice' as being unnatural and the straight-toned pop style as natural, it is in fact the other way round – although many would disagree. A pop singer or early music singer, who for artistic reasons employs a straight tone, is doing so by using tensions in the throat and face muscles. These tensions are, vocally speaking, 'unnatural' and the opera singer seeks to eliminate them in order to increase the resonance and size of the voice.[1] That's not to say that it's wrong to sing with a pop voice but if longevity can be considered an indicator of 'the right way' to sing, then opera singers definitely have the edge. Pavarotti retired in his sixties and Plácido Domingo is still singing at 69 years of age (albeit slightly lower than before). Name me one pop singer who sounds nearly as good at 60 as they did in their in their twenties.

Old rock singers regularly give the high notes to the crowd to sing. This is not generosity on their part – they simply can't hit the notes any more because the small muscles of the neck and face will no longer support the voice. Paul McCartney, Robert Plant and Jon Bon Jovi cannot sing top notes in the way they

could in their youth, whereas Ben Heppner (b. 1956) is still banging out the top notes in his fifties. I experience pangs of regret on
behalf of young rock singers who sound like they are traumatis-
ing their voices. The instrument that is giving them and others so
much pleasure will eventually fail if pushed to its limits. So
who's singing in the right way?

Some poorly trained singers 'apply' vibrato deliberately in
what can only be described as a bad impression of an opera
singer. In the best examples the vibrato is inoffensive, in the
worst examples it sounds like a bad joke. Judicious use of a
vibrato which arises from a natural, open and honest singing
technique will never sound unpleasant in the concert hall,
backed by a full orchestra, although I'm not sure how well this
sound translates to a recording.

## Surtitles: neon words projected above the stage

If you go to most major opera houses they have surtitles for all
their performances (including ones in English). For many purists
it's a matter of regret that English National Opera (who perform
everything in English) chose to use surtitles; it was thought to be
an admission of defeat. In reality it takes a remarkable singer to
create performances that can be beautifully sung, heard above an
orchestra and entirely understood. Plus the technology is cheap
and available to give the audience every single word with neon
brightness.

To my mind, I don't think it matters in the case of opera
because it's so different from watching a play. Much of the
dramatic interest is suggested by the orchestral music, the lyrical
lines of the voice and in the staging. It doesn't need to be quite as
audible as the dialogue in a Shakespeare play which would make
no sense whatsoever without the text – could you understand
*Henry IV* if it were recited in Chinese? But in opera this happens
all the time, when Rodolfo sings 'Che Gelida Manina' to Mimi as
he holds her hands and she shivers, we all know that he's fallen

in love with her and that she's cold without studying the libretto (words) beforehand.

Singing is about making beautiful sounds, not just getting the text across, and although the ideal is to have both, many singers have had huge careers despite having moments of unintelligibility. Joan Sutherland, who died in 2010, had a profoundly wondrous voice and sang with incredible musicianship, but was often criticised for her lack of diction. Her style was *Bel Canto* (Italian for 'beautiful singing') and she put clarity of the musical line above all other considerations. It hardly held back her career. However, I think the fashion has changed and singers are now required to be actors as well. It is not unusual to find in the performances of intelligent singers, like English baritone Simon Keenlyside, clarity of text, beauty of musical line and convincing acting. But if you can't understand what he sings you can glance up at the surtitles should you choose.

## Singing live from the heart: *you have to be there*

There are aspects of singing which are inexplicable and barely understood by scientists. How does our imagination imbue our voice with emotion and colour? How can we put our 'heart' into our singing? And yet any listener can hear if a singer is possessed of these qualities. Classical songs exist as a showcase for the artist's skill but the artist puts their skill at the service of the songs; it's a symbiotic relationship and when it works I defy anyone to be disinterested. To hear Renée Fleming, Cecilia Bartoli, Plácido Domingo, Thomas Quasthoff, Bryn Terfel or any other master of their trade singing live is an unforgettable experience. Their voices explode from the stage and you can sense their humanity in every phrase.

I'm not denigrating the art of recording – after all, it's how most of us experience music on a daily basis and it enables us to hear singers who are no longer with us. But it is merely a shade or spectre of the real thing. If you've ever ridden a horse through the countryside and then watched the horse racing live on TV or perhaps been present at a football match and then listened via Radio 5 Live on a crackly old medium-wave wireless, then you'll understand the difference in experience. Voices physically resonate in the singer's body and set up sympathetic resonance in the bodies of the audience. People who haven't heard classical singing live haven't heard classical singing at all.

# Chapter 11

# Taking Up the Baton: Conductors

66 *God tells me how the music should sound, but you stand in the way.* 99

Conductor ARTURO TOSCANINI
to members of the orchestra

'Why is that man waving his arms around?' is a question I hear children ask at family concerts, and although adults stop asking the question some may not fully know the answer. I will come to the nuts and bolts of baton waving later in the chapter, but first let's look at the typical life of a conductor, what he or she actually does and what he or she is responsible for. I've left the conductor until this late in the book because the role only developed recently in musical history. It was only when music became more complex and the orchestra so large that one person was essential to run the rehearsals and keep time in the concert, but now this arm-waving has become an art-form.

Conducting can be a lonely business. At most venues the conductor is given a huge backstage room with a piano and a sofa, whereas the instrumentalists are all crammed into shared, noisy dressing rooms. At the top levels conductors fly in a few days before the concert and are put up in a hotel for the duration of the rehearsals. From then on all their concentration is on the piece. That means discussions in the break backstage over a coffee with a member of the orchestra's backstage team: Could we move the harp a little so I can see the percussionists? Is there any chance the stage lights could be dimmed a little? The choir are a little out of tune at bar 158, could they sort that out please? And many other sundry musical matters that must be ironed out before the concert. They may be accompanied by a member of their management team or an assistant conductor but their families are likely to be in a different city or country.

During rehearsals the mood is businesslike but friendly – you'll hear the sort of small talk that you'd expect in any office before a meeting. Once the orchestra manager has made any small announcements it's over to the conductor who will usually have three hours, with a short break, to get through the material for the concert as they see fit. If they want to they don't have to play through every note; it's up to them, and most conductors will spend more time focusing on the difficult bits. Rehearsals are workaday and everybody knuckles down to getting things right – this can take a couple of goes as people make small fluffs even with familiar pieces; these are mostly self-corrected. As the break approaches the players get twitchy and stare at their watches; the conductor must be attentive to this because it's hard work for the players to concentrate for a long time without a break – plus union rules are clear on these matters. If a player is only playing in one movement, as can be the case with solo instruments, then the conductor may permit them to leave once their piece has been done, otherwise they may have to sit with a well-hidden newspaper on the music stand. I know one violinist who learnt Japanese during the short breaks in rehearsals while the conductor was addressing the other sections of the orchestra. Some players are on their BlackBerrys; others may even dare to get on to Twitter and tweet details of the concert.

From then on the conductor must keep themselves calm before the big event. The orchestra will get something to eat and avoid alcohol. Then they'll change into their concert outfit. For me this is a crucial stage in preparing for a concert, the equivalent of putting on armour before battle; it makes you feel ready. Some conductors will look over the score; some will meditate; and Sir Colin Davis will do a few lines of knitting.

The concert manager – a non-playing member of the orchestra's team – claps his or her hands loudly through the backstage area which is the signal for the orchestra to go to the platform. The atmosphere is energised and jovial but underneath there is a deadly serious sense of purpose; nevertheless discussions about TV, food, schools, children and politics continue through the door into the auditorium that wouldn't sound out of place at a middle-class dinner party.

The conductor meanwhile is alone. There is always a mirror backstage for a last-minute vanity check (including the all-important check that your trousers are zipped up for the men and that there is no danger of a Judy Finnigan moment for the ladies). The stage manager receives 'clearance' from front of house, which means the audience are in place and growing impatient in their seats. It is time. After a final deep breath, a lackey starts the applause backstage to indicate to the audience that the maestro is entering. The concert has begun.

Is the conductor really all that important? It's a moot point. There's no doubt that mythologising of the conductor is of benefit to the marketing departments of orchestras. Many a brooding A1 size poster of a conductor leers at you from billboard hoardings – when Sir Simon Rattle arrived in Berlin for a new appointment they put his picture up at every bus stop; this rarely happens for a lowly member of the viola section. But what is the benefit of the conductor to the orchestra, and does it actually make any difference to the sound? Explaining to non-musicians what a conductor does isn't easy – it's like explaining what a film director or producer does, so we need to step back a little. Before I look at the conductor it's necessary to explain how music came to be written down: the interpretation of the musical score is what a conductor concerns themselves with and without a score they'd have nothing to do.

## The evolution of the score

Once upon a time there was only singing and banging sticks against other sticks. Once *Homo sapiens* developed the ability to remember short phrases, repetition and inculcation over millennia brought music to a crucial stage of development that mirrors the move from an oral society to a literate one.

Religious chanting in churches became notated (written down) from around the ninth century. In non-Western cultures there were earlier attempts at notation but the Western classical tradition is about 1,000 years old. Prior to the invention of notation, the methods by which one musician would entrain another

Plainchant – a relatively simple form of musical scoring.[1]

would have been through a mixture of copying, speech and gesture. Select members of the Church would hold hundreds of melodies in their minds and pass them on to the next generation, a process which is less reliable than writing it down. After all how many people can remember the words to the second verse of the national anthem ... and the third verse?

At first the notation was simple – denoting movement up or down the scale – but it developed into a complex system of *fixing* a melody, and subsequently its rhythm. The score has evolved into one of the most visually beautiful aspects of music. At Handel House, a museum in London in the building where Handel lived, they have copies of the composer's handwritten opera scores. In one of the exhibits you can listen to the music played on CD and follow the dots and squiggles as he wrote them by candlelight. There was a telling page where he finished one

A section from the autograph score of Handel's *Jeptha*.[2]

opera on 24 December and the start date for the next opera was 26 December on the next page; clearly he was a workaholic and you can see that energy and passion in his notation. There are frequent crossings out and the angle that the notes are written at suggests that the music was pouring out of his head on to the paper.

Modern performers can sing music going back 1,000 years because today's notation is merely a more complex version of those early dots and squiggles. The system is pretty simple to understand; when the dots go up, the notes go up, when the dots go down, so do the notes. Whether a note has a tail or a dot after tells the musician how long to play it for. That way a musician can recreate the music on the page as if it had just been composed.

Prelude from Bach's Cello Suite No. 1.

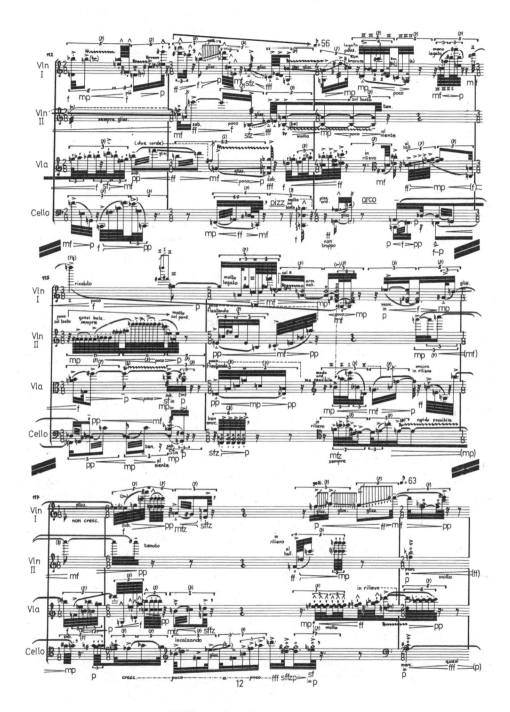

Mr Ferneyhough ...

Oh, and a page from Cornelius Cardew's opus magnus 'Treatise', a 193-page graphic score, written between 1963 and 1967 ...

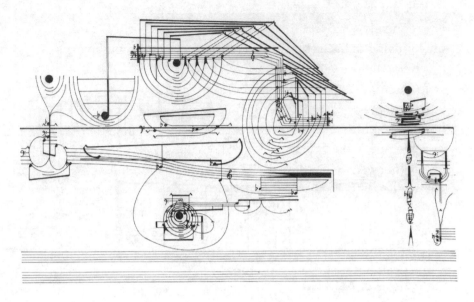

Excerpt from Cornelius Cardew's 'Treatise' (1963–67).

So what does the conductor do with the score if the players themselves can read the notes? I suspect that as long as there has been singing there have been hand movements to indicate pitch and dynamics. It's impossible to say exactly how it was done but conducting is an extension of two very natural human impulses: to communicate with gesture and to move to music or rhythm. From this natural basis, conducting has become formalised concomitantly with advances in musical notation. It was not until the nineteenth century that music reached a level of complexity that necessitated the role of the conductor. As music became more organised and reliant on the written page rather than memory or improvisation, so performers were required to learn the discipline of score reading. In addition music began to have more changes of speed which require one person to dictate the *tempo* (Italian for 'speed'). The necessity of a conductor became inevitable: there is a point in every team where one person has to take overall responsibility. As in all walks of life, the style and manner of their leadership depend greatly on the individual. For a long time this would have been one of the players themselves, a violinist shaking their head or a keyboard player using their eyebrows at important moments, but eventually it *had* to be a separate role.

In the modern musical world of international concert tours where orchestras play different concert programmes every few nights, a conductor is essential in keeping music together and running rehearsals. Many orchestral musicians probably wish it were otherwise when they are dealing with conductors they do not respect, but on the other hand they wouldn't know how to do without the ones they love. Most musicians would agree that somebody has to take the lead, and having this person be a non-playing member of the musical team gives them greater mental scope to attend to the overall sound.

I will explore how the role of conductor became the megalith that it is today later in the chapter. First, let's clear up what they actually *do.*

## How do the hand movements relate to the music?

In the simplest terms, big hand movements mean loud and small ones mean soft. In addition to that, one hand keeps the pulse going. A conductor may also signal to members of the orchestra when it's their turn to play and the manner in which they should do so, when to start and when to stop; and that's it.

If it's that simple why is so much fuss made of them? Well, perfecting this art is extremely complicated. They aim to communicate with an economy of gesture so that the players can easily understand what is intended – not as easy as it might sound. A conductor will practise their hand gestures until they communicate with efficiency. If a player can't detect a pulse amongst a conductor's wild gesticulations then it's as good as useless. It may appear as if they are waving their hands around theatrically (and some do!) but the best conductors make no movements by accident; everything has a meaning and is of use to the musicians, helping them to make music. It's a more technical and less flouncy profession than it looks.

" *With a good conductor musical contact can be so strong that musicians react to the slightest movement of his hand, his finger, his eye or his body. If the orchestra is at one with the conductor, they play differently if he stands up straight, or bends forward, or sideways or backwards. They are influenced by every movement.*[3] "

DANIEL BARENBOIM

That said, it's not a mathematical process and a conductor must react to the instrumentalists in front of him instead of merely imposing a predetermined vision upon them.

## Keeping time

Let's lift the lid of the orchestra and look inside. The conductor's most important role is in keeping all the musicians in time. This is not as easy as it sounds. Because of the size of modern orchestras and the delay caused by the relatively slow speed of sound travelling from the back of the orchestra to the front, discrepancies in timing can easily emerge. It's also nearly 100 people all playing different parts; that's a giant juggernaut to keep on the road.

To combat the distance problem many conductors began to use a white stick called a 'baton'. Although there is a reference to the use of a 'slender and well-polished wand' by nuns in San Vito

Lo Capo in 1594, it really became commonly used in the nineteenth century. This enabled players at the back of the orchestra to clearly see the beat out of the corner of their eyes. That's why most of the time it appears that the orchestra is not watching the conductor. Musicians become adept at keeping the beat in their peripheral vision whilst still reading the musical score. It's not easy, but drivers display a similar skill using their peripheral vision to watch the side of the road. It's not always a conscious activity and it's a skill that is learnt over years.

Percussionists, who are nearly always at the back of the orchestra, are able to play according to what they see, not what they hear. That means in practice that from a percussionist's perspective it might *sound* as if they are playing slightly early, but by the time the sound has travelled to the audience along with the sound of the rest of the orchestra it all evens out. Imagine the courage it takes to play your instrument *earlier* than might sound correct to you, having faith that it will sound right to the audience. That level of musical chutzpah is required of all orchestral musicians. This is teamwork to the finest degree. Its football equivalent is knowing exactly when to cross the ball so that the centre forward will be able to time his attack. We are talking about milliseconds. Most listeners will be unaware that this process is going on all the time in the orchestra, and to be honest it should be that way.

More complex music requires the musicians to speed up and slow down together – a feat almost impossible without one person setting the pace. If the musicians were to guess it could easily descend into chaos.

All quite simple so far. But then comes the advanced part: orchestral conductors show the pulse ahead of the beat. That means that they conduct fractionally early. Non-musicians can find this befuddling and I must admit I struggled with the logic for a long time. The reason for this apparent madness is that when beating ahead a conductor can show the orchestra how the music is about to change; this gives the players milliseconds to react and speed up and slow down accordingly. If they were beating and playing at exactly the same moment there would be no way to show how the music was changing until it had already changed, by which point it would be too late. If you were to remove the yellow light from a set of traffic signals you'd have the same effect – it would be impossible for drivers to know the precise moment that the lights go from green to red without advance warning.

Try to watch a conductor carefully next time you are at a concert (not one on television because sometimes the sound and the picture are not exactly together and very often the camera moves from the conductor at the crucial moment). You will notice that 99 per cent of their job is in anticipating the changes in the music, whether in speed or in other aspects such as dynamics or mood. That means that a conductor must know the music better than anybody else in the orchestra. They must be able to predict how the music is going to shift from one moment to the next and demonstrate that with their hands; they literally lead the orchestra through the music. Often conductors will learn the music by heart, allowing them to focus on the musicians more directly. This is why they get the big bucks.

In rehearsal of works for a very large orchestra and choir, a conductor will often have an assistant sitting in the audience seats. This person fulfils a crucial role. Their ears help determine whether the sound of all the instruments of the orchestra and singers will reach the listeners. In some cases this is very difficult to achieve – where a large number of loud instruments (especially the brass instruments) are playing at the same time as quieter ones (violins, singers, etc.) the result can be that one is obscured by the other. The responsibility for this lies with the conductor. They must *balance* the sounds to create a homogeneous whole. This can change with different concert halls because of the difference in acoustic. A few weeks ago I rehearsed my South Oxhey Choir in a church with a full orchestra. The sound was perfectly balanced and from the front I could hear everything. Once we got to the venue (Central Hall, Westminster) it became obvious that there were balance issues. These were caused by the domed roof which reflected the sound of the orchestra to the audience but not the sound of the choir. It was simple to remedy – I asked the orchestra to play quieter and the choir to sing up. Had we not had a short 'balance rehearsal' in the hall then we'd only have found out when it was too late: after the concert. As it was, the balance was fine.

Balance can go wrong when musicians get carried away with their own part, for instance if it's technically demanding or a really big tune that they enjoy playing very loudly. They then lose concentration on the overall sound of the orchestra; if your section of the orchestra is providing accompaniment to another section then it is vital that you don't play too loudly. A conductor will try to achieve the correct balance during rehearsal by asking players to listen to other parts at certain points (in a solo, for example). The player will often scribble a mark on their music score as a reminder (this is why you'll see pencil scribbles all over sheet music) and if that fails in the heat of the moment, as players get carried away and do not notice that the fragile balance has slipped, a quick hand gesture usually sorts it out. This can also be an error in the composition, where the composer's grasp of the relative volumes of the instruments is not as sharp as it should be and their beautiful piccolo melody is obscured by twelve horns. A conductor will make the necessary adjustments so that we can hear what the composer intended (or at least what the conductor *thinks* the composer intended).

## The amateur chorus: 'Just sing the notes'

Most of my conducting experience is with amateur singers and I've found them to be very different from professional musicians. You'd expect the musical standards of professionals to be higher and that is most often the case except in some rare examples of formidable amateur/semi-pro ensembles. But what I've found is that teaching people to be in a choir when they have never sung before reveals just how complex a business classical music is. Before any singing is attempted I have to get people used to reading the score, explaining how to follow the many dots and squiggles. It can take people about a year to grow accustomed to reading music but it's definitely worth the effort; in South Oxhey there was real panic about the sheet music at first and people demanded lyrics instead. Now they have become used to sheet music I don't think they'd want to go back to the lyric-only approach because it's actually *easier* to read a score once you know how. For amateurs the most important factor is inspiration; they have to *want* to sing the music, and that means exciting them first. I try to sing some of the piece or play them a CD and then talk to them about the composer – just enough to whet the appetite. Finally there's nothing like setting a challenge to get everyone pulling in the right direction: 'In six weeks you'll be singing this at …'

Amateur choral societies are required to sing in diverse languages: German, French, English, Italian, Latin, Russian, Czech, Hungarian and so on. They tackle music by composers from throughout musical history. If they are frightened of the piece then a choir will simply stare balefully at the sheet music, hoping for divine intervention. This is exactly what a conductor does not want, and it's the reason that whenever possible conductors love choirs to sing from memory. Sir Georg Solti was a famously fiery character and when conducting the London Philharmonic Choir he ran into this problem, as recalled by choir member Sheila Lewis in a book about the choir's long and colourful history:

We were on our own [*without Solti*] when we rehearsed Bartók's *Cantata Profana* in Hungarian. Hungarian isn't like any other language and it was impossible to memorise the words. At the […] rehearsal Solti was horrified to find that the choir weren't watching his beat because they had their heads down in their scores. Finally he could bear it no longer. 'Never mind the bloody Hungarian,' shouted the furious Hungarian, 'just sing the notes!'[4]

Conductors are like racehorses. They are highly trained and in constant demand. They are used to working with professional musicians of the highest standard. This works well for them as they buzz all over the world conducting the orchestral repertoire. There is a different skill involved in working with one of Britain's many amateur choral societies.

The formation of the great Victorian choral societies, such as the Huddersfield Choral Society formed in 1836, the Royal Choral Society in 1871 and the Bach Choir in 1876, led to a huge fashion for amateur singing. The building of the Royal Albert Hall is evidence of the desire for really whopping choirs: there are 450 seats in the choir section. For a conductor to handle that many amateur singers requires an inspiring manner and incredible diplomacy because amateur singers are there for the love of music and not for their day job: their perspective is completely different. To sing at their best they need to be inspired, cajoled and encouraged, whereas professional players are expected to give of their best automatically.

Conductors must deal with singers and players differently. In my early days of singing with the Bournemouth Symphony Chorus we were performing at the Bridgewater Hall in Manchester under the baton of an orchestral conductor (it's often referred to as *under the baton* and rarely *with the conductor*). In rehearsal we were prepared by the then chorus master, Neville Creed, whose conducting style was ideal for us nervous amateurs who were singing from memory, in German and in a strange town. His every gesture communicated faith in our singing; he breathed with us, his face was fully turned towards us and his arms showed all 150 of us exactly when to sing.

When the concert approached, as is normal, the orchestral conductor took over from the chorus master. This conductor was more used to dealing with instrumentalists and brought us in for our big moment in Mahler's Second Symphony as if we were the second violins. He did this with the tiniest gesture I have ever seen, so nobody in the choir knew when to breathe or sing. In the concert we were on the edge of our seats, waiting for this tiny gesture. Now that may have been the conductor's intention – to make us all watch very, very carefully – but I can still remember the terror of that moment. There is a story of a foolhardy American orchestral musician who brought binoculars to a rehearsal with a particularly unclear conductor. When asked why he had binoculars, the musician joked that he was looking for the beat. He was fired.

Joking aside, a professional musician must have absolute faith in their ability and play with a great degree of confidence, given only the slightest encouragement from the conductor. Even if the conductor forgets to bring them in, professional musicians will still play – they read the score with authority and derive a feeling of collective fortitude from the other players. This is not always the case in amateur choirs, especially with difficult new works. During my final concerts with the Bournemouth Symphony Chorus we tackled John Adams's *Harmonium*, a Minimalist piece that requires a high degree of rhythmic assurance and the ability to count accurately because the time signature (the number of beats in the bar) changes regularly. The choir were in near revolt over this seemingly impossible task and it took all Neville Creed's skill to reassure us that we *could* sing this music. However, I still remember staring fixedly at my score, counting the beats furiously through the music; it was a white-knuckle ride.

66 *You must have the score in your head, not your head in the score.* 99

HANS VON BÜLOW

For me conducting has always been a tool born out of my music education work for trying to get more out of people than they believe they can give. I think that's true, whatever level you are working at. Sometimes this is best done with humour, gently teasing a response from a choir. Sometimes I have to be tough and make people work harder – it's a balance that takes years to master. When I came down too hard on them they'd all go home despondent, so I used to try to keep everybody happy at all times. But I quickly learnt that this is part of the process – many times singers have spoken to me after eight weeks of rehearsal and said that they had been worried about a piece when we first started. Without the worry they won't work hard to learn it: scaring them is sometimes necessary and in the end the means are justified by the final performance where hopefully everyone is elated by their achievement. Conductors have to be cruel to be kind.

## What did the composer mean?
## What is interpretation?

This may sound like an easy question to answer – a waltz is a waltz, right? In reality there are many variables in music that must be agreed on by the conductor and the orchestra. How much energy does a piece require? How should you articulate the melody? (You can vary the stresses in the same way that you can in speech.) What is the precise mood of the music? How does the mood of one section affect the mood of the next (going from dark to light, joyous to elegiac, for example)? – and so on.

These are not mathematical certainties, neither are they entirely matters of personal taste on the part of the conductor. They are human decisions, revealing much about the conductor's musical influences, character and musicianship. This is the art of interpretation. It means looking at the dots and squiggles of a musical score and deciding how it should sound.

## 'IT'S STARTING TO SOUND LIKE MOZART'

During my six years as conductor of the London Symphony Orchestra St Luke's Community Choirs I had occasion to give a lot of feedback to the singers. One very sneakily wrote some of them down and sent me this list.

- Broadly speaking, there was a lot right with that.
- All there is to singing is vowels and consonants. If you get that, the rest will follow … I hope.
- You've got to sing before you're singing. [*explaining how to start a line with a consonant*]
- It doesn't matter what G it is, but it's got to be the same one within the choir.
- It's starting to sound like Mozart.
- Five points for pitch. I won't tell you how many points you got for rhythm.
- You are the carpet upon which they sit. [*to the basses*]
- It had the quality of people who are rushing to get to the pub.
- Maybe it's because it's ten past eight, but every note is flat, consistently flat.
- Think King's Singers, not Britney Spears.
- That was a bit approximate.
- Yes, there's an in tune version in there.
- Good. If we could just tune that last bit, it'd be great.
- Hey, that's lovely, that aaah moment, almost, almost in tune.
- Lots of bass, with floating ladies over the top.
- Half of it's down the plughole, and half of it's great.
- That was stinkingly good.
- There's a whole world of rhythmical pain in that.
- That's like the flight of the wounded bumblebee. [*when singing zzzz*]
- That's a change, and a change is as good as a nightmare. [*after changing the way to sing a phrase*]
- I have a feeling you'll be conducted for this, because otherwise you've got no chance.

## QUOTES FROM OTHER CONDUCTORS

❝ [To a musician]: *Why do you always insist on playing when I'm trying to conduct?* ❞

❝ *I never say what I mean but I always manage to say something similar.* ❞

❝ [To the orchestra]: *Let me say what I do here. I don't want to confuse you more than absolutely necessary.* ❞

❝ Musician: *Is that a G or a G sharp?*
Ormandy: *Yes.* ❞

❝ Ormandy: *Percussion, a little louder!*
Percussion: *We don't have anything.*
Ormandy: *That's right, play it louder!* ❞

❝ *Did you play? It sounded very good.* ❞

❝ Ormandy: *Did you play?*
William Smith: *Yes.*
Ormandy: *I know. I heard you.* ❞

EUGENE ORMANDY, PHILADELPHIA ORCHESTRA

❝ *The conductor has the advantage of not seeing the audience.* ❞

ANDRÉ KOSTELANETZ

❝ *I never use a score when conducting my orchestra. Does a lion tamer enter a cage with a book on how to tame a lion?* ❞

DIMITRI MITROPOULOS

> 66 *A conductor should guide rather than command.* 99
>
> RICCARDO MUTI

> 66 *If anyone has conducted a Beethoven performance, and then doesn't have to go to an osteopath, then there's something wrong.* 99
>
> SIMON RATTLE

> 66 *Can't you read? The score demands* 'con amore' *and what are you doing? You are playing it like married men!* 99
>
> TOSCANINI

## Who programmes the orchestral concert?

Since it's the conductor who will have to learn the music, the ultimate decision as to the content rests in their hands. I was discussing the programming of a concert with a player from the LSO following a concert by a visiting conductor. He was the director of a Russian ballet company and so knew the dance repertoire intimately. Given what was for him a chance for a musical holiday playing with the LSO, he programmed works that he normally didn't get to play. Of course both the orchestra and the audience wanted to hear him conduct ballet works. The resulting concert was a compromise: half ballet music and half orchestral repertoire. In that instance it was the ballet music that for me really shone; it spoke immediately of the conductor's wealth of experience where the other pieces lacked quite the same sparkle. It's a question of agreement between the orchestra and the conductor.

It is difficult to create a concert that is both entertaining and thought-provoking. Although a conductor may have areas of specialism, they will be expected to have the major symphonies under their belt: Brahms, Beethoven, etc. Concerts will often be themed or at least contain works that balance each other so you might expect works by composers that influenced each other, works for the same size of ensemble or pieces that follow on from each other in history. It's important to have variety in a concert so you can often expect three or four pieces in a concert – a short work followed by a concerto then perhaps a major symphony in the second half.

## Why is one conductor hot and another not?

Why are some conductors in constant demand all over the world, commanding high fees and working with only the very best orchestras? Why does putting the name of Sir Simon Rattle on the ticket sell better than any number of other talented conductors? Do they really have magic in their fingers, and what makes them hot properties? I've sat in on many orchestral rehearsals and there is a huge difference in atmosphere depending on who is at the helm.

In reality it's not magic but there's undoubtedly something of the sorcerer about a good conductor. It is rare to find someone with the necessary technical know-how and experience along with the artistic vision and feeling for the music. This makes those at the top of their game extremely sought after. As well as a broad range of ages there are many approaches from the convivial to the dictatorial: from Alan Titchmarsh to Alan Sugar in leadership style, and everything in between. These are human relationships and conductors can have high opinions of their own worth, so developing a relationship with them takes years.

Conductors have different techniques in rehearsal; not all of them are jovial yet they still get results – like a strict headmaster. I sat in on a rehearsal with one conductor where there was considerable tension as he picked over a section of the double basses' music, yet the concert was fantastic. As Goddard Lieberson, one-time head of Columbia Records, said: 'Show me an orchestra that likes its conductor and I'll show you a lousy orchestra.' That very friction between players and maestro can cause players to play better, even if it doesn't make for very pleasant rehearsals. Others are like elder statesmen or a kindly old music professor. As they have worked with an orchestra for many years, they command respect and know each player as individuals. It's a joy to watch that sort of relationship in rehearsal; natural charm and ebullience connects immediately with the orchestra.

The female conductors whom I have met, Marin Alsop in particular, are fed up with being asked what it's like to be a female conductor. Marin is respected for her work on the podium, not for the novelty factor, and it's not even a novelty any more. There are an increasing number of female conductors in a profession still dominated by men. In any other profession within music it would hardly be worthy of note as women are now to be found running and playing in all the major organisations. But conducting has been the last bastion of male supremacy, associated for a long time with bombastic male dictators. But fear not: we now have bombastic female dictators too.

At the beginning of their careers conductors talk too much in rehearsal. I witnessed one conductor give a short musical lecture to an orchestra – imagine the expression of glazed disinterest as the maestro prattles on, the players waiting to get on with the music. As they improve their technique they let their hands do the talking. The more experienced conductors have more faith in their hands to communicate their musical intention than in their tongue. A violinist friend of mine awarded the highest accolade to a conductor she said had 'beautiful hands', by which she meant that his gestures were very clear but also beautiful to watch. This is a boon for a conductor. Orchestral musicians are adept at watching for cues and rarely need them spelt out they also see conductors all day long waving their hands in their face, and so one with interesting gestures is always going to be more welcome.

The difference in experience of watching a young firebrand and a seasoned veteran is the difference between a fine aged wine and a new one bursting with young undeveloped character. The apprenticeship of the conductor is long and arduous. Most begin by learning one or more instruments and will often play these professionally alongside their nascent conducting careers (for example, Daniel Barenboim is still as much in demand as a pianist as he is on the podium) before going on to study conducting. When they are young they display mental brilliance, musical skill and the confidence of youth. As they mature they learn to deal with people and their experience of the music deepens. However, there is sometimes a law of diminishing returns: I once heard a player comment on the conducting of the venerable gentleman on the podium, who appeared less vigorous than in his youth, at the end of a long, tiring concert: 'His batteries have run down.'

As much as the job is a practical one, behind the scenes it involves a great deal of academic rigour. You cannot stand in front of an orchestra without having a strong idea about the work in question, and that means study. Looking for a new angle on the piece is very important and especially so for young conductors for whom it is imperative to be seen to move things along. It has become difficult to make your mark, especially in the modern climate where CD recordings are so abundant. Barenboim:

> What Furtwängler said is still true – the correct tempo is that which, at the moment of playing, cannot be imagined any other way. This is now becoming far more difficult since people compare live music with records.[5]

There is no merit for a young conductor in simply emulating the careers of his or her predecessors: they must make an impact. This posturing can sometimes be thrilling. At best a new reading of a piece can open up a piece to an audience as never before, although there is a slight danger that it can be innovation for innovation's sake.

A recent example can be found in the young conductor Vladimir Jurowski, Principal Conductor of the London Philharmonic Orchestra (at 38 years old still just considered young in his profession). He has the vision and talent to create recordings and performances that have this quality of difference. His is an energetic style and he approaches music with freshness and without an inhibiting over-reverence. But this doesn't always work with the larger works which take conductors years to master: I saw his 2009 London Philharmonic Orchestra performance of Mahler's Second Symphony (one of my all-time favourite works). I barely recognised sections of it because he had such a crisp and, to my ear, overly technical approach that was very far from the grander, more heartfelt style of some of the more traditional 'Mahlerians' and I was left with the feeling that it will probably be years before he has the experience for this titanic work. I'm sure he'll get there and every conductor must perform a work like than dozens of times before it becomes second nature. That's not to say he did anything wrong; it just lacked the depth of meaning that it's possible to elicit from this piece in the hands of an old master.

When he gets it right Jurowski can be very exciting. He was recently asked to tackle a piece of music very unfamiliar to him but hugely popular with British audiences: *The Planets* by Gustav Holst (if you don't know it then I recommend you listen to it). The concert version (and subsequent live recording) display his readiness to innovate. His version of 'Mercury' goes at a hell of a lick, faster than is usual, and it really has wings. Jurowski's interview in *Gramophone Magazine* about the project reveals a desire to create 'must see' concert experiences.

It can be advantageous not be bound [*sic*] by too many traditions but at the same time it's good to know what the tradition is. I listened to Holst's own recording and that was an inspirational experience, his is a very down-to-earth approach but at the same time it's very exciting – the tempi [speeds] are much faster than usual. The one thing I wanted to avoid was playing the way British orchestras have over the last 30 years. It took some time but the LPO were absolutely receptive. They found the speeds difficult but fascinating. They told me that they heard the piece with different ears.[6]

I love his gentle but telling use of the phrase 'it took some time'. It reveals much about the process and the relationship between this conductor and his orchestra. It is his job to push, cajole and persuade the orchestra into experimentation. There will often be resistance to new speeds and new approaches from players who know the repertoire well and have played it a thousand times. Sometimes there will be glorious failures but on those occasions when it works the palpable sense of inspiration in the orchestra communicates itself to the audience viscerally.

A great conductor, a Toscanini, Furtwängler, Rattle, Barenboim, Gergiev or Haitink, has an energy about them which inspires the most jaded of players. It's not just about precision, it's about creating excitement and passion. A technically perfect performance can be dull if it lacks feeling; an imperfect performance can keep you on the edge of your seat if it has energy and life. If you see a junior conductor you may get lucky and find them on form with a repertoire that suits them, but a seasoned conductor will never play repertoire that they are unsure about and they bring the crackle of electricity to the concert hall.

## Conducting levels

There are different degrees of conductor with a major orchestra. From the tea boy to the conductor in chief. Simon Rattle's rise to one of the top jobs in music is a great example of the steps necessary as a conductor navigates the various levels.[7]

### Assistant conductor

It's likely that this will be a young conductor. Many notable great conductors started in this apprentice role. Simon Rattle began his career in my home town of Bournemouth aged only nineteen years old. From there he took up an assistant role in Liverpool.

### Guest conductor

As a guest conductor you'd be expected to fulfil a certain number of concert obligations every season but there'd be no expectation of leading the orchestra in its overall artistic direction. Simon Rattle began guest conducting with the Los Angeles Philharmonic in 1979.

### Principal guest conductor

It's clear that Rattle quickly built a rapport with LA because he became Principal Guest Conductor in 1981. Despite being given a 'day job' in 1980 he maintained this role for thirteen years. Imagine the air miles.

### Principal conductor/music director

Rattle was appointed Principal Conductor of the Birmingham Symphony Orchestra in 1980 at the age of 25. This is young by any standards and was considered to be a daring appointment.

Having established himself in the great symphonic repertoire, Rattle brought the regional orchestra to international fame through a number of highly successful recordings. He then spearheaded the building of a new concert hall in Birmingham which revolutionised music in the Midlands. His youthful dynamism combined with a prodigious musical ability quickly matured into the skill necessary for Music Director of the Berlin Philharmonic, one of the world's finest orchestras.

In the latter stages of their careers before they retire, a distinguished conductor may be made either *conductor laureate* or *president,* or *conductor emeritus.* Many conductors never retire and some die in the act of making music. Munich has the unlucky distinction of having two conductors die during performances of the same piece, Wagner's *Tristan und Isolde* – Felix Mottl in 1911 and then Joseph Keilberth in 1968.

## New works and commissions – do something different

The mainstream orchestral repertoire has already been recorded many times over. You can also see any of the world's major conductors performing at venues all over the country. This doesn't leave much room for new kids on the block. So it is easy to see why young conductors like Nicholas Collon are now making their name seeking out far-flung corners of the repertoire or increasingly turning to new works on which they can stamp their authority. Nick is conductor of the Aurora Orchestra, a lithe ensemble which reaches 'new audiences with virtuosic performance, innovative programming and inspiring cross-arts partnerships'[8], according to its website. This is a sentiment of the moment: it reflects an acknowledgement across the world of music that the ivory tower of classical music for some time seemed unwelcoming and that creative 'event' concerts which catch the eye of the media is a good way to get people to concerts. Nick's wit and personality have become part of the appeal of the ensemble.

The traditional concert is not dead but it's great to see examples of smaller ensembles working in novel ways. Aurora recently performed music by Rameau, Stravinsky, Balakirev and Pärt with a *capoeira* group (a Brazilian fusion of dance and martial arts). Listening to music while half-naked sportsmen throw themselves around the stage may not be your idea of a concert but it sure marks a readiness to experiment.

A contemporary music ensemble is also a must-have part of the modern conductor's portfolio. Alongside positions with major orchestras, having the opportunity to do things their way is probably a welcome relief and keeps them plugged into new work.

Classical music has the rather unfair reputation of being a pursuit of the middle-aged. In fact many concertgoers are young and I went to more concerts between the ages of 21 and 26 than in the rest of my life put together. There is a fascination with youth even in this profession which is so much associated with the wisdom of age. There are many examples of child prodigies who excited audiences before others have begun to master their instruments, e.g. Chloe Hanslip, Daniel Barenboim, Yehudi Menuhin and of course Mozart.

The same cannot be said of conductors. It's only with experience that they become fully formed artists. There are those who in their twenties create a stir and who we then watch with interest. Will they, like Simon Rattle, ascend to the great heights or will they fail to live up to their early promise?

Seeing a particular conductor is part of the reason I go to a concert. Certainly I choose the music carefully but if there's a conductor I know is going to be exciting then it really adds to the experience. In the presence of Valery Gergiev the whole room feels different – like being inside the cage with a lion.[9] You can't get that watching at home or listening on a CD. When an exciting conductor walks to the podium there's a thrill in the air. Finding a conductor whose personality and communication you like means that you have a direct line to the music. A conductor is there to squeeze every last drop out of the performance.

## DEATH ON THE PODIUM

Musical deaths while conducting are more common than one would imagine ... not everyone immediately abandoned sticks on health and safety grounds and there are many baton-related injuries from the world of conducting.

- 1687 – **Jean-Baptist Lully (1621–87):** court musician to Louis XIV of France, would bang a stick on the ground to keep his musicians in time; this worked well until he stuck it through his foot and died of the resulting gangrene.
- 1911 – **Felix Mottl:** an Austrian conductor, died in 1911 while conducting Wagner's *Tristan und Isolde.*
- 1943 – **Albert Stoessel:** was conducting an orchestra for the American Academy of Arts and Letters in New York when he died of a heart attack.
- 1959 – **Eduard von Beinum:** conductor at the Royal Concertgebouw in Amsterdam, was taken ill after the second movement of a Brahms symphony in 1959. He died immediately after stepping off the podium.
- 1968 – **Joseph Keilberth:** conductor, died in Munich, 1968, after collapsing while conducting Wagner's *Tristan und Isolde* in exactly the same place as Felix Mottl had done in 1911.
- 1997 – **Sir Georg Solti:** was so vigorous in his conducting that he managed to skewer his head with the baton during a royal gala performance at the Royal Opera House. He bled on through the rest of the opera but fortunately this didn't kill him – he died of a heart attack in 1997.
- 2001 – **Giuseppe Sinopoli:** collapsed at the podium of a heart attack in 2001 while conducting an emotionally charged scene in *Aida.*

### … and off

- 1695 – **Henry Purcell:** died aged 36 which is far too young for such a brilliant composer. Theories vary from pneumonia to chocolate poisoning, which sounds more fun. That's the way to go.
- 1791 – **Frantisek Kotzwara:** composer, died from erotic asphyxiation – allegedly.
- 1893 – **Pyotr Ilyich Tchaikovsky:** drank a glass of unboiled water in a St Petersburg restaurant and contracted cholera.
- 1935 – **Alban Berg:** was stung to death by a bee.

Chapter

# 12

# How to Survive a Concert

66 *The concert is a polite form of self-induced torture.* 99

HENRY MILLER

A few years ago I stood at the bar after a particularly splendid night at the BBC Proms and was aghast at how many perfectly intelligent, articulate people apologised for not understanding music. One well-known TV presenter in particular (who gives his opinion on a wide range of topics for a living) refused to pass comment until I (a supposed expert) had passed judgement.

'Wasn't it loud?' I said.

'Yes ... er ... loud ... yes that's what I thought ... loud!' etc.

But to my mind there is no need to apologise for not knowing about classical music.

## Be prepared

When going to a concert it's always worth knowing what you are getting into. My wife recounts with horror the time a friend of hers, without any explanation and in an effort to expand her musical horizons, took her to a concert of Ligeti (1923–2006). Ligeti was an exponent of *polyrhythm* which is when a composer juxtaposes two rhythms that don't really fit in the traditional sense. Imagine the sort of rhythmic contradictions made by your car's indicators and windscreen wipers when they are slightly out of time with each other. Add to that the chugging of the bus in front and the ringing of a bicycle bell and you are approaching the rhythmic language of Ligeti. He fuses the harmonic developments of Schoenberg with complex rhythms and some strange instrumental choices: toy ocarinas appear on the platform alongside shouting conductors and swanee whistles. Much of his music can be impenetrable to say the least, and to my wife's ear, more attuned to music of the nineteenth century, the evening was largely incomprehensible. Had she known perhaps she'd have gone to the cinema instead [Sound Link 70]. A little preparation might have helped – as it was she sat in her seat and was immediately assaulted by music she couldn't understand.

I've made the same mistake at operas by not reading anything of the plot beforehand. It is quite common in opera for the male lead to be played by a woman (a practice known as 'trouser roles' for obvious reasons). If you don't know that one of the two women singing a love duet on stage is playing a man, it can lead you to draw very different conclusions about the nature of the plot! All you need to know to appreciate opera is the story and a smattering of the music. If you are watching an opera in a foreign language this is doubly important. If there are no surtitles then it's critical. Some operas go on for hours and knowing who's who can unlock the wonders within. I *always* try to listen to the music before I go. This is much easier in the internet age as you can always find at least a few bars of a composer's music lurking somewhere in the recesses of the web. Unless you are going to see a world première.

## If it's such an ordeal, why go?

When a concert is good, it's very, very good. There's nothing quite like getting lost in the sound world of a symphony for taking you outside yourself. It's not quite the same listening at home to a recording of the music. That can be like looking at a painting whilst wearing sunglasses: simply not as it was intended. If you've never been to a classical music concert then it's time to book a ticket.

Let me be straight with you: not all concerts are good. As a child I went to what I thought were *very* long concerts. Because even then I wished to appear sophisticated and knowledgeable I made it my mission not to let on when I was bored. In the slow movements I'd stare at the ceiling, count the lights or think about what I'd do when I got home. Then the music would pick up and I'd be absorbed once again. It's a tactic that later came in useful during early-morning university lectures.

Most people who have been to a concert may have found part of it less than 100 per cent engaging. I remember the first time I went to see a concert of Bruckner. As I may have mentioned before, his symphonies are long; it's not unusual to find a Bruckner symphony takes up a whole CD and doesn't leave room for a stocking filler. After about twenty-five minutes of music I *swear* I saw the conductor turn back about 30 pages in his score and *repeat* a large section of the music. I stared into the abyss.

Not every concert you ever attend can be a transformative, uplifting experience. Some will be, at best, bearable. I'm just trying to manage your expectations here. In an entire football season of matches how many will feel like the FA Cup Final? So picking the right concert for you is vital. There are two ways to approach this. You could look for a performance of a work with which you are familiar. Or in the same way as you pick different offerings from the same supermarket, you could go for a concert venue that you know and see what's coming up.

If you live within reach of a major city then it's likely you'll be spoilt for choice. In London, Edinburgh, Glasgow, Cardiff, Birmingham and Manchester there are music venues all offering excellent deals as they compete to get your bum on their seat.

## Getting it right on the day

Chris gets it wrong:

> 66 *Why is it that my wife and I are the only people who arrive at the opera five minutes before curtain up? Everyone else appears to have been there for hours.* 99

MY FRIEND CHRIS, AN IT SPECIALIST

You can help yourself by knowing what you are going to see and doing some homework, as mentioned earlier in this chapter.

Concerts can be long and in the UK they usually start at 7.30 p.m., although there is an increasing trend to buck this tradition – a new innovation of late-night proms can last 45 minutes and start around 10 p.m. But for most concerts that means you might not be leaving the building until around 10 p.m. (and then there's the queue in the car park). It's really important to factor this into your planning. If you have a busy day before the concert, forget to eat and you wear something too hot for the hall, then you'll be one of those people who snore through the slow movement or shift in your seat uneasily. At London concerts many people leap out of their seats on the final note of the concert to get to their car, missing the chance to applaud the musicians – I think this is very bad manners. Hrrrmph.

Despite the best of intentions when I go to a concert the evening often takes roughly the same shape: I rush there from work, eating a sandwich at the station. I can't find my wife in the concert hall so I'm late to my seat. To get to seat J47 I have to push past a whole line of people, all of whom have just got comfortable and don't want to let me past. Bashed, bruised and weary, I slump down. The music begins. I look at the programme and fall asleep. An angry lady in the row behind taps me on the shoulder and I splutter loudly. 'You're snoring!' hisses my wife, digging an elbow in my ribs. I go home in shame. This is to be avoided, yet I see many in this state at every concert.

### Where to sit and how much to pay for your seat

Ask yourself this: are you the sort of person who wants to sit slap bang in front of the orchestra, getting a crick in your neck in exchange for being cheek by jowl with the artists, or do you mind being behind a pillar but paying half price? Do you like to be in the swanky seats or would you rather be by the door so you can sneak out to the bar if the going gets too tough? Where you sit also affects the sound. Sit in some seats in the Royal Albert Hall, for example, and you get the impression that certain instruments are playing louder than the others. Sit too close and you don't get the overall balance, sit too far away and in some venues the sound, and thus the experience, loses its immediacy.

What we see affects how we listen because we tend to hear with our eyes: if you see the violins pick up their instruments and get ready to play then you are likely to tune in to the sound that they make. The brain has a great ability to filter sound, ignoring unwanted noise and seemingly amplifying or focusing on what we see. (Think about having a conversation in a noisy street: you don't focus on the background sounds.)

Here's sound artist Bill Fontana (b. 1947):

> We learn not to listen by visual cues. If you walk down a street, you're not going to listen to the traffic, but if you heard a recording of the traffic in the woods, you would listen. So the eyes can switch off the ears …[1]

When the conductor turns to the 'cellos with an expressive gesture then you instinctively watch them to see how they respond. These subtleties may be lost if you can't see them. Many people like to be up close and personal with the orchestra so that they can see the beads of sweat and the effort involved in playing. For my money it's always worth spending as much as you can afford and avoiding the cheapest seats if possible, but people enjoy listening to music on the radio so it's not the end of the world if you end up at the back of the hall.

Some people don't care about the view as they like to shut their eyes for the whole concert. If this is the case then in a good concert hall it won't matter where you sit.

### How to book

If you want to get a ticket for the best available music this coming weekend then you are already too late: the really hot tickets are spotted by aficionados before they are released. However, if you are lucky you can sometimes get day tickets from the major opera houses, but some element of queuing will be necessary.

Most music organisations have newsletters or email bulletins which notify you as soon as tickets become available to the public. Some organisations have a club which gives you priority booking – although entrance to these can have a long wait – years in the case of Glyndebourne (where, like the MCC, you need to think about signing up your unborn children). But it's worth signing up for advance notifications as sometimes one of them will catch your eye.

People talk about the dearth of audiences for classical music but in my experience the very best classical music sells pretty healthily. In a city like London there are usually tickets for concerts that are really worth seeing. Elsewhere you may have to be more selective.

See below, Appendix II (Useful Information), for a list of concert venues with their contact details.

## Where to go for recommendations

It is tough to find a reliable source for a good recommendation. The classical music reviews are (naturally) written after the event. I find it maddening to read five-star reviews of concerts when the concert happened last week and there is no chance of ever catching it again. Nevertheless, these reviews are helpful in learning who are the hot properties in music. Like fine wine has its *terroir* (characteristics of the land and environment) every conductor has repertoire at which they excel. It's good to know this sort of information – as a result of reading reviews I had put Sir Charles Mackerras conducting Mozart on my list of things to do before I die; to my great regret he died first. However, by keeping my ear to the ground in this way I saw the colourful 'cellist/conductor Mstislav Rostropovich at the height of his powers and the mellifluous English tenor Anthony Rolfe Johnson before he succumbed to Alzheimer's. I'm so glad now that I made the effort to see these musical giants while they were still performing because I cannot remember what I might have been doing otherwise, but I don't regret missing it … whatever it was.

## Prices

Classical music is not expensive. It's not even relatively expensive. It's cheap. I don't know why people think of it as something they can't afford when they spend so much money on other forms of entertainment. I spend a lot of my time defending classical music against this sort of attack, and what classical music offers you simply can't find anywhere else. At the time of writing, tickets for:

o Arsenal (season tickets) cost from around £950 (25 games), depending on area of stadium; price per match: roughly £50–£100, depending on fixture
o National Theatre tickets cost from £15 to £50

- Train tickets from London to Leeds cost from £11.50 (advance) to £223 (fully flexible); both standard class, one-way
- Cinema tickets in the West End of London cost from £9.50 to £15
- Gig tickets at the O2 Arena in London cost around from £25 to £85 (depending on the gig and when you book)
- Sheffield Crucible snooker tickets cost from £15

Top-price tickets for a concert hall can be as much as £50 a ticket at the moment. But the cheapest tickets are around £10. To sit behind the goal (the cheapest ticket) at Arsenal for a category B match is £33. The top-price ticket is £94, and with football you'd have an expectation of going every few weeks.

In opera the difference in price is greater, though at some opera houses you can find 'restricted view' seats for a very reasonable sum. For example English Touring Opera currently charge as little as £16 when on tour to Worcestershire whilst you can sit in the 'Upper Slips' of the Royal Opera House for just £8.50.

Let's take a moment to consider what you are paying for. In a symphony orchestra there can be around 100 players in a big piece. Each player will have learnt their instrument for an average of seventeen years (starting aged six and finishing postgraduate studies aged 23 or 24 at the earliest). That's 1,700 years' worth of collective study and expertise sat in front of you. Add to that the years that some of them will have been playing in the orchestra and you are talking about thousands more hours of experience. Compare that with a Lady Gaga concert.

If you want to splash out, you can get yourself in the prime spot – centre of the stalls at the Royal Opera House for £200. If you are spluttering into your tea then let me break down the difference in experience between the two options, what you get for your money and why it might be worth it. I have sat pretty much everywhere at the Royal Opera House: I stood at the back for the *Les Contes d'Hoffman*, sat in the box next to the royal box overlooking the orchestra for *La Traviata* and I've been lucky enough to sit in the stalls for a performance of Verdi's *Don Carlos*. Every time it's a totally different experience, but the performances I've enjoyed most were when I've sat in better seats. There is undeniably a feeling of prestige attached to having one of the best seats in the house. The usher gives you the deferential glance; you feel special because you have an unparalleled view. But that's not the reason that people pay to sit there (or at least it shouldn't be!). If you've ever turned the balance on your stereo so that only one speaker works then you'll appreciate why it's better to be in the centre of things. I don't like having to lean in to see the action from a side seat. I had to do this during the second section of Wagner's Ring Cycle, *Die Walküre*, which stretches to a leg-aching, neck-twisting four hours. After several rounds of osteopathy I can now walk straight.

You have to be careful with Wagner. My wife was locked out of the house while I was stuck in a performance of *Götterdämmerung*. In any other opera it wouldn't have mattered but *Götterdämmerung* is four and a half hours long. Plus an interval. Plus travelling time. Luckily a neighbour took pity on her and took her in from the snow.

### The Proms – back-breakingly satisfying

There are some people who view this sort of hardship as a boon, a musical hairshirt. Some of these masochists can be found at the world's biggest music festival, the Proms. They are such a particularly hardy breed that it would be reasonable to devote a whole chapter to them, if not a whole book.

The Proms began in 1895 at the Queen's Hall, a venue with an apparently superb acoustic which sadly was destroyed in the bombing of 1941. The founder conductor of these 'promenade' concerts, Sir Henry Wood, was determined to introduce new works to the public and charged them just one shilling (5p) for a standing ticket – hence 'promenade' as the audience could walk around. Today standing tickets for the Proms are only £5. The combination of low-cost tickets and a chance to see the very best music makes the Proms one of the most economical ways to see live performances.

A seasoned Prom enthusiast will begin the purgative process by taking public transport to the Royal Albert Hall, arriving in the middle of August in a heatwave on the hottest day of the year to South Kensington tube station (one of the busiest tourist stations in London). They are dressed for a concert – smart casual and most likely some all-weather gear just in case. They're carrying a Thermos flask and a picnic basket because it's not time for the concert yet: it's time for the queue.

Several hours of outdoor queuing later they purchase their cheap Promenader's ticket (even cheaper if they have a season ticket). Then the race is on. They're off – chasing each other to get to their favourite standing spot. Many of them like to stand underneath the conductor to catch any droplets of sweat that may fall. If you think this sounds like hell then you're wrong; it's actually great fun. The atmosphere among the 'Prommers' is electric and they are a friendly bunch, eager to share their thoughts on the upcoming concert. They are usually highly informed but since the whole *raison d'être* of the Proms is to introduce people to new music they wear this erudition as lightly as their Pac-a-Macs.

Some of the first concerts I attended were at the Proms. I stood through Mahler and had a great time. The thrilling musical atmosphere can be heightened with a sense of raw danger when a member of the audience collapses from sheer exhaustion (ushers are always ready with a glass of water).[2] Believe it or not there is great satisfaction in standing through a whole concert – it's hard work but when you finally get to move at the end there's an enormous sense of achievement. You can always sit on the floor if you're in real agony.

If you like a bargain and you don't mind standing, then this is an excellent option for you. Be warned: don't get on the wrong side of one of the pros. They don't appreciate queue jumpers (they are mostly British after all). There are some rituals that have obscure origins and the shady details are passed between members of the standing audience. They do not observe the same customs that exist in other concert halls. For example when stage hands enter to move a piano or bring in a new instrument the Promenaders will often applaud enthusiastically. Sometimes they communicate lessons from the annals of Proms history by arranging to shout in unison from the audience.

The Proms audience has a long collective memory. In 1974 one of the soloists, Thomas Allen, collapsed during a performance of Carl Orff's *Carmina Burana*.[3] There happened to be a singer in the audience who volunteered to take over and sang the whole work to rapturous applause. When I went to see the next performance of the work at the proms twenty years later in 1994[4] with the late Richard Hickox conducting, I remember the Prommers spontaneously announcing in unison to the waiting baritone before the start of the concert:

*'Arena to stage. Replacements are standing by.'*

I don't think it's likely that if you are a member of the Proms audience you'll be required to perform, but then again, anything can happen.

Promenaders raise money for charity, love the music and – somewhat perversely – genuinely seem to get a kick out of queuing. An obsessive-compulsive need to attend all of the concerts drives the hard core, including Sue Brady, who has hardly missed a single Prom since 1968. They come with their carrier bags, folding chairs and a series of rituals that often began as one-off jokes but have now become indelible tradition. They shout 'heave ho' when the piano is moved to the front for a soloist to perform. Every visiting orchestra is welcomed in its mother tongue, whether German, Finnish or Catalan. When the leader hits an A on the piano for the orchestra to tune up, it is greeted with bizarre enthusiasm. On the last night you may hear somebody shout 'Anyone for tennis?' at which the audience will call out 'ping', and is answered by a 'pong' from the people in the gallery. But for some all this is aggravating, to say the least. Here's Stephen Pollard, writing in the *Telegraph*:

> Somehow the myth has taken hold that the people who pay £4 to stand in the arena – the area that would normally have stalls seats, which is handed over to the Promenaders for the duration of the Proms – are the greatest audience on the planet … There is no other audience quite so noisy, fidgety, intolerant, smelly and plain bloody awful as the Promenaders. I know how bad they are because I used to be one of them …
>
> The real problem is that they are not there for the music, but to be part of a rather sad club that meets nightly at 7.30 and is defined by a series of inane rituals. So the highlight of their evening is not Martha Argerich playing Ravel, but the chance to chant 'heave' when the piano is shifted onto the stage, or their asinine mock applause when the orchestra leader plays a note on the piano for the orchestra to tune up to.[5]

If you don't fancy the free-standing delights of the Royal Albert Hall then the Royal Opera House offers an innovative alternative: the lean. You can stand but crucially there is a bar height leaning opportunity. Trust me, it makes all the difference.

## Seat wanted

If I've convinced you that the chair is a luxury you can afford then let's talk about where to sit. At a rock concert (so I'm told) the hardened fan gets as close to their idol as is possible without being on the stage. In the classical world it doesn't really work like that. Mostly because it's less of a personality cult and more about the sound quality, although this isn't true for everybody – some people love to get up close and personal with the orchestra, especially if there is an attractive soloist.

In an orchestral concert there is usually an area where the sound of the band comes together perfectly and where the balance between the instruments is optimal. Sit too close and you'll only hear the violins, sit too far away and you risk losing the presence and directness of the sound.

If you are about two-thirds of the way back in the stalls or near the front of the circle you are probably in the best seats for hearing clearly. It's acoustically engrossing in these seats because the sound seems to envelop you. The net effect of being absorbed in the sound over the two hours of a concert is qualitatively better than being at the back near the door. QED. The reason for this brings us to the magical world of acoustics. NB it's not magic: it's science.

## Acoustics

A 'good acoustic' is talked about in hushed, reverential tones by musicians. Buildings with a 'good acoustic' are cherished for their clarity and warmth (aural not literal!) by players and public alike. If you've ever been in a swimming pool, a Nissen hut, an underground bunker or an over-large school sports hall then you will have experienced a bad acoustic. Whenever we sit in a building and listen to music, what we are hearing is a combination of the direct sound from the musicians and a whole sea of sound formed from reflections off the walls, floors, ceilings and other members of the audience. The raw voice of a violin playing, whilst lovely on its own, is lent warmth by a decent acoustic. Because of this the hall itself plays as important a role in the concert as the players do.

Sound, as we perceive it, forms a mental image in our minds; that's why when you shut your eyes you can tell which direction the bus is coming from. It's almost as though you can see it. The brain does this by noticing how sound hits the ear at different times – a sound coming from the left will hit the left ear fractionally earlier than the right. The brain converts this into an accurate perception of sound in physical space. We are amazingly good at this and also barely aware that the process is going on, unless it goes wrong. It must be extremely difficult for people who are deaf in one ear to tell where sounds are coming from.

Reverb is the amount of time it takes for the reflections of a sound to finish. In a cathedral you'd expect a long reverb whereas in a small room you'd expect a short one. This is because in a cathedral the sound takes longer to travel to the walls and reflect back to your ears than in a room. Our brains can tell the difference in sound between indoors, outdoors, an oak-panelled library, a metal-roofed classroom and a stone cave without the evidence of our eyes by listening to the reverb. The reason for this is because sound moves in waves through the air; it doesn't travel like a laser beam straight to your ear, it moves out and reflects off different surfaces.

Some surfaces make excellent sound reflectors; others are too reflective and some absorb almost all the sound. Brick, for example, is an excellent sound reflector because the surface is coarse and unpolished; this creates complex reflections leading to a more natural-sounding acoustic. Flat metal or concrete surfaces are bad news in acoustics because they reflect all the sound in one direction and all at the same time. This gives a horrible flat and immediate reflection. If you've ever seen pictures of home-made recording studios you may have noticed egg boxes all over the walls to absorb the sound. It's OK for a recording studio to have no natural acoustics because in such an environment the sound dynamics can be controlled and generated electronically. Moreover, that element of directness for the microphones is required because that's what people are used to hearing now – very clever, close microphones.

So in a concert venue you need a balance between too much reverberation, which is the problem in many stone buildings – the sound just goes on and on – and not enough, which can sound incredibly dull. There should also be enough presence to the sound which means that to your ear it sounds nearby, not as though the musicians are playing a long way away – even though you might be sitting at the back. A 'warmth' to the sounds of the instruments or singers is also very important; under some circumstances only certain frequencies are absorbed and others reflected, giving either a tinny sound or a woolly sound with no definition. In a good acoustic it's easier to create a good balance between instruments. If an acoustic is not working then you might find that the trumpets seems to blare at you whilst the harp or strings are completely lost.

Musicians love to play in buildings with a great acoustic. There's a buzz about such places. The LSO has to rehearse in lots of different venues because the Barbican isn't always available during the day – other concerts may be happening or other groups rehearsing. Consequently I've been to rehearsals in all sorts of cramped conditions and there's a palpable sense of relief amongst the orchestral players and a sense that the music can breathe again when they get into the concert hall for which their music was written.

Until fairly recently acoustics were a mysterious business; it was pure luck as to whether a building would have a good acoustic. The Royal Festival Hall and the Barbican in London both suffered from bad acoustics for years, whereas the Symphony Hall in Birmingham had a great sound from the get-go.[6] Birmingham even has moveable sound chambers so that the acoustic can be adjusted according to the needs of the performance.

The City of London, who own the Barbican, spent £7 million on improving the acoustic of the concert hall. The project went about remedying the problems that had haunted the hall since its design:

> The Barbican Concert Hall was originally planned as a conference facility for 2000 people, with a design that emphasized audience proximity to the stage. Its reconception as a concert hall came too late in the design process to accommodate either the reduction in width or increase in volume that would have resulted in a more favorable geometry for music performance.

In 1991, Kirkegaard Associates completed a master planning document that discussed acoustics issues which included lack of intimacy, clarity and presence, poor low frequency response, anemic and uneven sound from the platform, poor ensemble conditions, and low reverberation time, particularly at low frequencies. The document also recommended acoustic improvements that would enhance technical facilities and performer and audience recommendation. Three phases of work have been completed to date.[7]

The final work was completed in 2001 and I was present at the final acoustic tests where they used innovative computer modelling to confirm how their alterations to the structure of the building had changed the sound for the audience. It might seem a lot of money to hang some acoustic reflectors and change the walls. These reflectors stretch across the roof of the stage and reflect sound from the orchestra directly to the audience. I have been told that before the baffles were hung you could not hear the strings when the full orchestra played. Today, although some complain that the acoustic is overly 'dry' (lacking in reverberation), I think the clarity of acoustic in the Barbican is second to none. And the stakes couldn't be higher: following their inaugural performance[8] at the Barbican, the Vienna Philharmonic, a world-class orchestra, vowed never to play there again. But now, following the reconstruction, the Barbican boasts an artist list of the world's greatest performers.

When you go to a concert hall, part of your ticket price is paying for the use of the venue. It makes a huge difference to how you listen to music. An orchestra playing in a packed St Paul's Cathedral has to contend with almost eight seconds of reverb. That muddies the waters immensely, and while that can be beautiful in choral music it's not what you want for complex orchestral pieces.

## Eating your greens and appreciating innovation

You may have to listen to a piece that you don't know and which you feel is too modern for your taste. Even some of the players roll their eyes at some of the more outlandish innovations: a trumpet-playing friend of mine was asked to march up and down across the stage whilst reciting text during one concert, which he hated – orchestral musicians can be surprisingly shy.

The spirit of education and discovery has always hovered around the concert hall. Through an introduction to different types of music an orchestra helps us become rounder human beings – that's the theory (although it didn't help Adolf Hitler, famously a huge fan of German classical music). I've always thought it akin to the 'Grand Tour of Europe' that young gentlemen used to take after university in the eighteenth century, traversing Europe to see the most important cultural wonders of the world (and getting mightily drunk at the same time): the Uffizi in Florence, the Palace of Versailles, the wonders of Paris and Venice. A concert can be seen as an exercise in self-improvement as it introduces us to works of cultural significance.

Whilst we may go to a concert because there is an element that is familiar to us, whether it's the hall itself, the work or a well-known composer, a good concert will broaden our horizons. Every time I go to a concert it's the pieces I don't know that I hope will pique my interest. Great discoveries can be made this way.

If the unfamiliar work is a new commission then there is often a definite tension in the audience. People hold their breath, preparing themselves for either an aural assault or a new and exciting work. If new work fills you with dread then it really shouldn't: because new commissions are expensive they are often short, so after a few minutes of battery by the avant-garde, the veterans of the concert hall may relax into more comfortable territory.

Attitudes to new work vary. Most acknowledge that music cannot stand still and hunger for a new gem. Some tolerate the new sounds whilst secretly believing that anything after Brahms is a travesty. Some view the experience as 'eating your greens': you can't have the dessert until you've swallowed what's good for you. Discovering the new is always thrilling. Humans are addicted to innovation, especially in our society, and it's a facet of music that after two listens the unfamiliar is made familiar. Without innovation we'd still be singing simple chants from the Middle Ages. The one constant in musical history is that upon the establishment of a set of musical conventions a composer of the next generation then smashes them to smithereens a few years later.

This desire to move forward marks out the brave composers from the humdrum, but never more so than when the composer risks their life with their artistic advances, not just their reputation. Dmitri Shostakovich (1906–1975) wrote music that railed against existing forms. He didn't always write the music that Joseph Stalin and his Soviet government wanted him to write and he was very nearly imprisoned for his 'anti-Soviet' piece *Lady Macbeth of Mtsensk*. The prevailing political atmosphere was essentially musically conservative, as summed up in 1947 by Soviet politician Andrei Zhdanov when he decreed that 'the people do not need music which they cannot understand'. From that point on, Shostakovich put codes into his music so that people could guess at the true meaning even though the style apparently pleased the Soviet government – a brave if hidden form of dissent. Imagine having Stalin in your audience.

Those who become steeped in the music of the past but fail to innovate are rarely remembered with such respect as those firebrands who broke the rules or pushed instruments and musicians beyond their limits at the time. Some composers take this idea to extremes, writing music which is a challenge to play and a challenge to listen to. A cursory glance by an untrained eye at a page of Brian Ferneyhough's score (see p. 249) is enough to tell you that this is adventurous music.

When abroad in Paris the composer Tchaikovsky first heard the celeste, a keyboard instrument which, though played like a piano, sounds like a glockenspiel.[9] The story goes that Tchaikovsky had the newly invented instrument smuggled into Russia in secrecy as he was worried that his contemporaries would use it before him. The badge of honour for being the first applies as much in music as it does in science. He used the celeste to miraculous effect in 'The Dance of the Sugarplum Fairy'. John Williams could not have written the theme to *Harry Potter*, which features a virtuoso celeste part, had the idea not been made available 109 years before. Without this (and other) expansions of the traditional pool of orchestral instruments the celeste might have gone the way of the Stylophone as brought to us by Rolf Harris. I long to see one of these in the concert hall. It could happen.

So remember that the greens are an important part of your diet and don't complain if it seems unfamiliar.

## What am I supposed to wear?

Don't worry about this. At most concerts there is no dress code. In cold churches people wear thick woollens and in concert halls there's everything from trainers to hand-made shoes. Glyndebourne is one of the last places to request that patrons wear evening dress and I applaud them for it – there is such a sense of style to an evening where everybody is dressed up to the nines. As discussed earlier, the Proms tend to be very informal because so many people have been queuing.

Basically if you are worried, then dress up; if you aren't worried, then dress down. If you are there for a sartorial appointment and not for the music then you've gone for the wrong reasons.

## What am I supposed to say?

When I take friends to concerts I'm always disheartened when they ask me if I thought it was 'good'. It reveals so much about their fear of classical music. I've been to concerts with highly articulate and educated people who when asked what they thought about the concert are left unable to comment. I'd struggle to talk to an art critic about Titian or Turner without using words like 'nice' or 'lovely'. So here are some easy platitudes to get you out of trouble.

- Firstly trust your own opinion: if you thought it sounded like cats screaming then it probably did.
- Talk about the skill of the musicians.
- Talk about the lush sound of the strings.
- Be impressed by how much energy was displayed by particular sections of the orchestra or the conductor.
- Find joy in one of the uplifting sections of music.
- Don't say that it was so relaxing that you fell asleep.
- Talk about the singer's high notes: pleasing, strained, strangulated, etc.

## Sit back and enjoy ... and please snore quietly if you must

So if you've got your ticket, made sure you've got to your seat in time, ideally done a bit of research beforehand, then you're ready for the concert hall. Ideally you will be able to sit back and enjoy, not worried about what you are supposed to be feeling, thinking or hearing. Be prepared to be enthralled, surprised, moved, uplifted or ravished by the experience. Of course you might be so bored that you fall asleep – don't worry, you won't be arrested – but do try not to snore during quiet passages, because I'll be behind you tapping you on the shoulder. The beauty of live music is that you never know how it's going to hit you. If you see ten live concerts then one of them may very well change your life.

# Coda

Hopefully by now you've put a few of those preconceptions behind you, learnt to listen more deeply and opened your mind to some new forms. This is the just the beginning of your new relationship with music. Now it's over to you: dig around in old secondhand record shops, check out the latest releases and, above all, go to live concerts if you are able. If the more technical sections of this book have left you feeling punchdrunk and baffled then don't worry, you are not alone; not everyone who listens to classical music is in full possession of all the knowledge. Enthusiasm comes from an initial curiosity which develops over time into a great passion, as I hope it will with you.

If you have children then start to introduce it to them at as early an age as possible. That doesn't mean merely putting on the radio – go to family music workshops, get to grown-up concerts once they're old enough and have musical instruments around the house which they feel free to make noise with. I had a piano in my house when I was growing up and it was always where I gravitated, even before I knew how to play it. As a result, I *asked* for piano lessons. This is crucial in learning about classical music: that the motivation comes from within. It cannot be put there.

This book will give you a starting point for conversation with any other classical enthusiast – so form groups, alliances and friendships around this music. Let it become the soundtrack to your life as it is mine. Classical music has been there through my entire life and I make new discoveries every time I switch on the radio. It's a joy to find a piece that you haven't found before and, as with any form of music, there is plenty still being written.

I sincerely hope this book helps you to feel that you know where to start with classical music. If you get half as much as I get from it then I believe your life will be considerably enriched; that's the point of classical music in the end. It's not frivolous – it's culture and it's art. If you've never experienced the pyrotechnics of a violin solo, shuddered at the assault of the full symphony orchestra or cried as the operatic heroine breathes her last, then make time to do it before you die. If someone makes you feel uncomfortable because they appear to know more about classical music than you do they may well be covering up for their own feelings of inadequacy – it's a *vast* subject and the appreciation of it is subjective.

Writing this book has given me great pleasure because of all the discoveries and re-discoveries that I've made over this six-month journey. It has made me evaluate *why* I love this music and has made me think about how to communicate my sense of excitement and wonder. It has been a learning experience for me as well, and one I've really enjoyed.

If you have felt unconfident about listening to this music, take heart from knowing that it does get easier and more familiar with practice. There may well have been pieces that I recommend to which you don't respond at first. Only with time will you find out what's going to become *your* classical music.

Make your own discoveries, share your enthusiasms and get to as many concerts as you can; over time you'll feel knowledgeable. This music belongs to you.

GARETH MALONE
February 2011
Kilburn, London

# Part 4
# APPENDICES

# Appendix 1

# Musical 'Starting Points'

## Pieces for romance (*not to be confused with Romantic pieces*)

What makes a piece 'romantic'? Hard to say, but the 'Habanera' has an aphrodisiac effect, whereas the Chopin Nocturne could make you better disposed to your partner's foibles.

- Bizet: *Carmen Suite No. 2*, 'Habanera'
- Tchaikovsky: *Romeo and Juliet Fantasy Overture*
- Chopin: Nocturne No. 2 in E flat Major, Op. 9
- Rachmaninov: *Vocalise*, Op. 34/14
- Rimsky-Korsakov: *Scheherazade*, Op. 35, 'The Young Prince and Princess'
- Khachaturian: *Spartacus Suite No. 2*: 'Adagio of Spartacus and Phrygia'

## Moving, sad and poignant

Many people associate 'classical music' with soporific and melancholic pieces served up extremely slowly. For those who are coming to this music from high-energy popular forms it can feel like either a slow, agonising death or a welcome chance to relax to music that isn't at a constant 160 beats per minute.

We each spend our first nine months listening to our mother's heartbeat and I think it's no accident that we find the slow pace soothing. All these pieces are all in minor keys, the musical equivalent of painting everything in sombre tones (for more of which see above, Chapter 2) and they could all be played at funerals without causing offence.

- Fauré: Pavane, Op.50
- Mozart: Requiem, K. 626, Lacrimosa dies illa
- Pietro Mascagni: *Cavalleria Rusticana*, Intermezzo
- Beethoven: 'Moonlight' Sonata, first movement
- Mahler: Symphony No. 5 in C Sharp Minor, fourth movement, Adagietto
- Albinoni: Adagio in G Minor
- Walton: *Henry V*, 'Passacaglia on the Death of Falstaff'
- John Williams: *Harry Potter and the Prisoner of Azkaban*, 'A Window to the Past'
- Chopin: Prelude in E Minor, Op. 28/4

## Uplifting, stirring and vital

Now this is the music that gets the blood pumping. It's not always the music that we'd put on after a hard day at the office but it can be extremely invigorating. The pulse is quicker and attitude more strident.

- Bizet: *L'Arlésienne,* Prelude
- Elgar: *Pomp and Circumstance*, Op. 39, 'Land of Hope and Glory' – one for the British
- Mozart: *The Marriage of Figaro*, Overture
- Handel: *Messiah*, 'Hallelujah' Chorus
- Prokofiev: *Romeo and Juliet*, 'Montagues and Capulets'
- Beethoven: Symphony No. 5 in C Minor, Op. 67, 'Fate', Allegro con brio
- Tchaikovsky: 1812 Overture, Op. 49, Finale

- Saint-Saëns: Symphony No. 3 in C Minor, Op. 78, ('Organ'), Maestoso
- Schubert: *Marche Militaire*, Op. 51, No. 1
- Holst: *The Planets*, Op. 32, 'Jupiter, The Bringer of Jollity'
- Walton: *Crown Imperial*
- John Williams: *Star Wars Episode 1: The Phantom Menace*, 'Duel of the Fates'
- Bach: Brandenburg Concerto No. 3 in G Major, BWV 1048, first movement, Allegro
- Handel: Concerto Grosso in D Major, Op. 6, No. 5, Allegro
- Smetana: *The Bartered Bride,* Overture
- Mozart: *The Magic Flute*, K. 620, Overture

## Quietly uplifting and energising

These pieces are not as outwardly upbeat as the previous section but they all have the ability to lift the spirits – and help get the dusting done in no time at all.

- Grieg: *Holberg Suite*, Op. 40, Prelude
- Stravinsky: *Pulcinella Suite*, first movement
- Beethoven: Symphony No.7 in A Major, Op. 92, second movement
- Mozart: *Eine Kleine Nachtmusik*: Serenade No. 13, first movement
- Bizet: *Carmen*, 'Toreador's Song'
- Rossini: *The Barber of Seville*, Overture
- Mozart: Symphony No. 40 in G Minor, K. 550, Allegro molto
- Handel: *The Arrival of the Queen of Sheba*
- Smetana: *Má Vlast* ('My Fatherland'), 'Vltava'

## Just beautiful for their own sake

Beauty may be in the eye of the beholder but it's also in the ear.
Here are some pieces which are simply delicious:

- Tchaikovsky: *Swan Lake*, Waltz
- Mozart: Piano Concerto No. 21 in C Major, K. 467, Andante
- Satie: *Gymnopédie* No. 1
- Schubert: Arabeske in C Major, Op. 18; Impromptus
- Mozart: Clarinet Concerto in A Major, slow movement
- Debussy: *Suite Bergamasque*, L. 75, 'Clair de Lune'
- Chopin: Nocturne No. 2 in E Flat Major, Op. 9
- Schumann: *Träumerei* ('Dreaming') from *Scenes from Childhood*, Op.15/7
- Grieg: *Peer Gynt Suite No. 1*, Op. 46, 'Morning'
- Handel: *Messiah*, 'I Know That My Redeemer Liveth'

## Magical or downright scary

These aren't necessarily pieces written for Hallowe'en but they
are all distinctively ominous or mysterious.

- Tchaikovsky: *The Nutcracker Suite*, 'Dance of the Sugar Plum Fairy'
- Richard Strauss: *Also Sprach Zarathustra*
- Copland: *Fanfare for the Common Man*
- Grieg: *Peer Gynt Suite No. 1*, Op. 46, 'In the Hall of the Mountain King'
- Mendelssohn: *A Midsummer Night's Dream*, Op. 61, Act II, Scherzo
- Khachaturian: *Maskarade*, Waltz
- Mozart: *Don Giovanni*, Overture
- Rachmaninov: Prelude in C Sharp Minor, Op. 3/2
- Grieg: Piano Concerto in A Minor
- Manuel de Falla: *El Amor Brujo*, 'Ritual Fire Dance'

- Bach: Toccata and Fugue in D Minor
- Sibelius: *Finlandia*, Op. 26
- Chopin: Piano Sonata No. 2 in B Flat Minor, Op. 35, 'Funeral March'

## Troubled, searching yet beautiful

- Brahms: Symphony No. 3 in F Major, Op. 90, third movement

## Spiritual (not necessarily religious)

- Bach: 'Jesu, Joy of Man's Desiring'
- Gounod/J.S. Bach: 'Ave Maria'
- Handel: *Water Music*, Air No. 6

## Old-fashioned fun

- Rossini: *William Tell*, Overture, Finale
- Johann Strauss II: Jockey-Polka, Op. 278 (*Polka schnell*), or pretty much anything by this composer
- Bach: Brandenburg Concerto No. 3 in G Major, BWV 1048, Allegro
- Offenbach: *The Tales of Hoffmann*, Barcarolle

## Pieces you wish you could play on the piano

- Mozart: Piano Sonata No. 11 in A Major, K. 331, Rondo alla Turca
- Beethoven: Bagatelle in A Minor ('Für Elise')
- Beethoven: 'Moonlight' Sonata, first movement
- Chopin: Étude in C Minor, Op. 10/2 ('Revolutionary')
- Mendelssohn: Spring Song, Op. 62, No. 2
- Chopin: Waltz in D Flat Major, Op. 64/1 ('Minute Waltz')
- Chopin: Étude No. 3 in E, Op. 10/3 ('Tristesse')

- ○ Dvořák: *Humoresque poco lento e grazioso*, G Flat Major
- ○ Gershwin: Prelude No. 1

## Toe-tapping brilliance

- ○ **Brahms:** Hungarian Dance No. 5 in G Minor
- ○ **Rimsky-Korsakov:** 'Flight of the Bumblebee'

## Pieces that have great tunes and only need one listen to 'get'

- ○ **Tchaikovsky:** *Swan Lake*, 'Dance of the Swans'
- ○ **Bach:** Orchestral Suite No. 3 in D Major, BWV 1068, 'Air on a G String'
- ○ **Johann Strauss II:** 'On the Beautiful Blue Danube', Op. 314
- ○ **Traditional:** 'Greensleeves'
- ○ **Jeremiah Clarke:** 'Trumpet Voluntary'
- ○ **Delibes:** *Coppélia* – Waltz

## Pieces you may either hate, love (in an ironic sense) or actually enjoy …

- ○ Hugo Alfvén: *Swedish Rhapsody* (I hated this on first listen but it's growing on me … I can imagine lots of little mice doing a dance to this music.) [Sound Link 71]
- ○ This is a very personal category. Add your own.

Appendix **2**

# Useful Information

## Major UK concert venues

### *London*

- **Artsdepot**
  5 Nether Street,
  Tally Ho Corner
  North Finchley
  London N12 0GA
  tel: 0208 369 5454
  www.artsdepot.co.uk

- **Barbican**
  Silk Street
  London EC2Y 8DS
  tel: 0207 638 8891
  www.barbican.org.uk

- **Blackheath Halls**
  23 Lee Road
  London SE3 9RQ
  tel: 0208 463 0100
  www.blackheathhalls.com

○ **Cadogan Hall**
5 Sloane Terrace
London SW1H 9DQ
tel: 0207 730 4500
www.cadoganhall.com

○ **Lauderdale House**
Highgate Hill
London N6 5HG
tel: 0208 348 8716
www.lauderdalehouse.co.uk

○ **London Symphony Orchestra**
St Luke's
161 Old Street
London EC1V 9NG
tel: 07490 3939
www.lso.co.uk/lsostlukes

○ **Royal Albert Hall**
Kensington Gore
London SW7 2AP
tel: 0845 401 5045
www.royalalberthall.com

○ **Royal Festival Hall**
Southbank Centre
Belvedere Road
London SE1 8XX
tel: 0207 960 4200
www.southbankcentre.co.uk/venues/royal-festival-hall

o **St John's**
Smith Square
London SW1P 3HA
tel: 0207 222 1061
www.sjss.org.uk

o **Wigmore Hall**
38 Wigmore Street
London W1U 2BP
tel: 0207 935 2141
www.wigmore-hall.org.uk

## Midlands and North

o **Bridgewater Hall**
Lower Mosley Street
Manchester M2 3WS
tel: 0161 907 9000
www.bridgewater-hall.co.uk

o **Curve**
Cultural Quarter
Rutland Street
Leicester LE1 1SB
tel: 0116 242 3560
www.curveonline.co.uk

o **Holmes Chapel Leisure Centre**
Selkirk Drive
Crewe CW4 7DZ
tel: 01270 529505
www.holmeschapel.org.uk

*o* **Leeds Town Hall**
The Headrow
Leeds LS1 3AD
tel: 0113 247 6647
www.leedstownhall.co.uk

*o* **Pacific Road Arts Centre**
1 Pacific Road
Birkenhead
Merseyside CH14 1LJ
tel: 0151 666 0000
www.pacificroad.co.uk

*o* **The Roundhouse**
Roundhouse Road
Pride Park
Derby DE24 8JE
tel: 0800 028 0289
www.derby-college.ac.uk

*o* **Royal Hall**
Harrogate International Centre
King's Road
Harrogate
North Yorkshire HG1 5LA
tel: 01423 537273
www.royalhall.co.uk

*o* **Sir Jack Lyons Concert Hall**
Heslington
York YO10 5DD
tel: 01904 432439
www.york.ac.uk/concerts

**o Symphony Hall**
Broad Street
Birmingham
W Midlands B1 2AE
tel: 0121 780 3333
www.thsh.co.uk/page/symphony-hall-birmingham

**o Town Hall**
Victoria Square
Birmingham
W Midlands B3 3DQ
tel: 0121 780 3333
www.thsh.co.uk/page/town-hall-birmingham/

### Northern Ireland

**o Ulster Hall**
1–7 Bedford Street
Belfast BT2 7FF
tel: 028 9033 4400
www.ulsterhall.co.uk

### Scotland

If you live near Edinburgh then the International Festival hand-picks artists of the highest quality every year. Just glancing at their website I can see that there wasn't a second-rate artist amongst the 52 concerts during the 2010 Festival. Internationally renowned singers from Simon Keenlyside to Magdelena Kožená, orchestras from the Royal Concertgebouw to the Cleveland Orchestra and some of the world's most exciting conductors – all in Scotland.

○ **Glasgow Royal Concert Hall**
2 Sauchiehall Street
Glasgow G2 3NY
tel: 0141 353 8000
www.glasgowconcerthalls.com

○ **Queen's Hall**
85–89 Clerk Street
Newington
Edinburgh EH8 9JG
tel: 0131 668 3456
www.thequeenshall.net

○ **Usher Hall**
Lothian Road
Edinburgh EH1 2EA
tel: 0131 228 1155
www.usherhall.co.uk

○ **Younger Hall**
North Street
St Andrews
Fife KY16 9AJ
tel: 01334 462226
www.st-andrews.ac.uk/music/Facilities/YoungerHall

*South*

○ **Assembly Hall**
Stoke Abbott Road
Worthing BN11 1HQ
tel: 01903 206206
www.worthingtheatres.co.uk

○ **Breinton**
Heath House Road
Woking GU22 0RD
tel: 0778 905 2028
www.breinton.com

○ **Civic Centre**
161 High Street
Berkhamstead
Herts HP4 3HD
tel: 01442 228925
www.dacorum.gov.uk/default.aspx?page=3970

○ **Princes Hall**
Princes Way
Aldershot
Hampshire GU1 1NX
tel: 01252 329 155
www.princeshall.com

## Wales
○ **Millennium Centre**
Bute Place
Cardiff Bay
Cardiff CF10 5AL
tel: 029 2063 6464
www.wmc.org.uk

## West
○ **Jacqueline du Pré Music Building**
St Hilda's College
Cowley Place
Oxford OX4 1DX
tel: 01865 276821
www.st-hildas.ox.ac.uk/index.php/What-s-on/whatson.html

*o*  **St George's Bristol**
Great George Street
Off Park Street
Bristol BS1 5RR
tel: 0845 4024001
www.stgeorgesbristol.co.uk

## Top 100 UK music venues

*Ranking based on the Performing Rights Society list of performing venues, 2009*

1. Southbank Centre, London
2. Wigmore Hall, London
3. The Sage Gateshead, Gateshead
4. St Martin-in-the-Fields, London
5. Royal Northern College of Music, Manchester
6. Stables, Milton Keynes
7. King Tuts Wah Wah Hut, Glasgow
8. Jazz Café, London
9. O2 Academy, Oxford
10. O2 Academy, Birmingham
11. 02 Academy, Newcastle
12. Bridgewater Hall, Manchester
13. O2 Academy, Islington
14. O2 Academy, Liverpool
15. Fairfield Halls, Croydon
16. Spa Complex, Scarborough
17. Philharmonic Hall, Liverpool
18. Underworld, London
19. Barbican Centre, London
20. Royal Scottish Academy of Music & Drama, Glasgow
21. Royal Albert Hall, London
22. St James's Church, London
23. Borderline, London

24. Norwich Arts Centre, Norwich
25. Cadogan Hall, London
26. Birmingham Conservatoire, Birmingham
27. Komedia Cabaret Bar, Brighton
28. Glasgow Royal Concert Hall, Glasgow
29. Koko, London
30. Kings Place, London
31. St Davids Hall, Cardiff
32. St Johns (Main Hall), London
33. Wedgewood Rooms, Southsea
34. Brighton Dome, Brighton
35. Glasgow ABC, Glasgow
36. Little Civic, Wolverhampton
37. Birmingham Town Hall, Birmingham
38. O2 Shepherds Bush Empire, London
39. St George's, Bristol
40. Turner Sims Concert Hall, Southampton
41. Night & Day Café, Manchester
42. Royal Academy of Music, London
43. Queen's Hall, Edinburgh
44. Rock City, Nottingham
45. Ronnie Scott's Club, London
46. Eden Court Theatre and Cinema, Inverness
47. The Junction, Cambridge
48. Anvil, Basingstoke
49. O2 Academy, Bristol
50. JB's Club, Dudley
51. International Convention Centre, Birmingham
52. City Halls, Glasgow
53. Customs House, South Shields
54. Colston Hall, Bristol
55. Strule Arts Centre, Omagh
56. Robin R'N'B Club 2, Bilston
57. Limelight Club, Crewe
58. Rescue Rooms, Nottingham

59. Royal College of Music, London
60. Seafront Bandstand, Eastbourne
61. Royal Concert Hall, Nottingham
62. The Brook, Southampton
63. Whitby Pavilion Complex, Whitby
64. Gala Theatre and Cinema, Durham
65. Pavilion Theatre, Bournemouth
66. Roadhouse, Manchester
67. City Hall, Sheffield
68. Dartington Hall – Great Hall, Totnes
69. Hawth Theatre Complex, Crawley
70. Embassy Theatre, Skegness
71. Huntingdon Arts, Worcester
72. The Met, Bury
73. Music Hall, Aberdeen
74. West Road Concert Hall, Cambridge
75. Scottish Exhibition & Conference Centre (Live), Glasgow
76. Bush Hall, London
77. Gordon Craig Theatre Cinema, Stevenage
78. Cox's Yard, Stratford-upon-Avon
79. Derngate, Northampton
80. The Point, Cardiff
81. Mr Kyp's, Poole
82. Waterfront Hall, Belfast
83. The Roundhouse, London
84. Sands Venue, Gainsborough
85. The Boardwalk, Sheffield
86. The Mill, Banbury
87. Farnham Maltings, Farnham
88. 21 South Street, Reading
89. De Montfort Hall, Leicester
90. Waterfront, Norwich
91. London Astoria 1, London
92. O2 Brixton Academy, London
93. Cliffs Pavilion, Westcliff-on-Sea

94. Epsom Playhouse, Epsom
95. Guildhall Complex, Preston
96. The Venue, London
97. Roses Theatre, Tewkesbury
98. Concert Hall, Perth
99. Carling Apollo, Manchester
100. South Hill Park Arts Centre, Bracknell

Appendix **3**

# Sound Links

These recordings can be found on Spotify unless a YouTube or other web address is given.

0 〜 Reich, Steve: *Music for 18 Musicians*, 'Pulses'

1 〜 *Trumpet:* London Symphony Orchestra – Mahler: Symphony No. 5 in C Sharp Minor, 'I. Trauermarsch' (Funeral March)

2 〜 *Flute:* Emmanuel Pahud – Debussy: *Syrinx*

3 〜 Nikolaus Harnoncourt – J. S. Bach: Cantata, BWV 61 'Nun komm der Heiden Heiland', I, Coro, 'Nun komm der Heiden Heiland'

4 〜 John Eliot Gardiner – J.S. Bach: St Matthew Passion, BWV 244, Part 2, no. 62 Choral, 'Wenn ich einmal soll scheiden'

5 〜 The London Oratory Junior Choir – J.S. Bach: St Matthew Passion, BWV 244, Part 2, no. 63, Evangelist, Chorus I/II, 'Und siehe da, der Vorhang im Tempel zerriss','Wahrlich, dieser ist Gottes Sohn','Und es waren viel Weiber da'

6 〜 Magdalena Koˇzená – J.S. Bach: St Matthew Passion, BWV 244, Part 2, no. 39. Aria (Alto), 'Erbarme dich'

7 〜 Magdalena Koˇzená/Claudio Abbado – Mahler: *Rückert Lieder*, 'Ich bin er Welt abhanden

gekommen' (http://www.youtube.com/watch?v=11m
fvRIKgUA&feature=related)

8 ～ Claudio Abbado – Mahler: Symphony No. 5 in C
   Sharp Minor, Adagietto (http://www.youtube.com/
   watch?v=HfXoADUoYy4)

9 ～ Mark-Anthony Turnage: Scherzoid

10 ～ Goetz: Piano Concerto, Op.18, III (1) (http://www.you
    tube.com/watch?v=MuhOwydioNQ&feature=related

11 ～ Anna Malikova – Schubert: *Die Schöne Müllerin*, D.
    795, no. 19, 'Der Müller und der Bach'

12 ～ Windows Startup Sounds: 95–Vista (http://www.
    youtube.com/watch?v=2RvoiyHJzzw)

13 ～ Cage: Music for Piano, Nos. 4–19 (http://www.
    youtube.com/watch?v=zQ4DmbuzJLQ)

14 ～ Cage: Concerto for Prepared Piano and Chamber
    Orchestra 1/3 (http://www.youtube.com/
    watch?v=BHFzu-X6Ruw)

15 ～ Elena Kats-Chernin – *Eliza's Aria* (http://www.
    youtube.com/watch?v=kwIFR6J1ylA)

16 ～ Django Bates – 'Interval Song' (http://www.youtube.
    com/watch?v=nl2d4zS56cY)

17 ～ Samson François – Mozart: 12 Variations, K. 265 (K.3
    00e) (http://www.youtube.com/
    watch?v=C0-U3PQPs3k)

18 ～ Rachmaninov: *Rhapsody on a Theme of Paganini*,
    Var. 18 (http://www.youtube.com/
    watch?v=DyPEiXkcI_E)

19 ～ Malcolm Martineau – Schubert: 'Gruppe aus dem
    Tartarus', D. 583, Op. 24, no. 1

20 ～ Terry Wogan – 'The Floral Dance' (http://www.
    youtube.com/watch?v=ElnCI1fkfFM)

21 ～ Arnold Schoenberg's Twelve-Tone Method (English)
    (http://www.youtube.com/watch?v=u5dOI2MtvbA)

22 ～ Dudley Moore – Britten and Weill parodies (http://
    www.youtube.com/watch?v=1n7BCUVJkhU)

55　〜　Olivier Messiaen: *Chronochromie*, Part 1

56　〜　Edgard Varèse: *Poème Electronique*

57　〜　Terry Riley: *In C* (2009, remastered)

58　〜　John Adams: *The Chairman Dances*

59　〜　Reich, Steve: *Music for 18 Musicians*, 'Pulses'

60　〜　The Sixteen – Britten: *A Hymn to the Virgin*

61　〜　Britten: *A Ceremony of Carols*, 'This Little Babe' (http://www.youtube.com/watch?v=BTyIP7m8Btg)

62　〜　James MacMillan: *Strathclyde Motets*, 'Mitte Manum Tuam'

63　〜　Gabrieli Consort and Players – John Tavener: *Song for Athene*

64　〜　Tenebrae – John Tavener: *The Lamb*

65　〜　Tan Dun: *Water Passion after St Matthew for Soloists, Choir and Instruments* (1999/2000), 'Death and Earthquake' (live recording)

66　〜　Gao Jian – Tan Dun: *The Banquet*, 2, 'Waiting'

67　〜　Mozart: Mass in C Minor, Kyrie (http://www.youtube.com/watch?v=zuFA3DmglwI)

68　〜　Malcolm Arnold: *A Grand Grand Overture for 3 Vacuum Cleaners, 1 Floor Polisher, 4 Rifles and Orchestra* (http://www.youtube.com/watch?v=HPsiVxUdkvo)

69　〜　Karlheinz Stockhausen: Helikopter String Quartet (http://www.youtube.com/watch?v=13D1YY_BvWU)

70　〜　Ligeti Project – Ligeti: *Mysteries of the Macabre*

71　〜　Hugo Alfvén: *Swedish Rhapsody* (http://www.youtube.com/watch?v=clvtQ34ay1Q)

# Appendix 4

# Bibliography

Barenboim, Daniel (2003) *A Life in Music.* Arcade Publishing.

Britten, Benjamin (2004) *Letters from a Life: The Selected Letters and Diaries of Benjamin Britten*, eds Donald Mitchell and Philip Reed. University of California Press.

Chapman, Janice (2005) *Singing and Teaching Singing: A Holistic Approach to Classical Singing.* Plural Publishing.

Chapman, Janice and Ron Morris, 'Phonation and the speaking voice'. In *Singing and Teaching Singing: A Holistic Approach to Classical Singing.* Plural Publishing.

Dürr, Alfred (2005) *The Cantatas of J.S. Bach*, transl. Richard Jones. Oxford University Preaa.

Fry, Stephen and Tim Lihoreau (2005) *Stephen Fry's Incomplete and Utter History of Classical Music.* Pan.

Grove, Sir George (2001) *The New Grove Dictionary of Music*, 2nd rev. edn, ed. Stanley Sadie and John Tyrrell. Macmillan.

Holmes, Paul (1991) *Debussy (Illustrated Lives of the Great Composers).* Omnibus.

Holst, Imogen (1963) *An ABC of Music.* Oxford University Press.

Keefe, Simon P. (ed.) (2003) *The Cambridge Companion to Mozart.* Cambridge University Press.

Kertesz, Elizabeth and Michael Christoforidis (2008). Confronting *Carmen* beyond the Pyrenees: Bizet's opera in Madrid, 1887–1888. *Cambridge Opera Journal*, 20: 79–110.

Kildea, Paul (ed.) (2003) *Britten on Music.* Oxford University Press.

Levitin, Daniel (2007) *This is Your Brain on Music: The Science of a Human Obsession.* Atlantic Books.

Mithen, Steven (2006) *The Singing Neanderthal: The Origins of Music, Language, Mind, and Body.* Harvard University Press.

Orenstein, Arbie (1991) *Ravel: Man and Musician.* Dover Publications.

Powell, John (2010) *How Music Works.* Penguin Books.

Priestley, J. B. (2009) *Delight* (60th Anniversary edn). Great Northern, ch. 15.

Rees, Jasper (2008) *I Found My Horn: One Man's Struggle with the Orchestra's Most Difficult Instrument.* Weidenfeld & Nicolson.

Sacks, Oliver (2007) *Musicophilia: Tales of Music and the Brain.* Picador.

Pleasants, Henry (ed.) (1989) *Schumann on Music: Selection from the Writings.* Dover Publications.

Snowman, Daniel (2007) *Hallelujah! An Informal History of the London Philharmonic Choir.* London Philharmonic Choir.

Walker, Alan (1988) *Franz Liszt: The Virtuoso Years, 1811–1847.* Cornell University Press.

# Appendix 5

# Notes

### 1. *You Love Classical Music* – Yes, You Do!

1. Since 2007 Transport for London has been piping classical music into underground stations to reduce anti-social behaviour. http://entertainment.timesonline.co.uk/tol/arts_and_entertainment/music/article3284419.ece

2. Arbie Orenstein (1991) *Ravel: Man and Musician.* Dover Publications, p. 200.

3. http://www.youtube.com/watch?v=13FrLGB_oK8

4. According to Jonathan Forster of Spotify AB, Spotify was supposed to be launched in the United States before the end of 2010 but has been pushed back for 2011 release. (http://en.wikipedia.org/wiki/Spotify)

5. *Repertoire* is the term used to describe pieces of music that are played or recorded as opposed to those which aren't and are currently gathering dust in the library. These forgotten pieces may at any time re-enter the repertoire, but the usual sense of the word refers to works in current circulation. It can also be used in reference to a specific period, for instance the Romantic repertoire, the Baroque repertoire, etc. All terms which will be explained later in the book.

## 2. Why, Why, Why?

1. Steven Mithen (2006) *The Singing Neanderthal: The Origins of Music, Language, Mind, and Body.* Harvard University Press, p. 46.

2. http://americanhistory.si.edu/collections/object.cfm?key=35&objkey=59

3. http://www.bbc.co.uk/pressoffice/pressreleases/stories/2010/09_september/10/proms.shtml

4. http://www.billboard.biz/bbbiz/content_display/industry/news/e3i3a15dfaab86484fb472afe06e7cf7171

5. http://www.telegraph.co.uk/culture/music/classicalmusic/7793334/Is-this-the-final-curtain-for-classical-records.html

6. http://www.guardian.co.uk/culture/2003/jan/10/artsfeatures.shopping

7. In 2003 Rutter told the US television programme *60 Minutes* that he was not particularly a religious man, yet still deeply spiritual and inspired by the spirituality of sacred verses and prayers (http://en.wikipedia.org/wiki/John_Rutter).

8. If you want to know just many there are, see http://en.wikipedia.org/wiki/List_of_female_composers_by_birth_year

9. Daniel Levitin (2007) *This is Your Brain on Music: The Science of a Human Obsession.* Atlantic Books, pp. 152–4.

10. 'Whenever J. S. Bach would sit at the console outside of the congregational church services, which he was often asked to do by visitors, he would select a theme at random and work it out in all forms of organ pieces in such a manner that it would always remain his material, even though he might play for two or more hours without a break. First he would use this theme in a Prelude and Fugue for full organ. Then he would display his mastery of registration in a trio, a quartet, and the like, always using the same theme. He would follow this with a chorale, the melody of which was surrounded by the first theme in three or four voices in the

most varied manner. He would conclude with a fugue for full organ in which either only a new treatment of the original theme would dominate, or one or, according to its nature, two others would be intermingled.' http://www.oldandsold.com/articles02/jsbach5.shtml

11. Robert Levin, *Improvising Mozart*. 'Improvisation in Mozart's case requires an intensive character study of the entire work from within, for a spontaneous elaboration of the written text' (www.aam.co.uk/features/9705.htm)

12. http://www.bbc.co.uk/programmes/p00c2byb

13. *Ein Mönchsleben aus der zweiten Hälfte des achtzehnten Jahrhunderts. Nach dem Tagebuche des Placidus Scharl*; see also Piero Melograni and Lydia G. Cochrane (2006) *Wolfgang Amadeus Mozart*. University of Chicago Press, p. 5.

### 3. How to Listen

1. http://www.bbc.co.uk/london/content/articles/2006/10/20/music_buses_feature.shtml

2. Janice Chapman (2005) *Singing and Teaching Singing: A Holistic Approach to Classical Singing*. Plural Publishing.

3. http://www.bbc.co.uk/news/uk-england-london-11932139

4. https://docs.google.com/viewer?url=http://www.ncbi.nlm.nih.gov/pmc/articles/PMC1690651/pdf/10885512.pdf

### 4. A Hot Date with Music

1. http://www.abc.net.au/news/newsitems/200208/s662739.htm

2. From Sir Ken Robinson's lecture to the Royal Society for the Encouragement of Arts, Manufactures and Commerce. http://www.youtube.com/watch?v=zDZFcDGpL4U

3. http://www.amazon.com/Bach-Cantatas-BWV-82-125/dp/B00004U5BF

4. See e.g. http://en.wikipedia.org/wiki/List_of_20th-century_classical_composers_by_birth_date

### 5. Exploding the Canon

1. The canon is, according to the Oxford English Dictionary, 'a list of literary or artistic works considered to be permanently established as being of the highest quality: *Hopkins was firmly established in the canon of English poetry.*' It's the must-haves in your record collection and the Shakespeare/Dickens/Austen of the music world.
2. http://www.stevereich.com/articles/Michael_Tilson_Thomas.html
3. http://www.franzschubert.org.uk/life/annl27.html and Grove entry on Schubert.
4. Paul Holmes (1991) *Debussy* (*Illustrated Lives of the Great Composers*). Omnibus, p. 83.
5. http://www.hyperion-records.co.uk/al.asp?al=CDA67791
6. http://www.hyperion-records.co.uk/dc.asp?dc=D_CDA67791&vw=dc
7. http://www.amazon.com/Songs-Schuberts-Friends-Contemporaries-Joseph/dp/B000ECXBMS
8. Alan Walker (1988) *Franz Liszt: The Virtuoso Years, 1811–1847.* Cornell University Press, p. 301.

### 6. The Secret of Melody

1. http://www.sfgate.com/cgi-bin/article.cgi?f=/c/a/1996/06/02/PK70006.DTL#ixzz1618
2. http://library.duke.edu/digitalcollections/gedney.CM0351/pg.1/
3. *Grove Dictionary of Music* – John Cage's entry.
4. Levitin, *This is Your Brain on Music*, op. cit. p. 29.
5. For more on melody, see http://www.cartage.org.lb/en/themes/arts/music/elements/elemofmusic/melody/melody.htm
6. Levitin, *This is Your Brain on Music, op. cit.,* p. 167.
7. http://www.guardian.co.uk/film/2002/feb/04/artsfeatures

8. Elizabeth Kertesz and Michael Christoforidis (2008). Confronting *Carmen* beyond the Pyrenees: Bizet's opera in Madrid, 1887–1888. *Cambridge Opera Journal*, 20: 79–110.
9. J. B. Priestley (2009) *Delight* (60th Anniversary edn). Great Northern, ch. 15, p. 58.
10. Paul Kildea (ed.) *Britten on Music*. Oxford University Press, p. 193.
11. Ibid., pp. 184–5.
12. Anyone contemplating the music of Richard Wagner must consider his attitude towards 'Jewishness in music' as propounded in his article of 1850, 'Das Judenthum in der Musik'. This is by any standards an objectionable article though it is probable that had Wagner's music and ideas not been appropriated by the Nazi party (Hitler was a fan) then this article would not be considered as significant as it now is. It causes problems for any lover of Wagner's operas. The sentiments expresses are small-minded, parochial, xenophobic, suspicious of difference, and it dresses anti-semitism in the clothing of respectability and pseudo-intellectual claptrap. I can find no justification for his fundamental lack of humanity in writing this repugnant article. So how can I (and many Jews as well, Daniel Barenboim being the most notable example) bear to listen to this man's music? There are two things to remember: firstly, however objectionable his ideas he did not, insofar as I am aware, go as far as the Nazi Party in calling for the extermination of the Jewish people (small comfort, perhaps, considering the tone of the article), and secondly, it should be seen within the context of the nineteenth century although this does not altogether mitigate his ideas. This was the era of German unification when the idea of a German cultural identity was hotly contested. Nevertheless to excuse Wagner on historical grounds is to ignore the unpleasant personal nature of his complaints about Jewish music. There is an astounding jealousy of the success of Felix Mendelssohn, a

Jewish convert to Christianity, and Meyerbeer, his one-time patron. That Wagner threw mud in the face of the man who had once helped him financially and encouraged him professionally cannot be justified by simply saying that it was the norm to be anti-semitic in those days. It throws up the question of exactly how much we need to know about the composer in order to appreciate his music. See also 'Richard Wagner's Anti-Semitism', http://www.cjh.org/p/52

### 7. The Magic of Harmony

1. For a definition of 'key' see above, 'How strange, the change …', Chapter 2.
2. It's only necessary to be able to name chords and chord progressions if you are planning to become a composer or performer. If that's the case then this is the wrong book for you.
3. For those with a modicum of musical training the chords are I V VI III IV I IV V I. The final cadence is IV–V–I which can be found in all musical forms throughout musical history. The V–I cadence is the most powerful; it's the most magnetic in music. because the V chord contains none of the notes of the I chord and seems to invite resolution.
4. There is a story in singer circles about a well-known soprano who, when rehearsing the music of Robert Schumann, was asked by the pianist, 'How does this song make you feel?' 'It makes me want to fuck,' was the reply. Whereupon they did. Or so legend has it. It's the sort of story that gets told by wishful-thinking young accompanists to soubrette sopranos in the vain hope it will inspire either passionate singing or just passion. And that's opera singers for you.
5. Elektra wants to avenge her father Agamemnon's murder by getting her brother Orestes to murder her mother, Klytemnestra. Upon satisfaction of this urge, she dies – it's not a comedy.

6. http://www.scena.org/columns/lebrecht/010708-NL-
   Schoenberg.html

## 8. Style and the Orchestra

1. *Grove Dictionary of Music* entry on 'Orchestra' *4. Lully and Corelli (1650–1715)*.
2. Ibid.
3. Observant people may notice that the bass is slightly differently shaped from the other members of the string family. This is because it is descended from a different branch of the string family; the viols. It is actually a bass viol. The viols were stringed instruments of the Renaissance and Baroque period. They have largely been superseded by the modern violin, except in historically informed performances.
4. http://aplaceforticketsblog.blogspot.com/2010/08/violinist-david-garrett-brings-his.html
5. Confusingly, despite looking like a brass instrument, the saxophone is a member of the woodwind family because it too has a single reed. It's essentially a metal clarinet. The saxophone is a recent addition to the musical world and is only heard in late-nineteenth- and early-twentieth-century music; Prokofiev put it to use in *Romeo and Juliet* written in 1936 (one of the pieces you may have heard as it was recently used on the BBC's *The Apprentice*) but it was in jazz that it found its raison d'être.

## 9. Grand Designs: The Structure of Music

1. Levitin, *This is Your Brain on Music*, op. cit., p. 155.

## 10. The Singers not the Songs

1. Janice Chapman and Ron Morris (2005) Phonation and the speaking voice. In *Singing and Teaching Singing: A Holistic Approach to Classical Singing*. Plural Publishing, p. 83.

### 11. *Taking up the Baton: Conductors*

1. Add.30014 ff.124v-125 The Virgin with angels, from the 'Hymn book of the St Saviour's Monastry, Siena', 1415 (vellum) by Italian School, (15th century) British Library, London, UK © British Library Board. All Rights Reserved/ The Bridgeman Art Library.
2. Autograph score of Handel's *Jeptha* © The British Library Board. R.M.20.e.8.
3. Daniel Barenboim (2003) *A Life in Music.* Arcade Publishing, p. 80.
4. Daniel Snowman (2007) *Hallelujah! An Informal History of the London Philharmonic Choir.* London Philharmonic Choir, p. 59.
5. Barenboim, *A Life in Music*, op. cit., p. 83.
6. Interview with Vladimir Jurowski, *Gramophone*, November 2010, p. 19.
7. http://www.gramophone.net/ArtistOfTheWeek/View/270
8. www.auroraorchestra.com
9. http://www.guardian.co.uk/music/2006/may/16/ classicalmusicandopera2; see also http://www.guardian. co.uk/music/2009/sep/20/ valery-gergiev-london-symphony

### 12. *How to Survive a Concert*

1. http://www.guardian.co.uk/music/2010/apr/15/ bill-fontana-interview
2. For a more guaranteed fainting experience go to the Globe Theatre on Bankside, London. Pick one of the really long Shakespeares. There will usually be a tourist who can't read English and so doesn't realise they'll be standing. Of course they'll have been busy all day and won't have eaten. Keep an eye on them and don't stand too close.
3. http://www.nytimes.com/2001/07/19/arts/bonkers-for- music-cheer-glory-for-britons-it-s-time-for-proms-that- exhilarating.html?pagewanted=3

4. http://www.schott-music.com/shop/leihwerke/
   show,154469,s.html?showOldPerformances=true
5. http://www.stephenpollard.net/001035.html
6. 'One of the earliest members of Artec's acclaimed family of
   world-class concert halls, Symphony Hall features a few of
   Artec's signature adjustable acoustic elements including a
   mobilised multi-piece canopy and acoustic control
   chambers', from http://www.artecconsultants.com/03_
   projects/performing_arts_venues/international_
   convention_centre/symphony_hall_birmingham.html
7. http://www.kirkegaard.com/arts/concert-halls
8. http://www.independent.co.uk/arts-entertainment/music/
   news/barbican-hall-acoustics-win-critical-
   applause-568023.html
9. http://tedmuller.us/Piano/SugarPlumFairy.htm

# Index

# Acknowledgements

Writing this book is the culmination of every music project I've been involved with over the last ten years, during which many people have helped, influenced and educated me. My passion for music is a direct result of all the brilliant people I've met and performed with during that time.

For asking all the right questions: Chloë Barnett, Claire Underwood, Cesca Eaton, Chris Needham, Jenny Farn, Liz Jones, Iestyn Davies, Catherine Hopper, Gabriella Swallow, Tim Carleston, Norman Lebrecht, Jamie Inverne, Catherine De Sybel, Jill Sutherland; for writing down everything I said in rehearsals, Ana De Moraes, and my mother-in-law Ruth for helping with the list of composers.

Many thanks to all the musicians of the London Symphony Orchestra who have provided the inspiration for most of my work, especially Matt Gardner, Gareth Davies, Matt Gibson, Bindi Macfarlane, Jonathan Lipton and Liz Burley. Thanks to those who gave me the opportunity to work in orchestral education: Richard McNicol, Karen Irwin, Katie Tearle from Glyndebourne and Paul Reeve of the Royal Opera House, along with all their brilliant animateurs who tirelessly promote music. Thanks to all my teachers: Muriel Levin, Margaret Glynn, Aiden Fairlie, Stephen Carleston, Sheila Olsen, Janice Chapman and Jonathan Papp.

Thanks to Suzi Digby and Voce Chamber Choir for letting me sing in their Christmas concert.

Thanks to Gordon Wise, Jacquie Drewe and everyone at Curtis Brown for support above and beyond. Pascal Wyse for his sense of fun and great ideas. Hannah MacDonald, Craig Adams and Kathy Dyke at HarperCollins. For sheer incisive brilliance, Martin Noble. Thanks also to Tom Lewis and Dickon Stainer at Decca Records.

Huge thanks to all the people who have sung in my choirs, been to my workshops and those who have written to me to say they enjoy what I do. I do too.

Constant thanks to my parents Siân and Jamie for giving me the gift of music, my bookish grandmother Patricia, who gave me the confidence to write, and my grandfather Teddy for buying me *Peter and the Wolf* when I was seven and for giving me the gift of the gab.

I couldn't possibly have written this book or frankly any book without the sharp editorial eye and all-round intelligence of my brilliant wife Becky, to whom this book is dedicated, along with my four-month-old daughter Esther who helped with her complicit quietness and precocious interest in the music of the Second Viennese School.

G.M.